Linguistically Motivated Statistical Machine Translation

Deyi Xiong · Min Zhang

Linguistically Motivated Statistical Machine Translation

Models and Algorithms

 Springer

Deyi Xiong
Soochow University
Suzhou
Jiangsu
China

Min Zhang
Soochow University
Suzhou
Jiangsu
China

ISBN 978-981-10-1365-2   ISBN 978-981-287-356-9   (eBook)
DOI 10.1007/978-981-287-356-9

Springer Science+Business Media Singapore Pte Ltd. is part of Springer Science+Business Media
(www.springer.com)

To my daughter Keke

Deyi Xiong

To my daughters Gege and Tongtong

Min Zhang

Acknowledgments

The first author is grateful to his wife Chiara for her endless love and support. He is also very grateful to his parents for their decades of hard work. This book serves as a testament to the considerable effort they've put into raising him. He appreciates loving phone calls from his grandfather-in-law for his kind encouragements and practical support from his parents-in-law. He dedicates this book to his angel Keke, the new joy of his life! The second author is grateful to his family for their great love and support.

This work was supported by National Natural Science Foundation of China (Grant No. 61373095, 61403269 and 61432013), Natural Science Foundation of Jiangsu Province (Grant No. BK20140355).

The first author would like to thank his friends and mentors from Institute of Computing Technology, China. We would like to express our gratitude to our former colleagues from Institute for Infocomm Research, Singapore. We cherish the friendship and memory of working with them. We also thank our colleagues from School of Computer Science and Technology, Soochow University, for their immense practical help. Finally, we are grateful to numerous individuals for their insightful comments on the earlier drafts of this book and many of our colleagues and friends in the research community for their encouragements and helps along the way of tens of years.

February 2015

Deyi Xiong
Min Zhang

Contents

Chapter 1
Introduction

Abstract This chapter introduces the basic concept and architecture of SMT and the various linguistic challenges for SMT, which are the reasons that we introduce linguistically motivated SMT. We also describe the scope and contributions of this book in this chapter.

Statistical machine translation (SMT) is a machine translation paradigm that relies on statistical models learned from parallel text corpora and decoding algorithms to automatically translate one natural language (e.g., Chinese) into another (e.g., English). With the rapid development of computing power and easy access to large-scale parallel corpora, we have witnessed substantial progress in SMT during the last two decades: a shift from word-based SMT developed by IBM researchers in the early 1990s to phrase- and syntax-based SMT.

Word-based SMT. Brown et al. (1993) proposed the well-known IBM models that produce source words from target words through a noisy channel. They introduce a *fertility*[1] attribute for each target word to allow one target word to connect with multiple source words. However, each source word can only be aligned with one target word or the *null* word. This restriction obviously disables word-based SMT to translate a single source word into multiple target words, which is not true in real-world bitexts.

Phrase-based SMT. In order to enable one-to-many or many-to-many translations, we should change translation units from words to *phrases* that contain a number of consecutive words. Such a change signals the shift from word-based SMT to phrase-based SMT. In phrase-based SMT, a source sentence is segmented into a sequence of phrases which are then translated into target counterparts and reordered to form a fluent target sentence.

Syntax-based SMT. The former two SMT formalisms can only model linear elements of language such as words and phrases. However, the inherent structure of a language is hierarchical. Syntax-based SMT is exactly the machine translation formalism that is able to build hierarchical mappings between the source and target language.

---

[1] The number of source words that a target word can generate.

© Springer Science+Business Media Singapore 2015
D. Xiong and M. Zhang, *Linguistically Motivated Statistical Machine Translation*, DOI 10.1007/978-981-287-356-9_1

Although translation quality is significantly improved in phrase- and syntax-based SMT due to their capacities of non-compositional translation and structural reordering, various challenges at different linguistic levels make machine-generated translations not yet comparable to human translations. A wide variety of efforts have been devoted to dealing with such linguistic challenges. This book reflects one of these efforts: linguistically motivated SMT that incorporates various linguistic knowledge to handle linguistic challenges for statistical machine translation.

1.1 Statistical Machine Translation

We first present the basic concept and architecture of statistical machine translation. This background knowledge will enable us to establish and discuss linguistically motivated SMT from the broad perspective of SMT in Sect. 1.4.

Given a source sentence f, most SMT systems find the best translation $\hat{e}$ among all possible translations as follows:

$$
\begin{aligned}
\hat{e} &= \operatorname*{argmax}_{e} P(e|f) \\
&= \operatorname*{argmax}_{e} \left\{ \frac{\exp\left[\sum_1^K \lambda_k M_k(f, e)\right]}{\sum_{e'} \exp\left[\sum_1^K \lambda_k M_k(f, e')\right]} \right\} \\
&= \operatorname*{argmax}_{e} \left\{ \exp\left[\sum_{m=1}^K \lambda_k M_k(f, e)\right] \right\}
\end{aligned}
\tag{1.1}
$$

where $M_k(f, e)$ is a feature function defined on the source sentence f and the corresponding translation e, λ_k is the weight of the feature function. Since the normalization $\sum_{e'} \exp\left[\sum_1^K \lambda_k M_k(f, e')\right]$ is constant for all possible translations e', we do not need to calculate it during decoding.

The weighted model in the Eq. (1.1) is a log-linear model. The feature functions $M_k(f, e)$ are also referred to as sub-models[2] as they are components of the log-linear model. In Table 1.1, we show the most widely used feature functions in SMT. Most of them can be easily factored over translation rules, which facilitates the application of dynamic programming in decoding. *Translation rules* are bilingual segments[3] that establish translation equivalences between the source and target language. They are widely used in statistical machine translation with various representations ranging

---

[2] This notation is used when we want to emphasize that a sub-model is a component of the log-linear model. Otherwise we just call them models, such as a language model, a reordering model, and so on.

[3] Here a segment is defined as a string of terminals and/or nonterminals.

Table 1.1 The most widely used sub-models of statistical machine translation

Sub-models	Descriptions
$\sum_1^I \log P(\bar{e}_i\|\bar{f}_i)$	Direct translation probabilities
$\sum_1^I \log P(\bar{f}_i\|\bar{e}_i)$	Inverse translation probabilities
$\sum_1^I \log \text{lex}(\bar{e}_i\|\bar{f}_i)$	Direct lexical translation probabilities
$\sum_1^I \log \text{lex}(\bar{f}_i\|\bar{e}_i)$	Inverse lexical translation probabilities
$\sum_1^{\|e\|} \log P(e_i\|e_1 \dots e_{i-1})$	Language model
$\sum_1^I \log \psi(\bar{e}_i, \bar{f}_i)$	Reordering model
$\log\|e\|$	Word count
$\log I$	Translation rule count

I is the number of translation rules that are used to generate the target sentence e given the source sentence f. $\bar{e}_i$ and $\bar{f}_i$ are the target and source side of a translation rule r_i

from word pairs to bilingual phrases and synchronous rules in word-, phrase-, and syntax-based SMT respectively.

The first four features in Table 1.1 can be grouped into a translation model as they all estimate translation probabilities of equivalences from different perspectives. Most SMT systems include the following three essential components:

1. A translation model that measures translation probabilities of equivalences in translation rules.
2. A language model that captures the fluency of generated sentences in the target language.
3. A reordering model that deals with word/phrase order differences between the source and target language.

If we only use $P(f|e)$ and $P(e)$ as features, and set the weights of both features to be equal, we have the noisy-channel model for SMT as follows:

$$\hat{e} = \underset{e}{\text{argmax}}\, P(e|f)$$

$$= \underset{e}{\text{argmax}}\, P(f|e)P(e) \tag{1.2}$$

Comparing with the noisy-channel model, the log-linear model allows us to integrate arbitrary useful features other than the translation and language model into SMT.

In the log-linear model of SMT, all sub-models are trained separately and combined under the assumption that they are independent of each other. The associated weights λs can be tuned using minimum error rate training (MERT) (Och 2003) or the Margin Infused Relaxed Algorithm (MIRA) (Chiang et al. 2008). Figure 1.1, adapted from (Och and Ney 2002), shows the architecture of the log-linear model-based SMT systems.

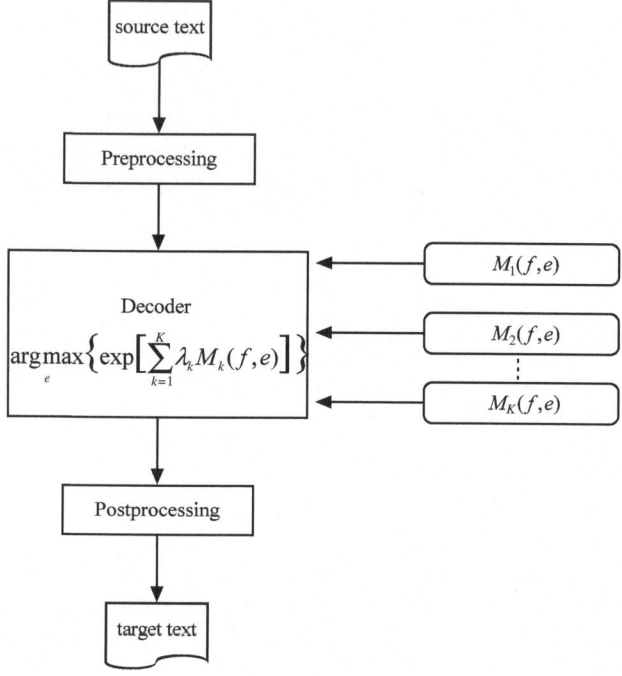

Fig. 1.1 The architecture of the log-linear model-based SMT

1.2 Phrase- and Syntax-Based SMT

Two major SMT formalisms have been developed in the SMT literature after word-based SMT: phrase- and syntax-based SMT. The fundamental difference between these two formalisms lies in translation rules. Phrase-based SMT adopts bilingual phrases as translation rules, while syntax-based SMT uses translation rules built on some form of synchronous grammar to generate hierarchical mappings between the source and target language.

In phrase-based SMT, normally a source sentence f is translated into a target sentence e in the following steps.[4]

- Segmenting f into a sequence of phrases $\bar{f}_1, \ldots, \bar{f}_J$ (not necessarily syntactic phrases);
- Translating each segmented source phrase f_j as a whole unit into its counterpart $\bar{e}_i$.
- Reordering target phrases $\bar{e}_i$.

---

[4] Note that we describe this process from a "direct" rather than a noisy channel perspective.

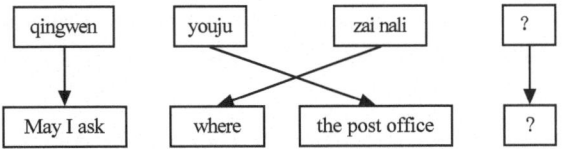

Fig. 1.2 A Chinese-to-English translation example which visualizes the process of phrase-based SMT

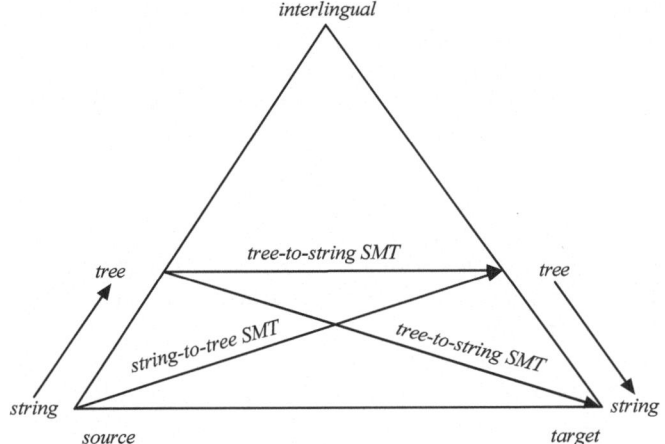

Fig. 1.3 Tree-based SMT

Figure 1.2 visualizes these three steps (phrase segmentation, translation, and reordering) with a Chinese-to-English translation example.[5] Correspondingly, we can use three models, namely segmentation model, translation model, and reordering model, to capture probabilistic properties of these three steps respectively.

Syntax-based SMT explores some form of synchronous grammar to translate a source sentence into a target sentence. Adopted synchronous grammars can be either formally syntactic or linguistically syntactic (Chiang 2005). Correspondingly, syntax-based SMT is divided into formally syntax-based and linguistically syntax-based SMT. For example, Chiang's hierarchical grammar-based SMT (2005) is formally syntax-based SMT. Yamada and Knight's work (2001) is both formally syntax-based and linguistically syntax-based SMT as it uses a linguistic synchronous grammar.

More powerful synchronous grammars that extend the domain of locality of synchronous context-free grammars can be also used in SMT. This develops various tree-based SMT formalisms. Based on which side (source or target) trees are built, tree-based SMT can be categorized into tree-to-string, string-to-tree, and tree-to-tree SMT, which are visualized in Fig. 1.3. For example, Liu et al. (2006) proposed a tree-to-string template model to capture the process of translating a source parse tree

---

[5] In this book, we use Chinese phonetic "pinyin" to represent Chinese characters.

into a target sentence. Galley et al. (2004, 2006) introduced string-to-tree translation models that build target trees for source sentences.

1.3 Linguistic Challenges for Machine Translation

On the one hand, we are witnessing more and more powerful SMT models that are being proposed, such as the combination of phrase-based and syntax-based SMT, which explores both syntactic reordering and non-syntactic phrases for machine translation (Quirk et al. 2005; Marcu et al. 2006). On the other hand, we notice that some linguistic phenomena, such as word sense ambiguity, long-distance reordering, co-reference, and so on, cannot yet be efficiently modeled or not modeled at all in these SMT systems. Such linguistic phenomena should be seriously considered and statistically modeled because they pose big challenges for machine translation. If we fail to deal with them, meanings of source sentences may not be correctly conveyed, or generated target sentences may be ungrammatical. Such failures will also cause many other translation errors.

We refer to the challenges posed by these linguistic phenomena as linguistic challenges. They come from different linguistic levels. We classify them into four major categories according to their linguistic level: lexical challenge, syntactic challenge, sentence-level semantic challenge, and document-level semantic challenge.

1.3.1 Lexical Challenge

This challenge is posed by the phenomenon in which a translation pattern is triggered by specific linguistic items at the lexicon level. Particularly, the lexical challenge causes machine translation issues that are related to *lexical selection* and *lexicalized reordering*.

1. Lexical selection is a task where appropriate target lexical items for source words are selected according to context information. The challenge of lexical selection is normally brought by words that have different meanings in different contexts. For example, the word "bank" has two significantly different meanings in the following two sentences.

   Example 1.1.
   We pedalled north along the east *bank* of the river.
   She withdrew money from her *bank* account.

   SMT system should translate them appropriately via lexical selection according to their meanings.
2. Lexicalized reordering handles cases in which particular lexical items trigger a specific reordering pattern. For instance, the Chinese particle "de" often triggers

a swapping where the modifier constituent to its left is moved towards its right after translation.

1.3.2 Syntactic Challenge

This challenge is posed by syntactic mismatches between the source and target language. Two particular cases of this challenge are:

1. Syntactic category divergence where syntactic relations are changed after translation (Dorr 1994). For instance, a noun phrase as a verbal object in the source language might be translated into a prepositional phrase in the target language.
2. Syntactic order divergence where syntactic constituents are reordered according to their syntactic patterns. For example, a Chinese VP constituent "VP → PP VP" is frequently translated into "VP → VP PP" in English.

1.3.3 Sentence-Level Semantic Challenge

Words and phrases in a sentence are not only syntactically correlated but also semantically connected. Sentence-level semantic challenge arises in cases where semantic relations influence translations. The thematic divergence discussed by Dorr (1994) is one case of this challenge, where for instance a subject argument of a verbal head is repositioned as an object argument after translation.

1.3.4 Document-Level Semantic Challenge

Sentences of a text are not randomly selected. They are logically and semantically connected to one another. This connection can be either a surface connection or an underlying meaning connection. The surface connection can be established via lexical choice. For example, we can use a synonym of word w in a sentence that succeeds the sentence where w occurs the first time. Such a synonym can help build a surface link between these two sentences. In contrast to the surface links among sentences, underlying meaning connectedness concerns the gist of a document or semantic relations between sentences such as causality. For example, if the gist of document is about finance, the probability that English word "bank" is translated as a finance institution is larger than that of river bank. These surface and underlying connections of a text pose document-level semantic challenges for SMT as they require SMT systems to translate the text in accord with its document-level semantic properties.

1.4 Linguistically Motivated SMT

Conventional phrase- and syntax-based SMT models are not yet adequate to deal with
the four major linguistic challenges discussed in the previous section. In order to suf-
ficiently handle these challenges, we should integrate linguistic knowledge that is not
embedded in bilingual phrases or synchronous grammars, such as lexical, syntactic,
and semantic knowledge, into SMT. We call this enhanced SMT *linguistically motivated SMT*. It should neither refer to nor be limited to only one specific SMT formalism. Any SMT formalisms can be enhanced with linguistic knowledge. For example,

- We can integrate syntactic knowledge into phrase-based SMT in order to strengthen
  its capability of long-distance reordering.
- We can also make formally syntax-based SMT linguistically syntax-based by
  incorporating syntactic knowledge into it.
- Syntax-based SMT can also be improved with fine-grained lexical knowledge or
  high-level semantic knowledge.

From this perspective, linguistically motivated SMT can be considered as a hybrid
SMT as it explores hybrid linguistic knowledge.

The log-linear architecture of SMT described in Sect. 1.1 facilitates this hybridiza-
tion of different linguistic knowledge in linguistically motivated SMT. Therefore, we
can also adapt the log-linear architecture for linguistically motivated SMT, which
is shown in Fig. 1.4. In this architecture, we incorporate linguistic knowledge into

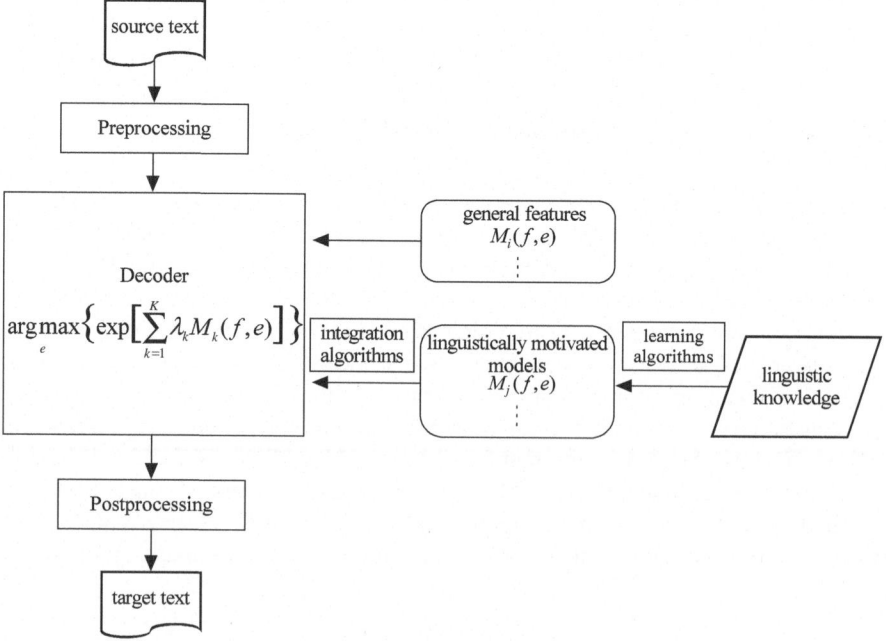

Fig. 1.4 The architecture of linguistically motivated SMT

linguistically motivated models via *learning algorithms*. The built linguistically motivated models are then integrated into the decoder through *integration algorithms*, which factor the linguistically motivated models over translation rules so that they can be efficiently calculated in a dynamic programming fashion during decoding.

1.5 What This Book Is

The major focus of this book is linguistically motivated SMT, particularly algorithms and models that incorporate linguistic knowledge into SMT. Because linguistically motivated SMT especially enhances the following three essential components of SMT, we introduce linguistically motivated models and algorithms correspondingly from these three aspects.

1. *Translation Model.* Measuring the probability that a source unit is translated into its target equivalence given surrounding contexts is one of the most important tasks for SMT. Although translation units may vary from word, phrase, to tree fragment, the importance of appropriately estimating translation probabilities for transla- tion units remains the same. The accuracy of translation probability estimation, to a great extent, determines whether meaning can be correctly conveyed from the source language to the target language. The estimation accuracy is closely related to two major factors. One is the estimation method, which can be generative or discriminative. The other is the context in which translation probabilities are con- ditioned. It ranges from local context to sentence- and document-level context. This book is devoted to the context factor of translation model and presents a semantically motivated translation model which explores document-level seman- tic knowledge, particularly the gist of a document, to constrain translation rule selection.
2. *Reordering Model.* As word order differences prevail among different lan- guages, the ability to capture such order differences (i.e., the reordering ability) is absolutely necessary for machine translation systems. Generally, reordering approaches can be roughly divided into three categories: (1) reordering the source language in a preprocessing step before decoding begins (Collins et al. 2005; Wang et al. 2007; Khalilov and Sima'an 2011); (2) estimating word/phrase move- ment with reordering models (Tillman 2004; Kumar and Byrne 2005; Al-Onaizan and Papineni 2006; Xiong et al. 2006); and (3) capturing reorderings by synchro- nous grammars (Chiang 2005; Wu 1997; Marcu et al. 2006; Liu et al. 2006). The preprocessing approach applies manual or automatically extracted reorder- ing knowledge from linguistic structures to transform the source language sen- tence into a word order that is closer to the target sentence. The second reordering approach moves words or phrases under some reordering constraint and estimates the probabilities of movement with various information. In the third approach, reordering knowledge is included in synchronous rules. The last two categories reorder the source sentence during decoding, which distinguishes them from the

first approach. We dedicate to the second approach: reordering models. This book introduces two linguistically motivated reordering models for SMT which integrates lexical, syntactic, and semantic knowledge to capture reordering patterns.

3. *Bracketing Model.* The translation and reordering models are the most widely investigated topics in the SMT community. The translation model is to find the best equivalence for a source unit given the contexts around it. The reordering model is to detect the correct position for a source unit on the target side after translation. Yet another important issue is to determine whether a sequence of source words should be translated as a whole unit, i.e., their translations remain continuous on the target side. This issue is known as a *segmentation* problem in phrase-based SMT (Chiang 2005). Compared with the translation and reordering issues, the segmentation problem is much less explored since most SMT systems assume a uniform distribution over segmentations. However, this is not true because not all segmented source phrases can be translated as a whole unit into the target language. We recast this issue as a *bracketing* problem: whether a consecutive sequence of source words should be bracketed and translated together. This book provides two bracketing approaches which integrate linguistic knowledge (lexical, syntactic, and semantic knowledge) to enable the decoder to make correct bracketing decisions on appropriate source segments.

For some linguistically motivated models introduced in this book, we use Bracketing Transduction Grammar (BTG)-based SMT as the platform to demonstrate how we implement these models and integrate them into SMT. We will elaborate BTG-based SMT in the next chapter. This does not mean that these linguistically motivated models and related algorithms are limited to BTG-based SMT. Actually, they can be applicable to many other SMT formalisms.

This book is not about general knowledge of statistical machine translation, such as a thorough survey of a number of SMT approaches, details of training and decoding used by those approaches. For these aspects, we refer the readers to Philipp Koehn's excellent textbook "Statistical Machine Translation" (2009).

The significance of this book lies in three basic grounds. Above all, the major purpose of this book is to discuss linguistically motivated SMT, particularly on various linguistically motivated models and related algorithms. Second, the book also serves the purpose of promoting our deep understanding on the impacts of linguistic knowledge on machine translation. Finally, the book provides a systematic introduction to BTG-based SMT, one of state-of-the-art SMT formalisms, as well as a case study of linguistically motivated SMT on BTG-based platform.

1.6 Organization

The first chapter introduces the basic concept and architecture of SMT and various linguistic challenges for SMT, which are the reasons that we introduce linguistically motivated SMT. We also describe the scope and contributions of this book in this chapter.

The second chapter systematically introduces *BTG-based SMT*. In this chapter, we first introduce the Bracketing Transduction Grammar and a unified framework for BTG-based SMT, including the model and decoding algorithm that does not integrate language model. We then present an algorithm to integrate standard *n*-gram language models into the decoder. Following that, we describe two extensions to these traditional language models: a backward language model that augments the conventional forward language model, and a mutual information trigger model, which captures long-distance dependencies that go beyond the scope of standard *n*-gram language models. Using these two models, we attempt to enhance the ability of conventional *n*-gram language models in capturing richer contexts and long-distance dependencies. Finally, we thoroughly compare BTG-based SMT with other SMT formalisms, such as (hierarchical) phrase-based and linguistically syntax-based SMT so that we can clearly understand the strengths and weaknesses of BTG-based SMT.

Chapter 3 presents a *syntactically annotated reordering* approach for SMT. We first present a lexicalized reordering model that uses boundary words as reordering features. The philosophy behind the model is that reordering under the ITG constraint is considered as a binary classification problem. We therefore build a maximum entropy classification model (Berger et al. 1996) to predict the order $o \in \{straight, inverted\}$ whenever we apply a BTG bracketing rule to merge two neighboring phrases. As syntax knowledge can provide high-level information for reordering, especially for long-distance reordering, we further extend the maximum entropy-based lexicalized reordering model to a syntactically annotated reordering model. The new model annotates each BTG node with syntactic knowledge by projecting binary trees generated by BTG onto source-side parse trees. The challenge, however, is that BTG hierarchical structures are not always aligned with the linguistic structures in syntactic parse trees of the source or target language. Therefore, we introduce an annotation algorithm to label both syntactic phrases and non-syntactic phrases that are not aligned with any syntactic constituents in source-side parse trees with syntactic elements. The annotated syntactic elements are then used as reordering features for the syntactically annotated reordering model. In order to investigate the impacts imposed by syntactic knowledge on phrase reordering, we also introduce a syntax-based reordering analysis method and conduct a thorough study on the impacts of syntactic knowledge on phrase reordering with this method.

Chapter 4 elaborates yet another reordering approach: *semantically informed reordering* that incorporates semantic knowledge from predicate-argument structures into reordering. Predicate-argument structure contains rich semantic information about which current statistical machine translation has not taken full advantage. Due to this semantic insensitiveness, one common error in statistical machine translation is about argument reordering: arguments are placed at incorrect positions after translation. In order to reduce such errors, we introduce a semantically informed reordering model that uses the position of a predicate as the reference axis to estimate positions of its associated arguments on the target side. In this way, the model predicts moving directions of arguments relative to their predicates with semantic features.

Chapter 5 describes a *lexicalized bracketing* approach to the bracketing issue. We automatically learn lexical features from word-aligned training data and use them to detect source segments that can be bracketed and translated as a unit. In particular, we build two classifiers to predict the beginning and ending positions for such source segments. In the penalty model, we output the best sequence of beginning and ending positions from the two classifiers and then build a penalty feature that penalizes translation hypotheses whenever they cross those source segment beginning and ending positions. In order to take full advantage of the classifiers learned from training data, we extend the penalty model to the lexicalized bracketing model that integrates the whole classifiers into the decoder rather than the best sequence of beginning and ending positions generated by the classifiers.

Instead of using two classifiers to detect the beginning and ending positions for a source segment that can be bracketed and translated together, we introduce a *linguistically motivated bracketing* approach in Chap. 6 that directly determines whether a source segment can be bracketed and translated as a unit or not. We achieve this by using high-level information: syntactic and semantic structure knowledge. In the syntax-driven bracketing model, we employ syntactic knowledge from source-side parse trees to determine whether a source segment is bracketable. In the semantically informed argument bracketing model, we focus on argument translations and use semantic features from predicate-argument structures to predict whether an argument can be translated as a unit.

Chapter 7 presents a framework for translation rule selection based on document-level semantic knowledge, particularly the gist of a document. Translation rule selection is the task of selecting appropriate translation rules for an ambiguous source-language segment. We represent the gist of a document as the topic of the document. Therefore, we introduce two topic-based models for translation rule selection, which incorporates global topic information into translation disambiguation. We associate each synchronous translation rule with source- and target-side topic distributions. With these topic distributions, we propose a topic dissimilarity model to select desirable (less dissimilar) rules by imposing penalties for rules with a large value of dissimilarity of their topic distributions to those of given documents. In order to encourage the use of non-topic-specific translation rules, we also present a topic sensitivity model to balance translation rule selection between generic rules and topic-specific rules. Furthermore, we project target-side topic distributions onto the source-side topic model space so that we can benefit from topic information about both the source and target language. We integrate the proposed topic dissimilarity and sensitivity model into hierarchical phrase-based machine translation for synchronous translation rule selection.

Chapter 8 discusses translation error detection with linguistic features. Automatic error detection is desired in the post-processing to improve machine translation quality. The previous work is largely based on confidence estimation using system-based features, such as word posterior probabilities calculated from N-best lists or word lattices. We propose to incorporate two groups of linguistic features, which convey information from outside machine translation systems, into error detection: lexical and syntactic features. We use a maximum entropy classifier to predict translation errors by integrating word posterior probability feature and linguistic features.

Chapter 9 concludes this book with a review of linguistically motivated SMT, especially those linguistically motivated models and algorithms introduced in this book from a linguistic perspective. We also discuss the future directions for linguistically motivated SMT in this chapter.

Chapter 2
BTG-Based SMT

Abstract This chapter systematically introduces *BTG-based SMT*. We first introduce the Bracketing Transduction Grammar and a unified framework for BTG-based SMT, including the model and decoding algorithm that does not integrate language model. We then present an algorithm to integrate standard n-gram language models into the decoder. Following that, we describe two extensions to these traditional language models: a backward language model that augments the conventional forward language model, and a mutual information trigger model which captures long-distance dependencies that go beyond the scope of standard n-gram language models. By these two models, we attempt to enhance the ability of conventional n-gram language models in capturing richer contexts and long-distance dependencies. Finally, we thoroughly compare BTG-based SMT with other SMT formalisms, such as (hierarchical) phrase-based and linguistically syntax-based SMT, so that we can clearly understand the strengths and weaknesses of BTG-based SMT.

BTG-based SMT is one of state-of-the-art SMT formalisms, which is comparable to hierarchical phrase-based and syntax-based SMT in terms of BLEU-measured translation quality (He et al. 2008). BTG-based SMT possesses the following characteristics.

- It is capable of long-distance and hierarchical reordering.
- It is built upon the minimum case of synchronous context-free grammars, which avoids extracting a large number of rarely used translation rules.
- It is both phrase-based and formally syntax-based SMT. It is phrase-based SMT because it uses phrases as translation units, while formally syntax-based SMT in that it constructs hierarchal structures during translation. From this perspective, BTG-based SMT is a natural bridge that connects both phrase-based and syntax-based SMT.

Because of these properties of BTG-based SMT, we select it as the base platform to discuss linguistically motivated SMT in some chapters.

D. Xiong and M. Zhang, *Linguistically Motivated Statistical Machine Translation*, DOI 10.1007/978-981-287-356-9_2

   This chapter serves the purpose of systematically introducing BTG-based SMT. The remainder of this chapter proceeds as follows.

- Section 2.1 provides a gentle introduction of Bracketing Transduction Grammar.
- Section 2.2 describes a unified framework for BTG-based SMT, including the whole log-linear model, CKY-style decoding algorithm, and reordering model.
- Section 2.3 elaborates the n-gram language model integration algorithm.
- Section 2.4 presents two extensions to the standard n-gram language model: (1) a backward language model that augments a conventional forward n-gram language model with succeeding words and (2) a trigger language model that captures long-distance dependencies that go beyond the scope of the standard n-gram language model. We give details of these two extensions on modeling, training procedure, and decoding integration.
- Section 2.5 introduces two threshold pruning methods that speed up the CKY-style decoder of BTG-based SMT.
- In order to highlight the strengths and weaknesses of BTG-based SMT, we compare it with other SMT formalisms from various perspectives in Sect. 2.6.
- Finally, we summarize the chapter in Sect. 2.7 and provide additional readings.

2.1 Bracketing Transduction Grammar

The normal form of Bracketing Transduction Grammar is first proposed by Wu (1996) for word-based machine translation. It is formulated as follows:

$$
\begin{aligned}
X &\rightarrow [X_1, X_2] \\
X &\rightarrow \langle X_1, X_2 \rangle \\
X &\rightarrow e/f \\
X &\rightarrow \epsilon/f \\
X &\rightarrow e/\epsilon
\end{aligned}
\tag{2.1}
$$

The first two productions are *bracketing rules* which combine two neighboring items into a larger item in a *straight* or *inverted* order. Here we use "[]" to denote a straight order and "⟨⟩" an inverted order. The two bracketing rules can be also written as

$$
\begin{aligned}
X &\rightarrow X_1 X_2 / X_1 X_2 \\
X &\rightarrow X_1 X_2 / X_2 X_1
\end{aligned}
$$

This clearly explains the meaning of the straight/inverted orientation. In the straight order, the first nonterminal on the source side is aligned to the first nonterminal on the target side, the second to the second. In other words, the source and target side have the same word order. In the inverted orientation, however, the first nonterminal on the source side is aligned to the second on the target side and the second to the first. This means that on the target side, the word order is completely reversed.

The last three productions are *lexical rules* which respectively translate a source word f to a target word e, f to the null word ε and the null word to the target word e.

BTG is a simplified version of Inversion Transduction Grammar (ITG) (Wu 1997) because it only uses one single undifferentiated nonterminal. As it contains only one nonterminal and five productions, BTG can also be considered as the minimal case of synchronous context-free grammars (SCFG[1]) which can be used for machine translation or bilingual parsing. Even so, this grammar is able to cover the full range of reorderings generated by any ITG (Wu 1997). Furthermore, BTG can also model long-distance reorderings with a tractable polynomial time complexity (Wu 1996). This is the most important advantage that motivates the use of BTG in machine translation. We will discuss more about this in Sect. 2.6.

When we adapt BTG to phrasal translation, we only need the following three rules:

$$X \rightarrow [X_1, X_2]$$
$$X \rightarrow \langle X_1, X_2 \rangle \tag{2.2}$$
$$X \rightarrow e/f$$

In comparison with the normal form of BTG as formulated in the Eq. (2.1), two changes are made in the adapted BTG.

- First, e/f represent a target/source phrase which shares the same definition of "phrase" in phrase-based SMT (Koehn et al. 2003), rather than a word.
- Second, in order to be consistent with phrase-based SMT in which null translation is not used (Lopez 2008), we remove the last two rules that involve null translation ϵ in the Eq. (2.1).

We call the SMT formalism built on this adapted BTG as BTG-based SMT.

2.2 A Unified Framework for BTG-Based SMT

We establish a unified framework for BTG-based SMT in this section. We introduce a universal statistical model that estimates scores of the three kinds of BTG rules listed in the Eq. (2.2) with different features. We also describe a CKY-style decoder that does not integrate any language models. Finally, we briefly introduce reordering in BTG-based SMT.

---

[1] Readers who are interested in more details of SCFG application in machine translation can refer to Chiang (2006) and Lopez (2008).

Fig. 2.1 A BTG tree
example. The bar under
nonterminal nodes indicates
that the nodes are generated
using an inverted bracketing
rule

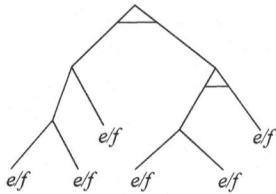

2.2.1 Model

Given the three BTG rules in the Eq. (2.2), we define a BTG derivation $\mathcal{D}$ as a set of independent applications of lexical and bracketing rules as follows:

$$\mathcal{D} = \langle r^l_{1..n_l}, r^b_{1..n_b} \rangle$$

where $r^l_{1..n_l}$ are lexical rules and $r^b_{1..n_b}$ are bracketing rules. Generally, a BTG derivation can be visualized as a binary BTG tree. Figure 2.1 shows a BTG tree example, where leaf nodes are generated by lexical rules and nonterminal nodes generated by bracketing rules.

We assign a score to each rule using the log-linear model (see Sect. 1.1 of Chap. 1) with different features and corresponding weights λs, then multiply them to obtain the statistical model $M(D)$. To keep in line with the common understanding of standard phrase-based SMT (Koehn et al. 2003), here we reorganize these features into the translation model (M_T), reordering model (M_R), and target language model (P_L) as follows:

$$M(D) = M_T(r^l_{1..n_l}) \cdot M_R(r^b_{1..n_b})^{\lambda_R} \cdot P_L(e)^{\lambda_L} \cdot \exp(|e|)^{\lambda_w} \qquad (2.3)$$

where $\exp(|e|)$ is the word penalty, λ_R, λ_L and λ_w are the weight of the reordering model, language model, and word penalty model, respectively.

The translation model M_T is defined as:

$$M_T(r^l_{1..n_l}) = \prod_{i=1}^{n_l} W(r^l_i)$$

$$W(r^l) = P(x|y)^{\lambda_1} \cdot P(y|x)^{\lambda_2} \cdot p_{\text{lex}}(x|y)^{\lambda_3} \cdot p_{\text{lex}}(y|x)^{\lambda_4} \cdot \exp(1)^{\lambda_5} \qquad (2.4)$$

where $W(r)$ is the weight of rule r, $P(\cdot)$ represent the phrase translation probabilities in both directions, $p_{\text{lex}}(\cdot)$ denote the lexical translation probabilities in both directions, and $\exp(1)$ is the phrase penalty. Obviously, the translation model is exactly the same as that in standard phrase-based SMT. In other words, the phrase pairs in the phrase table of phrase-based SMT can be directly used as the lexical rules in BTG-based SMT.

The reordering model M_R is defined on the bracketing rules as follows:

$$M_R(r^b_{1..n_b}) = \prod_{i=1}^{n_b} M_R(r^b_i) \qquad (2.5)$$

One of the most important and challenging tasks to build a BTG-based SMT system is to develop an appropriate reordering model $M_R(r^b)$ on the bracketing rule r^b. Section 2.2.3 will be devoted to various reordering models for BTG-based SMT.

2.2.2 The −LM Decoding Algorithm

Given an input sentence $f_1 \ldots f_J$, the decoder employs BTG rules (see the Eq. (2.2)) to generate derivations for each segment spanning from f_i to f_j. Our goal is to find the best derivation $\mathcal{D}^*$ that covers the whole input sentence. The final translation e^* is produced from the best derivation as follows:

$$\mathcal{D}^* = \operatorname*{argmax}_{f(\mathcal{D})=f_1 \ldots f_J} M(\mathcal{D})$$
$$e^* = e(\mathcal{D}^*) \qquad (2.6)$$

where $f(\mathcal{D})$ and $e(\mathcal{D})$ are the source and target yields of $\mathcal{D}$, respectively.

Because the integration of a standard n-gram language model into a CKY-style decoder is not as natural as the integration into a standard phrase-based decoder (Koehn et al. 2003), we separate the language model integration from the decoding algorithm in this section in order to provide a clear and preliminary understanding of the decoding process. Sections 2.3 and 2.4 will discuss more deeply on the integration of an n-gram language model and its variants into the decoder. We call the decoder without language model −LM decoder.

Following Chiang (2007), we use the deductive proof system (Shieber et al. 1995; Goodman 1999) to describe the −LM decoder. In a deductive proof system, there are two essential elements: weighted item and inference rule. A weighted item is defined as $\mathcal{I} : w$ where $\mathcal{I}$ represents a chart element in a cell, for instance, $[X, i, j]$ which is a nonterminal X spanning from source word i to j, and w is the weight of the element $\mathcal{I}$. We use inference rules to generate new items. For example,

$$\frac{X \to [X_1, X_2] \ [X_1, i, k] : w_1 \ [X_2, k+1, j] : w_2}{[X, i, j] : w_1 w_2 P(X \to [X_1, X_2])}$$

The meaning of an inference rule is that if all terms (items or productions) on the top line is true, we can obtain the item on the bottom line. Therefore, the example mentioned above means that if there are an item with weight w_1 spanning from i to k, and the second item with weight w_2 spanning from $k+1$ to i, we can use

$$\frac{X \to e/f}{[X,i,j] : w} \tag{2.7}$$

$$\frac{X \to [X_1, X_2] \quad [X_1,i,k] : w_1 \quad [X_2, k+1, j] : w_2}{[X,i,j] : w_1 w_2 (M_R(X \to [X_1, X_2]))^{\lambda_R}} \tag{2.8}$$

$$\frac{X \to \langle X_1, X_2 \rangle \quad [X_1,i,k] : w_1 \quad [X_2, k+1, j] : w_2}{[X,i,j] : w_1 w_2 (M_R(X \to \langle X_1, X_2 \rangle))^{\lambda_R}} \tag{2.9}$$

Fig. 2.2 The −LM decoding algorithm

the production $X \to [X_1, X_2]$ to combine these two items and generate a new item spanning from i to j with the weight $w_1 w_2 P(X \to [X_1, X_2])$.

The algorithm of the −LM decoder is shown in Fig. 2.2. The Eq. (2.7) generates an item by using the lexical rule $X \to e/f$ to translate the source phrase f spanning from i to j to the target phrase e. The weight of the item w is calculated as

$$w = W(X \to e/f) \exp(|e|)^{\lambda_w}$$

where $W(X \to e/f)$ is defined in the Eq. (2.4). The Eq. (2.8) combines two neighboring items into a larger item in a straight order and the Eq. (2.9) in an inverted order.

The actual CKY-style decoding procedure is given by the pseudocode in Fig. 2.3. It is easy to prove that the time complexity is $O(J^3)$. We organize all items spanning from i to j into an array $chart[X, i, j]$ (a.k.a. chart cell). First, the chart is initialized

```
1:  Procedure CKYDecode
2:  for all lexical rules X → e/f do
3:      add item [X, i, j] : w to chart[X, i, j]
4:  end for
5:  for span = 1 to J do
6:      for i = 1 to J-span+1 do
7:          j = i+span-1
8:          for k = i to j -1 do
9:              for all items [X, i, k] : w₁ and [X, k + 1, j] : w₂ do
10:                 add [X, i, j] : w₁w₂M_R(X → [X₁, X₂]) to chart[X, i, j]
11:                 add [X, i, j] : w₁w₂M_R(X → ⟨X₁, X₂⟩) to chart[X, i, j]
12:             end for
13:         end for
14:     end for
15: end for
```

Fig. 2.3 CKY decoding procedure for the −LM decoder

with items generated by applying lexical rules $X \rightarrow e/f$ in which f matches some part of the source sentence. Then for each chart cell that spans from i to j on the source side, all possible derivations over this span are generated. The algorithm guarantees that any subcells within (i, j), such as cell $chart[X, i, k]$ or $chart[X, k+1, j]$, have been filled with items before the chart cell $chart[X, i, j]$ is explored. We generate items for chart cell $chart[X, i, j]$ by using inference rules on items from its any two neighboring subcells $chart[X, i, k]$ and $chart[X, k+1, j]$. We enumerate all possible k so that we explore all combinations of neighboring subcells. These inference rules use the bracketing rules with a *straight* or *inverted* order to generate new items covering span (i, j). The score of a newly generated item is derived from the scores of its two subderivations and the reordering model score according to the Eq. (2.5). When the whole input sentence is covered by items, the decoding is completed.

2.2.3 Reordering

In BTG-based SMT, only two reordering orientations are allowed: either in a straight or an inverted order o when two neighboring nodes X_l and X_r are merged into a larger parent node X_p by a bracketing rule r^b. Therefore, it is natural to define the BTG reordering model $M_R(r^b)$ as a function as follows:[2]

$$M_R(r^b) = h(X_l, X_r, X_p, o) \tag{2.10}$$

where $o \in \{straight, inverted\}$.

Based on this function, various reordering models can be built according to different assumptions. For example, the early used flat reordering model in the original BTG (Wu 1996) assigns prior probabilities for the straight and inverted order assuming the order is highly related to the properties of language pairs. It is formulated as

$$M_R(r^b) = \begin{cases} p_s, & o = straight \\ 1 - p_s, & o = inverted \end{cases} \tag{2.11}$$

Supposing French and English are the source and target language, respectively, the value of p_s can be set as high as 0.8 to prefer monotone orientations since the two languages have similar word orders in most cases.

Similar to the distortion model described by Koehn et al. (2003), we can also define a distortion style reordering model for BTG-based SMT as follows:

$$M_R(r^b) = \begin{cases} \exp(0), & o = straight \\ \exp(\|X_p\|), & o = inverted \end{cases} \tag{2.12}$$

where $\|X_p\|$ denotes the number of words on the source side of node X_p.

---

[2] X_l, X_r, X_p are actually undifferentiated nonterminals. The subscripts (l, r, p) here are only for notation convenience.

There is a common problem of the flat and distortion reordering model defined above. They do not take any linguistic contexts into account. To be context-dependent, the BTG reordering model might directly estimate the conditional probability as follows:

$$M_R(r^b) = P_R(r^b) = P(o|X_l, X_r, X_p)$$

This probability could be calculated using the maximum likelihood estimate (MLE) by taking counts from training data in the way of lexicalized reordering model (Tillman 2004; Koehn et al. 2005).

$$P(o|X_l, X_r, X_p) = \frac{\text{Count}(o, X_l, X_r, X_p)}{\text{Count}(X_l, X_r, X_p)} \tag{2.13}$$

Unfortunately, this lexicalized reordering method usually suffers from the serious data sparseness problem because X_l, X_r, and X_p become larger and larger as we recursively generate them by combining their children nodes with the bracketing rules, and finally unseen in the training data.

To avoid data sparseness problem, yet be contextually informative, we take a new perspective of reordering in BTG-based SMT. Since our final purpose is to estimate the probability $P_R(r^b)$ of order $o \in \{straight, inverted\}$ for each bracketing operation, we treat reordering in BTG-based SMT as a binary classification problem where the possible order o between the two children nodes is the target class to be predicted. Statistical classifiers therefore can be used for this order prediction task. We use attributes of nodes X_l, X_r and X_p, instead of nodes themselves, as reordering features in the reordering classifier so that the data sparseness problem of the Eq. (2.13) can be avoided. Chapters 3 and 4 will give more details about this classifier-based reordering.

2.3 n-Gram Language Model Integration

The standard n-gram language model (Goodman 2001) assigns a probability to a hypothesis e_1^I in the target language as follows:

$$P(e_1^I) = \prod_{i=1}^{I} P(e_i|e_1^{i-1}) \approx \prod_{i=1}^{I} P(e_i|e_{i-n+1}^{i-1}) \tag{2.14}$$

where the approximation is based on the nth order Markov assumption: the prediction of word e_i is dependent on the preceding $n - 1$ words $e_{i-n+1} \ldots e_{i-1}$ instead of the whole context history $e_1 \ldots e_{i-1}$.

As we mention in Sect. 2.2.2, the integration of such a language model into the CKY-style decoder is not as trivial as the integration of other models such as the translation model. It is also different from the integration of the n-gram language model into the standard phrase-based decoder (Koehn et al. 2003) in that the preceding $n - 1$ words are not always fully available for words to be predicted when we integrate the n-gram language model into the CKY-style decoder. For example, when we use the lexical rule to translate a source phrase f_i^j into a target phrase e_*^*, the preceding words for the leftmost word of e_*^* are not available as we currently do not know where e_*^* will be placed in the final hypothesis. This section will introduce an algorithm that integrates the n-gram language model into the CKY-style decoder in polynomial time. We call the new decoder integrated with the n-gram language model +LM decoder. We also introduce various pruning methods to speed up the +LM decoder in Sect. 2.5.

Before we introduce the integration algorithm, we define three functions $\mathcal{P}$, $\mathcal{L}$, and $\mathcal{R}$ on a target string e_u^v ($u < v$). The function $\mathcal{P}$ is defined as follows:

$$
\mathcal{P}(e_u \ldots e_v) = \underbrace{P(e_u) \ldots P(e_{u+n-2}|e_u \ldots e_{u+n-3})}_{a}
$$

$$
\times \underbrace{\prod_{u+n-1 \leq i \leq v} P(e_i|e_{i-1} \ldots e_{i-n+1})}_{b} \tag{2.15}
$$

The Eq. (2.15) consists of two parts:

- The first part (a) calculates incomplete n-gram language model probabilities for words e_u to e_{u+n-2} which do not have complete $n - 1$ preceding words. That means, we calculate the unigram probability for e_u ($P(e_u)$), bigram probability for e_{u+1} ($P(e_{u+1}|e_u)$) and so on until we take ($n - 1$)-gram probability for e_{u+n-2} ($P(e_{u+n-2}|e_u \ldots e_{u+n-3})$). This resembles the way in which the language model probability in the future cost is computed in the standard phrase-based SMT decoder (Koehn 2012).
- The second part (b) calculates complete n-gram language model probabilities for word e_{u+n-1} to e_v.

This function is different from Chiang's p function in that the latter function p only calculates language model probabilities for complete n-grams. As we mention before, the preceding context for the current word is either yet to be generated or incomplete in terms of n-grams. The $\mathcal{P}$ function enables us to utilize incomplete preceding context to approximately predict words. Once the preceding $n - 1$ words are fully available, we can quickly update language model probabilities in an efficient way that will be introduced later in the integration algorithm.

The other two functions $\mathcal{L}$ and $\mathcal{R}$ are defined as follows:

$$
\mathcal{L}(e_u \ldots e_v) = \begin{cases} e_u \ldots e_{u+n-2}, & \text{if } |e_u^v| \geq n \\ e_u \ldots e_v, & \text{otherwise} \end{cases} \tag{2.16}
$$

$$
\mathcal{R}(e_u \ldots e_v) = \begin{cases} e_{v-n+2} \ldots e_v, & \text{if } |e_u^v| \geq n \\ e_u \ldots e_v, & \text{otherwise} \end{cases} \tag{2.17}
$$

They return the leftmost and rightmost $n - 1$ words from a string, respectively.

The integration algorithm is shown in Fig. 2.4. The item $[X, i, j; l|r]$ indicates a BTG node X spanning from i to j on the source side with the leftmost|rightmost $n-1$ words $l|r$ on the target side. One difference from the $-$LM decoder (see Fig. 2.2) is that we have to record the leftmost|rightmost $n-1$ words for each item in the $+$LM decoder. These $n-1$ terminal symbols in the target language can be considered as the language model state for an item.

In order to highlight how we integrate the language model, we only display the n-gram language model probability for each item, ignoring all other scores that are displayed in the $-$LM decoding algorithm (Fig. 2.2). The Eq. (2.20) in Fig. 2.4 shows how we calculate the language model probability for a BTG lexicon rule which translates a source phrase c into a target phrase e. The Eqs. (2.21) and (2.22) show how we update the language model probabilities for the two bracketing rules which combine two neighboring phrases in a straight and inverted order, respectively. The fundamental theories behind this update are,

$$\mathcal{P}(e_1 e_2) = \mathcal{P}(e_1)\mathcal{P}(e_2)\frac{\mathcal{P}(\mathcal{R}(e_1)\mathcal{L}(e_2))}{\mathcal{P}(\mathcal{R}(e_1))\mathcal{P}(\mathcal{L}(e_2))} \tag{2.18}$$

$$\mathcal{P}(e_2 e_1) = \mathcal{P}(e_2)\mathcal{P}(e_1)\frac{\mathcal{P}(\mathcal{R}(e_2)\mathcal{L}(e_1))}{\mathcal{P}(\mathcal{R}(e_2))\mathcal{P}(\mathcal{L}(e_1))} \tag{2.19}$$

Whenever two strings e_1 and e_2 are concatenated in a straight or inverted order, we can reuse their $\mathcal{P}$ values ($\mathcal{P}(e_1)$ and $\mathcal{P}(e_2)$) in terms of dynamic programming. Only the probabilities of boundary words (e.g., $\mathcal{R}(e_1)\mathcal{L}(e_2)$ in the Eq. (2.18)) need to

$$\frac{X \rightarrow e/f}{[X, i, j; \mathcal{L}(e)|\mathcal{R}(e)] : \mathcal{P}(e)} \tag{2.20}$$

$$\frac{\begin{array}{l} X \rightarrow [X_1, X_2] \\ [X_1, i, k; \mathcal{L}(e_1)|\mathcal{R}(e_1)] : \mathcal{P}(e_1) \\ [X_2, k+1, j; \mathcal{L}(e_2)|\mathcal{R}(e_2)] : \mathcal{P}(e_2) \end{array}}{[X, i, j; \mathcal{L}(e_1 e_2)|\mathcal{R}(e_1 e_2)] : \mathcal{P}(e_1)\mathcal{P}(e_2)\frac{\mathcal{P}(\mathcal{R}(e_1)\mathcal{L}(e_2))}{\mathcal{P}(\mathcal{R}(e_1))\mathcal{P}(\mathcal{L}(e_2))}} \tag{2.21}$$

$$\frac{\begin{array}{l} X \rightarrow \langle X_1, X_2 \rangle \\ [X_1, i, k; \mathcal{L}(e_1)|\mathcal{R}(e_1)] : \mathcal{P}(e_1) \\ [X_2, k+1, j; \mathcal{L}(e_2)|\mathcal{R}(e_2)] : \mathcal{P}(e_2) \end{array}}{[X, i, j; \mathcal{L}(e_2 e_1)|\mathcal{R}(e_2 e_1)] : \mathcal{P}(e_1)\mathcal{P}(e_2)\frac{\mathcal{P}(\mathcal{R}(e_2)\mathcal{L}(e_1))}{\mathcal{P}(\mathcal{R}(e_2))\mathcal{P}(\mathcal{L}(e_1))}} \tag{2.22}$$

Fig. 2.4 The $+$LM decoding algorithm

Table 2.1 Values of $\mathcal{P}$, $\mathcal{L}$, and $\mathcal{R}$ in a trigram example

Function	Value
e_1	$a_1 a_2 a_3$
e_2	$b_1 b_2 b_3$
$\mathcal{R}(e_1)$	$a_2 a_3$
$\mathcal{L}(e_2)$	$b_1 b_2$
$\mathcal{P}(\mathcal{R}(e_1))$	$P(a_2)P(a_3|a_2)$
$\mathcal{P}(\mathcal{L}(e_2))$	$P(b_1)P(b_2|b_1)$
$\mathcal{P}(e_1)$	$P(a_1)P(a_2|a_1)P(a_3|a_1 a_2)$
$\mathcal{P}(e_2)$	$P(b_1)P(b_2|b_1)P(b_3|b_1 b_2)$
$\mathcal{P}(\mathcal{R}(e_1)\mathcal{L}(e_2))$	$P(a_2)P(a_3|a_2)$
	$P(b_1|a_2 a_3)P(b_2|a_3 b_1)$
$\mathcal{P}(e_1 e_2)$	$P(a_1)P(a_2|a_1)P(a_3|a_1 a_2)$
	$P(b_1|a_2 a_3)P(b_2|a_3 b_1)P(b_3|b_1 b_2)$

be recalculated since they have complete *n*-grams after the concatenation. Table 2.1 shows values of $\mathcal{P}$, $\mathcal{L}$, and $\mathcal{R}$ in a 3-gram example which helps to verify the Eq. (2.18). These two equations guarantee that the +LM decoding algorithm can correctly compute the language model probability of a sentence stepwise in a dynamic programming framework.[3]

Because in the update parts in the Eqs. (2.18) and (2.19) both the numerator and denominator have up to $2(n-1)$ terminal symbols, the theoretical time complexity of the +LM decoding algorithm is $\mathcal{O}(J^3|T|^{4(n-1)})$ where T is the target language terminal alphabet. This is the same as the time complexity of Chiang's language model integration (Chiang 2007). Practically, this is very slow. Therefore, we have to use various beam search methods for search space pruning.

2.4 Two Extensions to *n*-Gram Language Model

Language model is one of the most important knowledge sources for statistical machine translation. It is commonly assumed that the quality of language model has great impact on the fluency of target translations. A great variety of methods can be used to improve the quality of language model. The following approaches are widely adopted in the literature of statistical machine translation.

- *Large language model*. More data is better data. Trillions of English words are used to construct a huge language model in a distributed manner (Brants et al. 2007).

---

[3] The start-of-sentence symbol $\langle s \rangle$ and end-of-sentence symbol $\langle /s \rangle$ can be easily added to update the final language model probability when a translation hypothesis covering the whole source sentence is completed.

- *Language model adaptation.* Language models are adapted to a new domain where an SMT system trained in a different domain is tested (Zhao et al. 2004).
- *Structured language model.* In order to capture long-distance dependencies, syntax-based language models are trained on constituent parse trees or dependency trees (Charniak et al. 2003; Shen et al. 2008; Hassan et al. 2008).

In this section, we focus on techniques that enable standard n-gram language models to capture rich contexts. Our goal is similar to that of structured language models. However, we do not resort to any additional language resources such as parsers. In particular,

1. We build a *backward n-gram language model* that augments a conventional forward n-gram language model with succeeding words.
2. We build a mutual information *trigger language model* which captures long-distance dependencies that go beyond the scope of standard n-gram language models.

The following two Sects. 2.4.1 and 2.4.2 elaborate the backward language model and trigger language model, respectively, with details on modeling, training procedure, and integration algorithm.

2.4.1 Backward Language Model

In this section, we will introduce the backward language model that predicts current words conditioning on their succeeding words, rather than preceding words. Conventional n-gram language models look at the preceding $n - 1$ words when calculating the probability of the current word. We henceforth call the previous $n - 1$ words plus the current word as *forward n-grams* and a language model built on forward n-grams as forward n-gram language model. Similarly, *backward n-grams* refer to the succeeding $n - 1$ words plus the currrent word. We train a backward n-gram language model on backward n-grams and integrate the forward and backward language models together into the decoder. In doing so, we are able to capture both the preceding and succeeding context of a word to be predicted.

2.4.1.1 Model

Given a sequence of words $e_1^I = (e_1 \ldots e_I)$, the backward n-gram language model assigns a probability $P_b(e_1^I)$ to e_1^I conditioning on the succeeding context as follows:

$$P_b(e_1^I) = \prod_{i=1}^{I} P(e_i|e_{i+1}^I) \approx \prod_{i=1}^{I} P(e_i|e_{i+1}^{i+n-1}) \tag{2.23}$$

This is different from the forward n-gram language model formulated in the Eq. (2.14) which instead uses the preceding context.

2.4.1.2 Training

For the convenience of training, we invert the order in each sentence in the training data, i.e., from the original order $(e_1 \ldots e_I)$ to the reverse order $(e_I \ldots e_1)$. In this way, we can use the same toolkit[4] that we use to train a forward n-gram language model to train a backward n-gram language model without any other changes. To be consistent with training, we also need to reverse the order of translation hypotheses when we access the trained backward language model. Note that the Markov context history of the Eq. (2.23) is $e_{i+n-1} \ldots e_{i+1}$ instead of $e_{i+1} \ldots e_{i+n-1}$ after we invert the order. The words are the same but the order is completely reversed.

2.4.1.3 Decoding

The decoding algorithm with a backward n-gram language model is similar to the algorithm shown in Fig. 2.4, which integrates a forward n-gram language model into the CKY-style decoder. The biggest difference is that all input strings of the backward language model are in a reverse order. Therefore, we need to redefine the three functions $\mathcal{P}$, $\mathcal{L}$, and $\mathcal{R}$ on a target string in a reverse order.

The function $\mathcal{P}$ is reformulated on a reversed string $e_v \ldots e_u$ ($u < v$) as follows:

$$\mathcal{P}(e_v \ldots e_u) = \underbrace{P(e_v) \ldots P(e_{v-n+2}|e_v \ldots e_{v-n+3})}_{a}$$
$$\times \underbrace{\prod_{v-n+1 \geq i \geq u} P(e_i|w_{i+n-1} \ldots w_{i+1})}_{b} \qquad (2.24)$$

The part (a) calculates incomplete backward n-gram language model probabilities for word e_v to e_{v-n+2}, while the part (b) estimates complete backward n-gram language model probabilities for word e_{v-n+1} to e_u (see Sect. 2.3 for more details about (a) and (b) on the forward language model).

The other two functions $\mathcal{L}$ and $\mathcal{R}$ are redefined as follows:

$$\mathcal{L}(e_v \ldots e_u) = \begin{cases} e_v \ldots e_{v-n+2}, & \text{if } |e_v^u| \geq n \\ e_v \ldots e_u, & \text{otherwise} \end{cases} \qquad (2.25)$$

$$\mathcal{R}(e_v \ldots e_u) = \begin{cases} e_{u+n-2} \ldots e_u, & \text{if } |e_v^u| \geq n \\ e_v \ldots e_u, & \text{otherwise} \end{cases} \qquad (2.26)$$

---

[4] For example, the SRI language modeling toolkit (Stolcke 2002).

The $\mathcal{L}$ and $\mathcal{R}$ function return the leftmost and rightmost $n-1$ words from a string in a reverse order, respectively.

The decoding algorithm with the backward language model is shown in Fig. 2.5, where $\bar{e}$ denotes the reversed e. Once again in (2.30) and (2.31), we calculate the backward language model probability for a reversed string in a dynamic programming manner based on the following equations.

$$\mathcal{P}(\overline{e_1 e_2}) = \mathcal{P}(\overline{e_1})\mathcal{P}(\overline{e_2})\frac{\mathcal{P}(\mathcal{R}(\overline{e_2})\mathcal{L}(\overline{e_1}))}{\mathcal{P}(\mathcal{R}(\overline{e_2}))\mathcal{P}(\mathcal{L}(\overline{e_1}))} \tag{2.27}$$

$$\mathcal{P}(\overline{e_2 e_1}) = \mathcal{P}(\overline{e_1})\mathcal{P}(\overline{e_2})\frac{\mathcal{P}(\mathcal{R}(\overline{e_1})\mathcal{L}(\overline{e_2}))}{\mathcal{P}(\mathcal{R}(\overline{e_1}))\mathcal{P}(\mathcal{L}(\overline{e_2}))} \tag{2.28}$$

Figure 2.6 displays a real-world example to show how we update the score of a five-gram backward language model when two items are merged. Let us take the item X_{01} for instance. This item is the combination of the item X_0 (with target string $e_1 =$ "understand") and X_1 (with target string $e_2 =$ "that Africa can no longer") in a straight order. The backward language model costs (i.e., $\log\mathcal{P}(\overline{e_1})$ and $\log\mathcal{P}(\overline{e_2})$) of item X_0 and X_1 are -4.52 and -9.67, respectively. The leftmost four words of $\overline{e_1}$ (i.e., $\mathcal{L}(\overline{e_1})$) comprise only the single word "understand," while the rightmost four words of $\overline{e_2}$ (i.e., $\mathcal{R}(\overline{e_2})$) are "no can Africa that". According to the Eq. (2.27), the backward language model cost of the item X_{01} should be $(-4.52) + (-9.67) + (-14.71) - (-4.52) - (-11.25) = -13.13$. Similarly, we can easily calculate the backward language model score of item X_{012} when we merge item X_{01} and X_2. Note that we

$$\frac{X \to e/f}{[X, i, j; \mathcal{L}(\bar{e})|\mathcal{R}(\bar{e})] : \mathcal{P}(\bar{e})} \tag{2.29}$$

$$\frac{\begin{array}{l} X \to [X_1, X_2] \\ [X_1, i, k; \mathcal{L}(\overline{e_1})|\mathcal{R}(\overline{e_1})] : \mathcal{P}(\overline{e_1}) \\ [X_2, k+1, j; \mathcal{L}(\overline{e_2})|\mathcal{R}(\overline{e_2})] : \mathcal{P}(\overline{e_2}) \end{array}}{[X, i, j; \mathcal{L}(\overline{e_1 e_2})|\mathcal{R}(\overline{e_1 e_2})] : \mathcal{P}(\overline{e_1})\mathcal{P}(\overline{e_2})\frac{\mathcal{P}(\mathcal{R}(\overline{e_2})\mathcal{L}(\overline{e_1}))}{\mathcal{P}(\mathcal{L}(\overline{e_1}))\mathcal{P}(\mathcal{R}(\overline{e_2}))}} \tag{2.30}$$

$$\frac{\begin{array}{l} X \to \langle X_1, X_2 \rangle \\ [X_1, i, k; \mathcal{L}(\overline{e_1})|\mathcal{R}(\overline{e_1})] : \mathcal{P}(\overline{e_1}) \\ [X_2, k+1, j; \mathcal{L}(\overline{e_2})|\mathcal{R}(\overline{e_2})] : \mathcal{P}(\overline{e_2}) \end{array}}{[X, i, j; \mathcal{L}(\overline{e_2 e_1})|\mathcal{R}(\overline{e_2 e_1})] : \mathcal{P}(\overline{e_1})\mathcal{P}(\overline{e_2})\frac{\mathcal{P}(\mathcal{R}(\overline{e_1})\mathcal{L}(\overline{e_2}))}{\mathcal{P}(\mathcal{L}(\overline{e_2}))\mathcal{P}(\mathcal{R}(\overline{e_1}))}} \tag{2.31}$$

Fig. 2.5 The +LM decoding algorithm with the backward n-gram language model

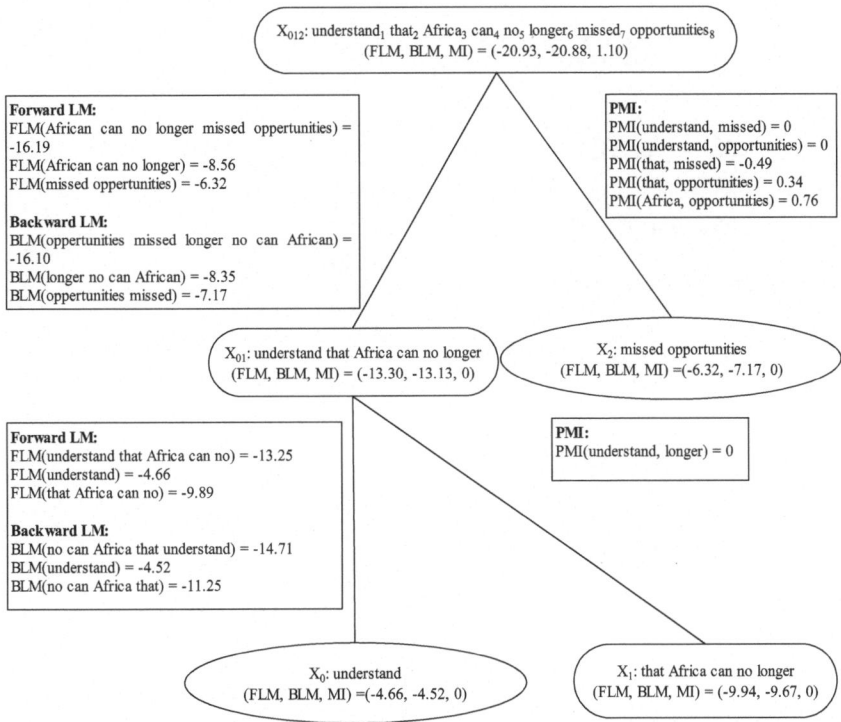

Fig. 2.6 A BTG tree fragment showing how the values of the forward (FLM), backward (BLM), and mutual information trigger (MI) language model are computed. The rectangles display the FLM/BLM costs (log (base-10) probabilities) of target strings as well as the PMI values of trigger pairs that are used to calculate the FLM/BLM/MI values of the item X_{01} (the combination of item X_0 and X_1) and X_{012} (the combination of item X_{01} and X_2)

can store the calculated backward language model scores of the leftmost/rightmost words of each item in practice to save time.

We can also integrate both the forward language model and backward language model into the CKY-style decoder at the same time. The decoding algorithm with the two language models is shown in Fig. 2.7.

2.4.2 Trigger Language Model

It is well-known that long-distance dependencies between words are very important for statistical language modeling. However, conventional *n*-gram language models can only capture short-distance dependencies within an *n*-word window. If the current word is indexed as e_i, the farthest word that a conventional forward *n*-gram includes is e_{i-n+1}. In this section, we introduce a *trigger language model* that is capable of

$$\frac{X \to e/f}{[X,i,j;\mathcal{L}(\overline{e})|\mathcal{R}(\overline{e})] : \mathcal{P}(e)\mathcal{P}(\overline{e})} \tag{2.32}$$

$$
\begin{array}{c}
X \to [X_1, X_2] \\
[X_1, i, k; \mathcal{L}(e_1)|\mathcal{R}(e_1)] : \mathcal{P}(e_1)\mathcal{P}(\overline{e_1}) \\
[X_2, k+1, j; \mathcal{L}(e_2)|\mathcal{R}(e_2)] : \mathcal{P}(e_2)\mathcal{P}(\overline{e_2}) \\
\hline
[X, i, j; \mathcal{L}(e_1 e_2)|\mathcal{R}(e_1 e_2)] : \mathcal{P}(e_1)\mathcal{P}(e_2)\dfrac{\mathcal{P}(\mathcal{R}(e_1)\mathcal{L}(e_2))}{\mathcal{P}(\mathcal{R}(e_1))\mathcal{P}(\mathcal{L}(e_2))} \times \\
\mathcal{P}(\overline{e_1})\mathcal{P}(\overline{e_2})\dfrac{\mathcal{P}(\mathcal{R}(\overline{e_2})\mathcal{L}(\overline{e_1}))}{\mathcal{P}(\mathcal{R}(\overline{e_2}))\mathcal{P}(\mathcal{L}(\overline{e_1}))}
\end{array}
\tag{2.33}
$$

$$
\begin{array}{c}
X \to \langle X_1, X_2 \rangle \\
[X_1, i, k; \mathcal{L}(e_1)|\mathcal{R}(e_1)] : \mathcal{P}(e_1)\mathcal{P}(\overline{e_1}) \\
[X_2, k+1, j; \mathcal{L}(e_2)|\mathcal{R}(e_2)] : \mathcal{P}(e_2)\mathcal{P}(\overline{e_2}) \\
\hline
[X, i, j; \mathcal{L}(e_1 e_2)|\mathcal{R}(e_1 e_2)] : \mathcal{P}(e_1)\mathcal{P}(e_2)\dfrac{\mathcal{P}(\mathcal{R}(e_2)\mathcal{L}(e_1))}{\mathcal{P}(\mathcal{R}(e_2))\mathcal{P}(\mathcal{L}(e_1))} \times \\
\mathcal{P}(\overline{e_1})\mathcal{P}(\overline{e_2})\dfrac{\mathcal{P}(\mathcal{R}(\overline{e_1})\mathcal{L}(\overline{e_2}))}{\mathcal{P}(\mathcal{R}(\overline{e_1}))\mathcal{P}(\mathcal{L}(\overline{e_2}))}
\end{array}
\tag{2.34}
$$

Fig. 2.7 The +LM decoding algorithm with the forward and backward n-gram language model

detecting long-distance dependencies that go beyond the scope of traditional forward n-grams, e.g., dependencies between e_i and words from e_1 to e_{i-n}.

2.4.2.1 Model

The trigger language model measures the dependency between two words of a trigger pair. Formally, a trigger pair is defined as an ordered two-tuple (x, y) where word x occurs in the preceding context of word y. It can also be denoted in a more visual manner as $x \to y$ with x being the trigger and y the triggered word.

We use pointwise mutual information (PMI) (Church and Hanks 1990) to measure the strength of the association between x and y, which is defined as follows:

$$\text{PMI}(x, y) = \log\left(\frac{P(x,y)}{P(x)P(y)}\right) \tag{2.35}$$

Zhou (2004) proposes a new language model that is also enhanced with trigger pairs. In his model, the probability of a given sentence e_1^m is approximated as

$$P(e_1^m) \approx (\prod_{i=1}^{m} P(e_i|e_{i-n+1}^{i-1}))$$

$$\times \prod_{i=n+1}^{m} \prod_{k=1}^{i-n} \exp(\text{PMI}(e_k, e_i, i-k-1)) \qquad (2.36)$$

There are two components in his model. The first component is still the standard *n*-gram language model. The second one is the mutual information (MI) trigger language model which multiples all exponential PMI values for trigger pairs where the current word is the triggered word and all preceding words outside the *n*-gram window of the current word are triggers. Note that his MI trigger language model is distance-dependent since trigger pairs (e_k, e_i) are sensitive to their distance $i - k - 1$ (zero distance for adjacent words). Therefore, the distance between word x and word y should be taken into account when calculating their PMI.

In order to avoid serious data sparseness, we adopt a *distance-independent* MI trigger language model as follows:

$$\text{MI}(e_1^m) = \prod_{i=n+1}^{m} \prod_{k=1}^{i-n} \exp(\text{PMI}(e_k, e_i)) \qquad (2.37)$$

We integrate the distance-independent MI trigger language model into the log-linear model of machine translation as an additional knowledge source which complements the standard *n*-gram language model in capturing long-distance dependencies. By the minimum error rate training (Och 2003), we are able to tune the weight of the MI trigger langauge model against the weight of the standard *n*-gram language model while Zhou (2004) sets equal weights for both models.

2.4.2.2 Training

We can use the maximum likelihood estimation method to calculate PMI for each trigger pair by taking counts from training data. Let $C(x, y)$ be the co-occurrence count of the trigger pair (x, y) in the training data. The joint probability of (x, y) is calculated as follows:

$$P(x, y) = \frac{C(x, y)}{\sum_{x,y} C(x, y)} \qquad (2.38)$$

The marginal probabilities of x and y can be deduced from the joint probability as follows:

$$P(x) = \sum_{y} P(x, y) \qquad (2.39)$$

$$P(y) = \sum_{x} P(x, y) \qquad (2.40)$$

Since the number of distinct trigger pairs is $\mathcal{O}(|T|^2)$, the question is how to select valuable trigger pairs. We select trigger pairs according to the following three steps.

(1) The distance between x and y must not be less than $n - 1$. Suppose we use a five-gram language model and $y = e_i$, then $x \in \{e_1 \ldots e_{i-5}\}$. This is because local dependencies within the n-word window are already captured by the standard n-gram language model. The trigger language model therefore focuses on long-distance dependencies outside the n-word window.
(2) $C(x, y) > c$. We set $c = 10$. This will remove noisy trigger pairs.
(3) Finally, we only keep trigger pairs whose PMI value is larger than 0. Trigger pairs whose PMI value is less than 0 often contain stop words, such as "the", "a". These stop words have very large marginal probabilities due to their high frequencies.

2.4.2.3 Decoding

We integrate the MI trigger model into BTG-based SMT system still in a dynamic programming fashion. In particular, we calculate MI trigger model scores for two strings e_1 and e_2 that are concatenated in a straight ($e_1 e_2$) or inverted ($e_2 e_1$) order as follows:

$$\text{MI}(e_1 e_2) = \text{MI}(e_1)\text{MI}(e_2)\text{MI}(e_1 \mapsto e_2) \tag{2.41}$$

$$\text{MI}(e_2 e_1) = \text{MI}(e_2)\text{MI}(e_1)\text{MI}(e_2 \mapsto e_1) \tag{2.42}$$

where $\text{MI}(e_1 \mapsto e_2)$ represents the PMI values for all trigger pairs in which a word in e_1 triggers a word in e_2. It is defined as follows:

$$\text{MI}(e_1 \mapsto e_2) = \prod_{w_i \in e_2} \prod_{\substack{w_k \in e_1 \\ i-k \geq n}} \exp(\text{PMI}(w_k, w_i)) \tag{2.43}$$

Similarly, we can obtain $\text{MI}(e_2 \mapsto e_1)$ as follows:

$$\text{MI}(e_2 \mapsto e_1) = \prod_{w_i \in e_1} \prod_{\substack{w_k \in e_2 \\ i-k \geq n}} \exp(\text{PMI}(w_k, w_i)) \tag{2.44}$$

The integration algorithm is shown in Fig. 2.8. The problem here is that the state of the MI trigger model involves all words in a string. It is different from the state of n-gram language model as the latter only considers the preceding or succeeding $n - 1$ words. If we define the MI trigger model state as the whole string involved, it results in an intractable integration algorithm as we cannot resort to hypotheses recombination for search space pruning. In order to make the integration algorithm tractable, we still use the outermost $n - 1$ words to define the MI trigger model state.

$$\frac{X \rightarrow e/f}{[X,i,j] : MI(e)} \tag{2.45}$$

$$\frac{X \rightarrow [X_1, X_2] \quad [X_1, i, k] : MI(e_1) \quad [X_2, k+1, j] : MI(e_2)}{[X, i, j] : MI(e_1)MI(e_2)MI(e_1 \mapsto e_2)} \tag{2.46}$$

$$\frac{X \rightarrow \langle X_1, X_2 \rangle \quad [X_1, i, k] : MI(e_1) \quad [X_2, k+1, j] : MI(e_2)}{[X, i, j] : MI(e_1)MI(e_2)MI(e_2 \mapsto e_1)} \tag{2.47}$$

Fig. 2.8 The decoding algorithm with the trigger language model

Although this will lead to search errors, we can benefit from the MI trigger model for long-distance dependencies in a tractable way.

Let us revisit Fig. 2.6 in order to get a clear picture of how we calculate the mutual information trigger language model. This time, we take the item X_{012} (the combination of item X_{01} and X_2) as an example. The MI trigger language model score of item X_2 (log value of the Eq. (2.37)) is 0 as there are no two words whose distance is equal or larger than 4. For item X_{01}, although the distance of the two words (understand, longer) is equal to 4, they are not selected as a trigger pair as the two words co-occur rarely. Therefore, the default MI value for these two words is set 0. When we combine item X_{01} and X_2 into item X_{012}, the MI trigger language model score of item X_{012} will be deduced from $MI(X_{01})$, $MI(X_2)$, and all trigger pairs (x, y) where x and y are in X_{01} and X_2, respectively, and their distance is not less than 4. The qualified trigger pairs therefore include (understand, missed), (understand, opportunities), (that, missed), (that, opportunities), and (Africa, opportunities). Their PMI values are shown in the PMI rectangle in Fig. 2.6. As we only use trigger pairs whose PMI value is larger than 0, the final MI trigger language model score of item X_{012} is calculated as $MI(X_{01}) + MI(X_2) + PMI(\text{that, opportunities}) + PMI(\text{Africa, opportunities}) = 1.10$ according to the Eq. (2.43).

2.5 Pruning

Search space pruning is very important for SMT decoders. Normally, the following four pruning methods are widely used in SMT systems. We introduce them in the context of BTG-based SMT.

- *Hypothesis recombination.* Whenever two partial hypotheses in the same cell are equivalent, we will recombine them by discarding the one with a lower score. By equivalence, we mean that the two partial hypotheses cover the same span on the source side and contain the same leftmost/rightmost $n - 1$ words on the target side. Recombination can safely prune hypotheses which will not be included in the final best translation.

- *Threshold pruning*. It discards partial hypotheses with a score worse than α times the best score in the same cell.
- *Histogram pruning*. It only keeps the top N best hypotheses for each cell.
- *Cube pruning*. Suppose we have 100 partial hypotheses exactly covering the source span (i, k) and 100 hypotheses for the source span $(k + 1, j)$. When we use the bracketing rules to combine the two neighboring spans, we will have $2 \times 100 \times 100 = 200{,}000$ new hypotheses which exactly cover the source span (i, j). Most of them will be immediately deleted if we only keep the top 100 best hypotheses for each span. A better way to generate new hypotheses is to only generate hypotheses that have a higher chance to be kept in the top 100. This is the philosophy behind cube pruning that sorts the hypotheses in two neighboring spans by their scores and selects top hypotheses to generate the most promising new hypotheses. This pruning method is first proposed by Chiang (2007).

In this section, we will introduce two variants on the conventional threshold pruning method, both of which speed up the decoding without degrading the performance. The first variant is the dynamic threshold pruning, in which the beam threshold varies with the length of source sequences covered by hypotheses. The second one incorporates a language model dependent probability into the threshold pruning, so that the interaction between a hypothesis and the context outside the hypothesis can be captured.

2.5.1 Dynamic Threshold Pruning

Generally, if we use a loose beam threshold to retain as many hypotheses as possible, the speed of decoding will be very slow, although the translation quality may remain high. On the other hand, if we use a tight beam threshold to prune as many hypotheses as possible, we can get a considerable speedup. However, it comes at a cost of degraded translation quality. Therefore, the question is how we can find an appropriate beam threshold to get the best trade-off between the translation quality and decoding speed. Unfortunately, we are not able to find such an ideal beam threshold since we do not know exactly the distribution of hypotheses beforehand.

Most researchers empirically select a beam threshold on a development set and then use it constantly on a test set. We call this strategy *fixed threshold pruning* (FTP). In order to guarantee a high translation quality, a loose beam threshold is usually used at the cost of slow decoding speed.

A better strategy is to dynamically adjust the beam threshold with a hidden variable. Here, we define the variable as a ratio r (seq/sent) between the length of a source sequence covered by a partial hypothesis and the length of the whole sentence to be translated. To investigate how we should vary the beam threshold with the length

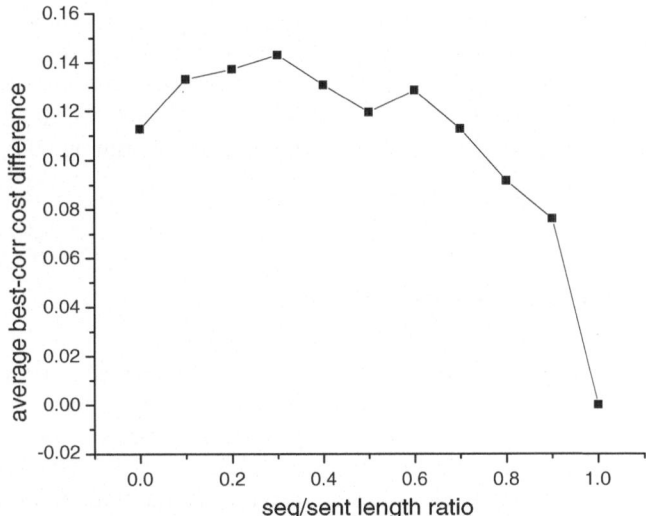

Fig. 2.9 Average best-corr cost difference versus seq/sent length ratio on the NIST MT-02

ratio r, we trace the cost[5] difference (best-corr) between the best hypothesis and the correct hypothesis[6] in chart cells on the NIST MT-02 test set (878 sentences, 19.6 words per sentence). We use a very loose beam threshold[7] to translate sentences on the test set. We plot the curve of average best-corr cost difference versus seq/sent length ratio in Fig. 2.9, which visualizes how wide we should set the beam, so that correct hypotheses fall inside the beam.

From this figure, we can observe that in most cases, the longer the source fragment covered by a hypothesis, the smaller the cost difference between the correct hypothesis and the best hypothesis. This means that we can safely use a tighter beam threshold for hypotheses covering longer source fragments. It is safe because correct hypotheses are still included in the beam, while incorrect hypotheses are pruned as many as possible. However, for hypotheses covering shorter fragments, we should use a looser beam threshold to include all possible candidates for future expansion, so that potential candidates can survive to become part of the finally best hypothesis.

According to this observation, we dynamically adjust the beam threshold parameter α as a function of the length ratio:

$$\alpha = \alpha_0 + (1 - \alpha_0) \cdot r \tag{2.48}$$

---

[5] The cost of a hypothesis is the negative logarithm of the score of it, estimated by the model shown in the Eq. (2.3). The higher the score, the lower the cost.

[6] The correct hypothesis is the hypothesis that is part of the best translation generated by the decoder. The best hypothesis is the hypothesis with the least cost in the current span. Note that the best hypothesis is not always the correct hypothesis.

[7] Here, we loosen the beam threshold gradually until the BLEU (Papineni et al. 2002) score is not changing. Then, we use the last beam threshold we have tried.

where α_0 is the initial value of the beam threshold parameter which is purposely set to a small value to capture most of the candidates during the early stage of decoding. We call this pruning strategy *dynamic threshold pruning* (DTP). DTP increases the parameter α to tighten the beam when more source words are translated. In theory, DTP runs faster than traditional beam threshold pruning FTP at the same performance level.

2.5.2 LM-Dependent Threshold Pruning

In the traditional beam threshold pruning used in SMT decoding, only the probability estimated from inside a partial hypothesis is adopted. This probability does not provide information about the probability of the hypothesis in the context of the complete translation. In A* decoding for SMT (Och et al. 2001; Zhang and Gildea 2006), different heuristic functions are used to estimate a "future" probability for completing a partial hypothesis. In CKY bottom-up parsing, Goodman (1997) introduces a prior probability into the beam threshold pruning. All of these probabilities are capable of capturing contextual information outside partial hypotheses.

In this section, we introduce an LM-dependent probability for threshold pruning. The basic idea behind the LM-dependent threshold pruning is to incorporate the (forward) language model probability of the boundary words of a hypothesis and neighboring words outside the hypothesis on the target side into the pruning process as early as possible. Since the exact neighboring words are not available until the partial hypothesis is completed, we obtain potential neighboring words in two steps as follows:

- *Step 1*: For each sequence of source words $f_i \ldots f_j$, we find its most probable translation $T(f_i \ldots f_j)$ with a monotone search, only considering the translation model and the language model probability. This can be quickly done with dynamic programming, similar to the method described by Koehn (2004). Then, we cache the leftmost/rightmost target boundary words $T^l(f_i \ldots f_j)/T^r(f_i \ldots f_j)$, which both include $n' = \min(n-1, |T(f_i \ldots f_j)|)$ (n is the language model order) words. Since there are only $J(J+1)/2$ continuous sequences for a source sentence of J words, the target boundary words for all these sequences can be quickly found and cached before decoding with a very cheap overhead.
- *Step 2*: for a hypothesis H covering a source span $f_i \ldots f_j$, we look up the leftmost/rightmost target boundary words of its neighboring spans:

$$T^l(f_1 \ldots f_{i-1})/T^r(f_1 \ldots f_{i-1}) \text{ and } T^l(f_{j+1} \ldots f_J)/T^r(f_{j+1} \ldots s_J)$$

which are cached in the first step. Although these boundary words are not exactly adjacent to H since there exist thousands of word reorderings, they still provide context information for language model interaction. We utilize them according to the following two reordering options.

Fig. 2.10 Two reordering options (straight (**a**) and inverted (**b**)) for language model dependent threshold pruning

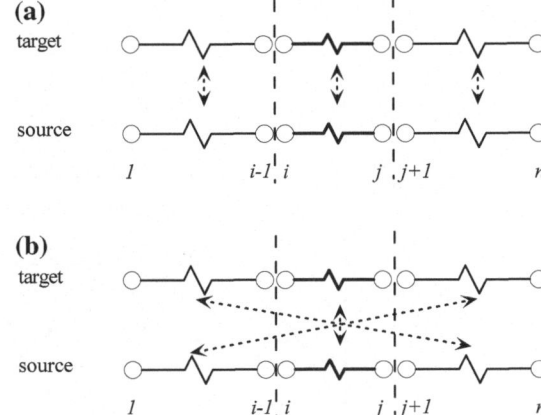

– If a straight order is preferred (Fig. 2.10a), the LM-dependent threshold probability $\pi_s(H)$ can be estimated as follows:

$$\pi_s(H) = \mathcal{P}(T^r(f_1 \ldots f_{i-1})H^l) \cdot \mathcal{P}(H^r T^l(f_{j+1} \ldots f_J)) \qquad (2.49)$$

where $H^{l/r}$ are the leftmost/rightmost boundary words of H, which both include $m' = \min(m-1, |H|)$ words, the function $\mathcal{P}$ is defined in the Eq. (2.15).

– If an inverted order is preferred (Fig. 2.10b), the LM-dependent threshold probability $\pi_i(H)$ can be estimated as follows:

$$\pi_i(H) = \mathcal{P}(T^r(f_{j+1} \ldots f_J)H^l) \cdot \mathcal{P}(H^r T^l(f_1 \ldots f_{i-1})) \qquad (2.50)$$

Since we do not know which order will be preferred, we take the maximum of the straight and inverted LM-dependent threshold probability for the hypothesis

$$\pi(H) = \max(\pi_s(H), \pi_i(H)) \qquad (2.51)$$

The final beam threshold pruning metric for H when compared to the best hypothesis within the same cell is,

$$M(H) = M_{\text{in}}(H) \cdot \pi(H)^{\lambda_L} \qquad (2.52)$$

where $M_{\text{in}}(H)$ is the model score estimated from inside the hypothesis H according to the Eq. (2.3), λ_L is the weight of the language model. Note that $M(H)$ is only used for beam threshold pruning.

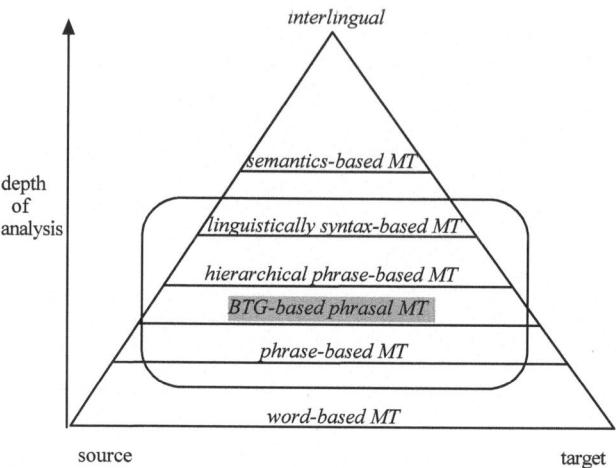

Fig. 2.11 *Triangle* of machine translation

2.6 Comparison with Other SMT Formalisms

In Sects. 2.2 and 2.3, we introduce BTG-based SMT from its inner perspectives: modeling and decoding. We will have a more clear picture of this SMT formalism by comparing it with other SMT formalisms in this section. Figure 2.11 projects BTG-based SMT onto the well-known machine translation triangle. In the figure, we highlight three alternative SMT formalisms: phrase-based SMT, hierarchical phrase-based SMT and linguistically syntax-based SMT. The rest of this section will discuss the differences between BTG-based SMT and the highlighted three alternative formalisms. By this comparison, we will understand more about the strengths and weaknesses of BTG-based SMT.

2.6.1 Comparison with Phrase-Based SMT

The biggest difference between BTG-based SMT and the standard phrase-based SMT (Koehn et al. 2003) is that the former uses two bracketing rules $X \rightarrow [X_1, X_2]$ and $X \rightarrow \langle X_1, X_2 \rangle$ in addition to the lexical rules (i.e., phrase pairs in phrase-based SMT). These two bracketing rules along with the CKY-style decoding endow BTG-based SMT (BTG-SMT) with several advantages over the standard phrase-based SMT (PB-SMT).

2.6.1.1 BTG-SMT Models More Reorderings Than PB-SMT Does

It has been verified that arbitrary reorderings make the decoding search for the best permutation an NP-complete problem, just like the Traveling Salesman Problem as shown by Knight (1999). Therefore, constrained reordering is widely adopted to make the translation decoding computationally tractable. The *ITG constraint* and *IBM constraint* are the two most popular reordering constraints. In the ITG constraint, as shown in Sect. 2.2.3, there are only two reordering options whenever two neighboring phrases are merged: either keeping them in the straight (monotonic) order or inverting the order on the target side. In the IBM constraint, only the k leftmost uncovered words (or phrases in PB-SMT) are allowed to be translated. Typically, k is set to 4.

It is known that the ITG constraint cannot model the so-called "inside-out" reorderings as shown in Fig. 2.12. Although these reorderings do occur in real translations (Wellington et al. 2006), the ITG constraint still allows more phrase reorderings than the IBM constraint if the number of phrases is larger than six according to Zens and Ney (2003). In addition, empirical results described by Zens et al. (2004) further show that the ITG constraint outperforms the IBM constraint in a phrase-based SMT system.

2.6.1.2 BTG-SMT Allows Long-Distance Reordering

As we mention above, the IBM constraint used by PB-SMT typically defines a four-phrase window for local reordering. If we want to allow long-distance reordering, we have to set a larger k or resort to arbitrary permutation, which however makes the decoding more computationally expensive or intractable. In contrast, BTG, as a simple case of SCFG, can easily model long-distance reordering in polynomial time through dynamic programming algorithms (Wu 1996; Lopez 2008).

2.6.1.3 BTG-SMT Facilitates the Incorporation of Syntax into SMT

As linguistic representations of syntax are hierarchical (Chomsky 1957) and BTG-SMT is capable of building hierarchical structures, it is convenient for BTG-SMT to incorporate syntax. However, this is not always true for PB-SMT as the incorporation of syntax into the formalism is mixed with failures (Koehn et al. 2003; Och et al. 2004) and successes (Collins et al. 2005; Wang et al. 2007). It seems that PB-SMT is generally not a good fit for syntax (Lopez 2008).

Fig. 2.12 The so-called inside-out reorderings that the ITG constraint does not allow

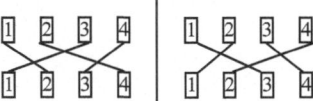

2.6.2 Comparison with Hierarchical Phrase-Based SMT

We call the grammar induced in hierarchical phrase-based machine translation (Chiang 2005, 2007) *hierarchical grammar*. There are two features of the hierarchical grammar that are also shared by BTG.

1. Only one single undifferentiated nonterminal X is used.
2. At most two nonterminals are permitted at the right-hand side of any productions. Therefore the grammar is an ITG as any SCFG of rank[8] two is an ITG (Wu 2010).

The difference between the hierarchical grammar and BTG is that rules of the hierarchical grammar may contain a number of terminals (words) on the right-hand side for both source and target language as shown in Fig. 2.13. This difference confers upon the hierarchical grammar more modeling power, such as lexicon-sensitive reordering, than BTG. But it comes at a cost of inducing a very large number of rules that are rarely used during decoding (He et al. 2009).

Since both the hierarchical grammar and BTG are an ITG, normally, statistical techniques that are used to improve one of them can be also applied to enhance the other in general.

2.6.3 Comparison with Linguistically Syntax-Based SMT

In recent years, a wide variety of linguistically syntax-based machine translation approaches have been proposed, for example, string-to-tree translation (Galley et al. 2006), tree-to-string translation (Liu et al. 2006), forest-based translation (Mi et al. 2008), dependency-based translation (Quirk et al. 2005; Xiong et al. 2007; Shen et al. 2008) and so on. All these linguistically syntax-based machine translation approaches employ linguistic theories and annotations, which have proven to benefit machine translation.

In contrast to linguistically syntax-based SMT, BTG-based SMT is a formally syntax-based SMT in that it does not depend on any linguistic theories or annotations. On the one hand, such an independence on linguistic theories enables us to train BTG-based SMT more efficiently than linguistically syntax-based SMT because

Fig. 2.13 Sample rules of the hierarchical grammar

$$X \rightarrow \text{grands } X_1/\text{jiyü } X_1$$
$$X \rightarrow \text{held talks } X_1 X_2/X_1 \text{ jüxing huitan } X_2$$
$$X \rightarrow \text{accept } X_2 \text{ from } X_1/\text{jieshou } X_1 \text{ de } X_2$$

---

[8] The *Rank* of an SCFG is the maximum number of nonterminals in the right-hand side of any productions of the synchronous grammar (Chiang 2006).

BTG-based SMT enjoys a much smaller number of synchronous rules. On the other hand, however, BTG-based SMT suffers from no explicit linguistic constraints.

2.6.4 Strengths and Weaknesses of BTG-Based SMT

After comparing BTG-based SMT with the three alternative SMT formalisms (phrase-based SMT, hierarchical phrase-based SMT and linguistically syntax-based SMT), we can summarize the strengths and weaknesses for BTG-based SMT as follows.

- *Strengths.* The formalism has sufficient and flexible reordering ability. It can represent long-distance reordering and build hierarchical structures in polynomial time. It can be trained efficiently.
- *Weakness.* It does not employ any lexical or linguistic syntax knowledge for modeling.

2.7 Summary and Additional Readings

This chapter systematically introduces BTG-based SMT, including the unified framework, reordering under the ITG constraint, the CKY-style −LM decoding algorithm that builds BTG trees from the bottom up, and the +LM decoding algorithm that integrates n-gram language models into the decoder for BTG-based SMT. Following this chapter, readers can implement a complete BTG-based SMT system.

This chapter also introduces two extensions to traditional n-gram language models, namely the backward language model which uses backward n-grams to predict the current word and the trigger language model which incorporates long-distance trigger pairs into language modeling. The decoding algorithms that integrate the two extended language models into the CKY-style decoder are described. Experiment results of these two extensions are included in "Enhancing Language Models in Statistical Machine Translation with Backward N-grams and Mutual Information Triggers" (Xiong et al. *Proceedings of the 49th Annual Meeting of the Association for Computational Linguistics*, Portland, Oregon, June 19–24, 2011; pp. 1288–1297.).

In order to speed up the decoder, two variants of threshold pruning, i.e., dynamic threshold pruning and LM-dependent threshold pruning, are also introduced. More details about the empirical evaluation of these two pruning methods are given in "Efficient Beam Thresholding for Statistical Machine Translation" (Xiong et al. *Proceedings of the twelfth Machine Translation Summit*, August 26–30, 2009, Ottawa, Ontario, Canada; pp. 363–370.).

Additional Readings. Zhang and Gildea (2005) propose a lexicalized BTG to obtain word alignments. Similarly, Saers et al. (2009) also present an agenda-based BTG biparsing algorithm with a novel pruning method to obtain word alignments. Sánchez and Benedí (2006) use a stochastic BTG to obtain bilingual phrases for phrase-based SMT. Su et al. (2010) extend the normal BTG to a dependency-based BTG and explore it for machine translation.

Duchateau et al. (2002) use the score estimated by a backward language model in a post-processing step as a confidence measure to detect wrongly recognized words in speech recognition. Finch and Sumita (2009) use a backward language model in their reverse translation decoder where target translations are generated from the ending to the beginning. The backward language model introduced here is different from theirs in that we access the backward language model during decoding (rather than after decoding) where target sentences are still generated from the left to the right.

Rosenfeld et al. (1994) introduce trigger pairs into a maximum entropy based language model as features. The trigger pairs are selected according to their mutual information. Raybaud et al. (2009) use MI triggers in their confidence measures to assess the quality of translation results after decoding. Mauser et al. (2009) propose bilingual triggers where two source words trigger one target word to improve lexical choice of target words.

Chapter 3
Syntactically Annotated Reordering

Abstract This chapter presents a *syntactically annotated reordering* approach for SMT. We first present a lexicalized reordering model that uses boundary words as reordering features. The philosophy behind the model is that reordering under the ITG constraint is considered as a binary classification problem. We therefore build a maximum entropy classification model to predict the order $o \in \{straight, inverted\}$ whenever we apply a BTG bracketing rule to merge two neighboring phrases. As syntax knowledge can provide high-level information for reordering, especially for long-distance reordering, we further extend the maximum entropy-based lexicalized reordering model to a syntactically annotated reordering model. The new model annotates each BTG node with syntactic knowledge by projecting binary trees generated by BTG onto source-side parse trees. The challenge, however, is that BTG hierarchical structures are not always aligned with the linguistic structures in syntactic parse trees of the source or target language. Therefore, we introduce an annotation algorithm to label both syntactic phrases and nonsyntactic phrases that are not aligned with any syntactic constituents in source-side parse trees with syntactic elements. The annotated syntactic elements are then used as reordering features for the syntactically annotated reordering model. In order to investigate the impacts imposed by syntactic knowledge on phrase reordering, we also introduce a syntax-based reordering analysis method and conduct a thorough study on the impacts of syntactic knowledge on phrase reordering with this method.

Reordering is crucial for translating languages with word order differences. Although phrase-based SMT is capable of local word reorderings within phrases, reorderings at the phrase level are still problematic as arbitrary permutation of phrases is intractable (Knight 1999). The ITG constraint makes phrasal reorderings tractable and endows the BTG-based SMT with abilities of long-distance and hierarchical reordering (see Sect. 2.6.1 of Chap. 2 for more details). However, the ITG constraint alone is not sufficient to move phrases to their correct positions. In order to detect correct positions for phrases, reordering models that observe the ITG constraint should be built to provide extra information.

© Springer Science+Business Media Singapore 2015
D. Xiong and M. Zhang, *Linguistically Motivated Statistical Machine Translation*, DOI 10.1007/978-981-287-356-9_3

This chapter presents a *Syntactically Annotated Reordering* model to capture reordering patterns under the ITG constraint with various syntactic features. We consider the reordering under the ITG constraint as a binary classification problem. In this perspective, the reordering model is actually a classifier that predicts the ITG orientation (straight or inverted) for any two neighboring phrases when they are bracketed together by the bracketing rules.

We select the maximum entropy (MaxEnt) classifier (Berger et al. 1996) as the reordering classifier as it is able to explore arbitrary features and train them discriminatively. In order to train the reordering classifier, we automatically extract training instances from word-aligned bilingual data. These training instances are annotated with syntactic information from source-side parse trees.

Interesting questions about the syntactically annotated reordering are as follows:

- To what extent the integrated syntactic knowledge will change phrase movement in an actual SMT system?
- And in what direction the change will take place?

Such investigations will enable us to have better comprehension of the relationship between phrase movement and syntactic context, and therefore explore syntactic knowledge more effectively in reordering.

In order to conduct the above investigations, we also introduce yet another reordering model that only uses phrase boundary words as features to predict the ITG orientations. We call it *Boundary Word Reordering* model. We compare translation results generated by the two different reordering models with a syntax-based reordering analysis method. The analysis method automatically detects constituent movement in both reference and system translations, and summarizes syntactic reordering patterns that are captured by the two reordering models.

The chapter is organized as follows.

- Section 3.1 formally defines reordering examples under the ITG constraint.
- Section 3.2 presents a reordering example extraction algorithm with various extraction strategies.
- Section 3.3 describes the boundary word reordering model. It also uses the model to empirically analyze the reordering example extraction algorithm and its different extraction strategies.
- Section 3.4 elaborates the syntactically annotated reordering model. We present the annotation algorithm, the model as well as methods that combine the boundary word reordering model and the syntactically annotated reordering model.
- Section 3.5 introduces the syntax-based analysis method. The method consists of 5 steps, which finally generates syntactic reordering patterns from system/reference translations.
- Section 3.6 provides the analysis results in details by comparing translations generated by the boundary word reordering model against those generated by the combination of the two reordering models with the analysis method.

3.1 Reordering Example

Since we consider reordering under the ITG constraint as a classification problem,[1] we need to obtain training instances to build a classifier. Here, we refer to a training instance as a *reordering example*, which is formally defined as a triple of (o, b_l, b_r) where b_l and b_r are two neighboring blocks and $o \in \{straight, inverted\}$ is the order between them.

The *block* is a pair of aligned source phrase and target phrase

$$b = (c_{i_1}^{i_2}, e_{j_1}^{j_2}) \tag{3.1}$$

b must be consistent with the word alignment M

$$\forall (i, j) \in M, \quad i_1 \le i \le i_2 \leftrightarrow j_1 \le j \le j_2 \tag{3.2}$$

By this, we require that no words inside the source phrase $c_{i_1}^{i_2}$ are aligned to words outside the target phrase $e_{j_1}^{j_2}$ and that no words outside the source phrase are aligned to words inside the target phrase. This definition is similar to that of bilingual phrase except that there is no length limitation over blocks. Figure 3.1 shows a word alignment matrix between a Chinese sentence and English sentence. In the matrix, each block can be represented as a rectangle, e.g., block (c_4^4, e_4^4), (c_4^5, e_4^5), (c_4^7, e_4^9) on the bottom left, and (c_2^3, e_3^3), (c_1^3, e_1^3) on the upper right.

3.2 Reordering Example Extraction Algorithm

In this section, we discuss two algorithms to extract reordering examples from word-aligned bilingual data. The first algorithm *AExtractor* (described in Sect. 3.2.1) extracts reordering examples directly from word alignments by extending bilingual phrase extraction algorithm. The second algorithm *TExtractor* (described in Sect. 3.2.2) extracts reordering examples from BTG-style trees which are built from word alignments.

3.2.1 AExtractor: Extracting Reordering Examples from Word Alignments

Before we describe this algorithm, we introduce a concept of *junction* in the word alignment matrix. We define a junction as a vertex shared by two neighboring blocks. There are two types of junctions: *straight junction* which connects two neighboring blocks in a straight order (e.g., dots J_1–J_4 in Fig. 3.1) and *inverted junction* which connects two neighboring blocks in an inverted order (e.g., dot J_5 in Fig. 3.1).

---

[1] Readers can refer to Sect. 2.2.3 of Chap. 2 for a general introduction of reordering models under the ITG constraint.

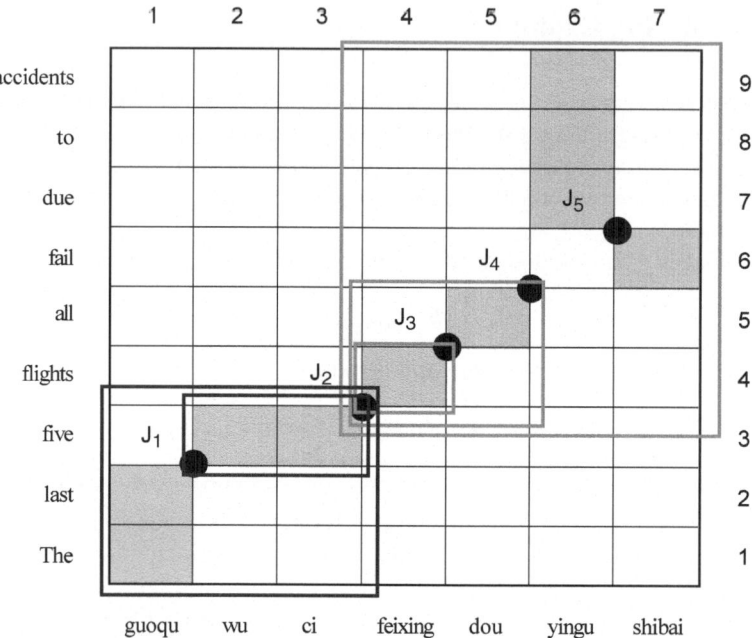

Fig. 3.1 A word alignment matrix between a Chinese sentence and English sentence. *Bold dots* represent *junctions* which connect two neighboring blocks. *Rectangles* are blocks which are connected by junction J_2 (Color figure online)

The algorithm is shown in Fig. 3.2, which completes three subtasks as follows.

1. Find blocks (line 4 and 5). This is similar to the standard phrase extraction algorithm (Och 2002) except that we find blocks with arbitrary length.
2. Detect junctions and store blocks in the arrays of detected junctions (line 7 and 8). Junctions that are included the current block can be easily detected by looking at previous and next blocks. A junction can connect multiple blocks on its left and right side. For example, the second junction J_2 in Fig. 3.1 connects two blocks on the left side and three blocks on the right side. To store these blocks, we maintain two arrays (left and right) for each junction.
3. Extract block pairs from each detected junction as reordering examples (line 12–16). This is the most challenging task of this algorithm. Since a junction may have n blocks on its left side and m blocks on its right side, we will obtain nm reordering examples if we enumerate all block pairs. This will quickly increase the number of reordering examples, especially those with the straight order. In order to keep the number of reordering examples tractable, we adopt various extraction strategies to heuristically extract special block pairs as reordering examples.

We can exploit the following four extraction strategies for AExtractor.

1. *strINV*. We extract the smallest (in terms of the target length) blocks for straight junctions, and the largest blocks for inverted junctions. Take the straight junction

1: **Input**: sentence pair (s, t), word alignment M and block extraction strategy r
2: $\Re := \emptyset$
3: **for** each span $(i_1, i_2) \in s$ **do**
4:     Find block $b = (s_{i_1}^{i_2}, t_{j_1}^{j_2})$ that is consistent with M
5:     Extend block b on the target boundary with any possible non-aligned target words to get blocks $E(b)$
6:     **for** each block $b^* \in b \bigcup E(b)$ **do**
7:         Detect possible junctions in b^*.
8:         Store b^* in the arrays of detected junctions.
9:     **end for**
10: **end for**
11: **for** each junction J in the matrix M **do**
12:     Select b_l and b_r from the left and right array of J respectively according to the extraction strategy r.
13:     **if** J is a straight junction **then**
14:         $\Re := \Re \bigcup \{(straight, b_l, b_r)\}$
15:     **else if** J is an inverted junction **then**
16:         $\Re := \Re \bigcup \{(inverted, b_l, b_r)\}$
17:     **end if**
18: **end for**
19: **Output**: reordering examples $\Re$

Fig. 3.2 AExtractor

J_2 in Fig. 3.1 as an example, the extracted reordering example is (*straight, wuci| five, feixing| flights*).

2. *STRinv*. We extract the largest (in terms of the target length) blocks for straight junctions, and the smallest blocks for inverted junctions. Still take the straight junction J_2, for example, this time the extracted reordering example is (*straight, guoqu wu ci| The last five, feixing dou yingu shibai| flights all fail due to accidents*).

3. *RANDOM*. For any junction, we randomly select one block pair from its arrays.

4. *COMBO*. For each junction, we first extract two block pairs using the extraction strategy strINV and STRinv. If there are unselected blocks, we randomly select one block pair from the remaining blocks.

In Sect. 3.3.2, we will compare these four strategies.

3.2.2 TExtractor: Extracting Reordering Examples from BTG-Style Trees

A potential problem of AExtractor is caused by using heuristic extraction strategies: keeping some block pairs as reordering examples, while abandoning other block pairs. The kept block pairs are not necessarily best training instances for tuning an ITG order predictor. To avoid this problem, we can extract reordering examples from BTG trees of sentence pairs. Reordering examples extracted in this way are naturally suitable for BTG order prediction.

There are various ways to build BTG trees on sentence pairs. One can use BTG to produce bilingual parses on sentence pairs, similar to the approaches proposed by Wu (1997), Zhang and Gildea (2005) but with more sophisticated reordering models. After parsing, reordering examples can be extracted from bilingual parse trees and a better reordering model is therefore induced from extracted reordering examples. Using the better reordering model, bilingual sentences are parsed again. This procedure is run iteratively until no performance gain is obtained in terms of translation or parsing accuracy. Formally, we can use expectation-maximization (EM) training in this procedure. In the expectation step, we first estimate the likelihood of all BTG trees of sentence pairs with the current BTG model. Then, we extract reordering examples and collect counts for them, weighted with the probability of the BTG tree where they occur. In the maximization step, we can train a more accurate reordering model with updated reordering examples. Unfortunately, this method is at high computational cost.

Instead, here we adopt a less expensive alternative method to produce BTG trees on sentence pairs. Supposing we have word alignments produced by GIZA++, we use the shift-reduce algorithm (SRA) introduced by Zhang et al. (2008) to decompose word alignments into hierarchical trees. The SRA can guarantee that each node is a bilingual phrase in the generated hierarchical tree.

Given an interval $[x, y]$ on the target side and a word alignment matrix M, we define the aligned interval $[u, v]$ on the source side as follows:

$$u = \min\{i | (i, j) \in M, j \in [x, y]\}$$
$$v = \max\{i | (i, j) \in M, j \in [x, y]\}$$

The core component of SRA is to determine whether words in $[x, y]$ on the target side and their aligned words in $[u, v]$ on the source side form a block as defined in Sect. 3.1. Zhang et al. (2008) perform this block test by calculating the number of links to positions in $[x, y]$ and the number of links to positions in $[u, v]$ in a dynamic programming manner. If these two numbers equal, $([u, v], [x, y])$ is a block or bilingual phrase pair. The shift-reduce algorithm is shown in Fig. 3.3. The algorithm runs in a left-to-right bottom-up fashion. Whenever it finds a block, it brackets the block. Once a target sentence is completely parsed, we can obtain a bracketed hierarchical decomposition tree.

If the fan-out of a node in decomposition trees generated by SRA is larger than 2, we binarize it from left to right: for two neighboring child nodes, if they are also neighboring at both the source and target side, we combine them and create a new node to dominate them. In this way, we can transform the decomposition tree into a BTG-style tree. Note that not all multibranching nodes can be binarized. We extract reordering examples only from binary nodes.

1: SRA (source sentence $[1, m]$, target sentence $[1, n]$ and word alignment matrix M)
2: $X := \{1\}$
3: **for** $y \in [2, n]$ from left to right **do**
4:      shift: push y to X
5:      **for** $x \in X$ from right to left **do**
6:          perform block test on $[x, y]$
7:          **if** $[x, y]$ and its aligned span on the source side form a block **then**
8:              bracket (x, y)
9:              Reduce: remove $[x + 1, y]$ from X
10:         **end if**
11:     **end for**
12: **end for**

Fig. 3.3 The shift-reduce algorithm

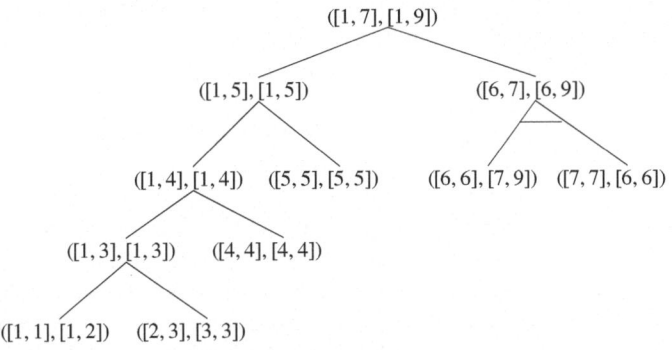

Fig. 3.4 The BTG-style tree built from the word alignment in Fig. 3.1. We use $([u, v], [x, y])$ to denote a tree node, where u, v and x, y are the beginning and ending index in the source and target language, respectively

Figure 3.4 shows the BTG-style tree which is built from the word alignment in Fig. 3.1 according to the method mentioned above. From this tree, we can easily extract 4 reordering examples in a straight order and 1 reordering example in an inverted order.

3.3 Boundary Word Reordering

After we extract reordering examples from word-aligned bilingual training data, we can train a classifier and use the classifier as the ITG reordering predictor. In this section, we develop a maximum entropy-based reordering model which adopts boundary words of reordering examples as features.

3.3.1 Model

Following the binary classification perspective of the ITG reordering, we formulate
the maximum entropy-based reordering model as follows:

$$P_{R_b}(r^b) = P_\theta(o|X_l, X_r, X_p) = \frac{\exp(\sum_i \theta_i f_i(o, X_l, X_r, X_p))}{\sum_{o'} \exp(\sum_i \theta_i f_i(o', X_l, X_r, X_p))} \qquad (3.3)$$

where the functions $f_i \in \{0, 1\}$ are reordering features and the θ_i are weights of these
features.

We use boundary words of source/target sides of both children $\{X_l, X_r\}$ as reordering features. Figure 3.5 shows the 8 boundary words (bold dots) in the two neighboring blocks $\{X_l, X_r\}$. Let us have a more concrete example. Supposing that we
have a reordering example (*inverted, yu 7yue 15ri\on July 15, juxing zongtong yu
guohui xuanju\—held its presidential and parliament elections*), the leftmost/
rightmost source words $\{yu, 15ri, juxing, xuanju\}$ and target words $\{on, 15, held,
elections\}$ will be extracted as boundary words.

Each boundary word will form a reordering feature as follows:

$$f_i(o, X_l, X_r, X_p) = \begin{cases} 1, & fn = \text{bval}, o = inverted \\ 0, & \text{otherwise} \end{cases}$$

where *fn* denotes the feature name (e.g., $X_l.s_l^r$), bval is the corresponding boundary
word. Since we have 8 boundary words for each reordering example, we can obtain
8 feature templates using these boundary words, which are shown in Table 3.1.

We call this reordering model *Boundary Word Reordering (BWR)* model. There
are two reasons why boundary words are used as important clues for reordering,
which are listed as follows.

1. Phrases cohere across languages frequently (Fox 2002). In cohesive phrase movement, boundary words directly interact with external contexts of phrases. This
   suggests that boundary words might contain information for phrase reordering.
2. The quantitative analysis by Xiong et al. (2006, p. 525) further shows that boundary words indeed contain information for order prediction.

We go through the following 3 steps to train a BWR model.

1. We extract reordering examples from word-aligned bilingual data using the algorithm described in the last section.

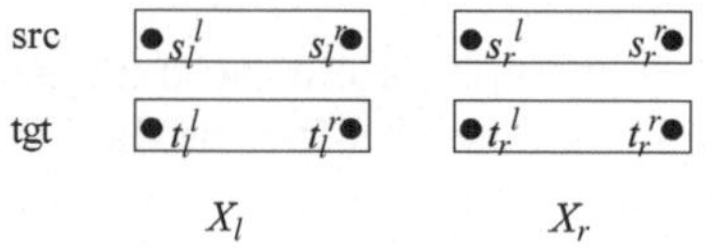

Fig. 3.5 Boundary words in the two neighboring blocks X_l and X_r (*black dots*)

Table 3.1 Feature templates for the boundary word reordering model

Template	$f(o, X_l, X_r, X_p) = 1$ if and only if
1	$o = \mathcal{O}$ and $X_l.s_l^l = \text{bval}$
2	$o = \mathcal{O}$ and $X_l.s_l^r = \text{bval}$
3	$o = \mathcal{O}$ and $X_l.t_l^l = \text{bval}$
4	$o = \mathcal{O}$ and $X_l.t_l^r = \text{bval}$
5	$o = \mathcal{O}$ and $X_r.s_l^l = \text{bval}$
6	$o = \mathcal{O}$ and $X_r.s_l^r = \text{bval}$
7	$o = \mathcal{O}$ and $X_r.t_l^l = \text{bval}$
8	$o = \mathcal{O}$ and $X_r.t_l^r = \text{bval}$

$\mathcal{O} \in \{straight, inverted\}$

2. Then, we generate reordering features using boundary words from extracted reordering examples according to the feature templates shown in Table 3.1.
3. Finally, we use an off-the-shelf maximum entropy toolkit to estimate feature weights.

Normally, the reordering model trained in such a way is much smaller than the lexicalized reordering model used in the standard phrase-based SMT (Koehn et al. 2005).

3.3.2 Analysis of Reordering Example Exaction Algorithms

In this section, we use the BWR model to conduct some analyses for the two reordering example extraction algorithms described in Sect. 3.2.

3.3.2.1 Bias in AExtractor

In Sect. 3.2.1, we introduce four different extraction strategies for AExtractor. Such heuristic strategies would naturally raise the following three questions.

1. Is it necessary to extract all reordering examples?
2. If not necessary, do the heuristic extraction strategies impose any bias on the reordering model? For example, if we use the strINV extraction strategy, meaning that we always extract largest block pairs for inverted reordering examples, does the reordering model prefer swappings on larger blocks to those on smaller blocks?
3. Does the bias have a strong impact on the performance in terms of BLEU score?

In this section, we conduct an in-depth analysis on the four extraction strategies with the boundary word reordering model. We extract several groups of reordering examples using the four extraction strategies. These extracted reordering examples are used to generate boundary word reordering features. We then train different boundary word reordering models using these features. According to our experiment results (Xiong et al. 2010a), we answer the three questions one by one.

The answer to the first question is no. Firstly, it is practically undesirable to extract all reordering examples because even a very small training set will produce millions of reordering examples if we enumerate all block pair combinations. Secondly, extracting all reordering examples introduces a great amount of noises into training and therefore undermines the final reordering model. According to our findings (Xiong et al. 2010a, p. 552), the AExtractor with the COMBO strategy extracts the largest number of reordering examples. However, it does not obtain the highest BLEU score compared with other strategies which extract a smaller number of reordering examples. This suggests that there is no need to extract all reordering examples.

To answer the second question, we trace the best BTG trees produced by the system with the BWR reordering model trained on reordering examples which are extracted with different strategies. Then, we calculate the average number of words on the target side which are covered by binary nodes in a straight order. We refer to this number as *straight average length*. Similarly, *inverted average length* is calculated on all binary nodes in an inverted order. Comparing these average numbers, we clearly observe that two extraction strategies indeed impose noticeable bias on the reordering model.

- The strINV extraction strategy, which always extracts largest block pairs for inverted reordering examples, has the largest inverted average length. This indicates that the strINV strategy biases the reordering model toward larger swappings.
- On the contrary, the STRinv extraction strategy, which extracts the largest block pairs for straight reordering examples and smallest pairs for inverted reordering examples, has the largest straight average length while a relatively much smaller inverted average length. This suggests that the STRinv strategy makes the reordering model prefer smaller swappings.

Note that the extraction strategies RANDOM and COMBO do not impose bias on the length of extracted reordering examples compared with strINV and STRinv. The latter two extraction strategies have special preferences on the length of reordering examples and transfer these preferences to reordering models.

Finally, for the last question, we observe that BLEU scores are not that much different, although we have quite opposite bias imposed by different extraction strategies. The changes in BLEU score, which happen when we shift from one extraction strategy to the other, are limited to a maximum of 1.2 % according to our experiments (Xiong et al. 2010a, p. 552). Among the four extraction strategies, the STRinv strategy achieves the highest BLEU score. The reason might be that the bias toward smaller swappings imposed by this strategy helps the decoder to reduce incorrect long-distance swappings (Xiong et al. 2008).

3.3.2.2 AExtractor Versus TExtractor

We further compare the two algorithms of reordering example extraction. According to our experiment results (Xiong et al. 2010a, p. 552), we find that TExtractor significantly underperforms AExtractor. This is because the transformation from decomposition trees to BTG trees is not complete. Many crossing links due to errors and noises in word alignments generated by GIZA++ make it impossible to build BTG nodes over the corresponding words. It would be better to use alignments induced by ITG and EM procedure described in Sect. 3.2.2 but with a very high cost.

Therefore, we suggest that AExtractor with the STRinv extraction strategy should be used to extract reordering examples for boundary word reordering as described in the this section and syntactically annotated reordering which will be introduced in the next section.

3.4 Syntactically Annotated Reordering

Experiments show that the boundary word reordering model is much better than the two context-independent reordering models shown in the Eqs. (2.11) and (2.12) of Chap. 2 (Xiong et al., 2006). However, only using boundary words is not adequate to move phrases to appropriate positions. Consider the example in Fig. 3.6. In this example, boundary words *zai* and *shi* are able to decide that the translation of the PP phrase *zai...shi* should be postponed until some phrase that succeeds it is translated. But they cannot provide further information about exactly which succeeding phrase should be translated first. If high-level linguistic knowledge, such as the syntactic context VP→PP VP, is given, the position of the PP phrase can be easily determined since the preverbal modifier PP in Chinese is frequently translated into a postverbal counterpart in English.

In order to incorporate such syntactic knowledge into the ITG reordering, we annotate each BTG node involved in reordering with syntactic elements by projecting the BTG node onto the corresponding source-side parse tree. The syntactic elements include: (1) head word *hw*, (2) the part-of-speech (POS) tag *ht* of head word, and (3) syntactic category *sc*. These annotated syntactic elements are then used as reordering features. We call the reordering model built upon such syntactic features *Syntactically Annotated Reordering (SAR)* model.

In the remainder of this section, we describe the algorithm that annotates BTG nodes with syntactic elements from source-side parse trees, the SAR model as well as the combination of SAR and BWR.

3.4.1 Annotation Algorithm

There are 2 steps to annotate a BTG node using source-side parse tree information: (1) determining the sequence on the source side which is exactly covered by the

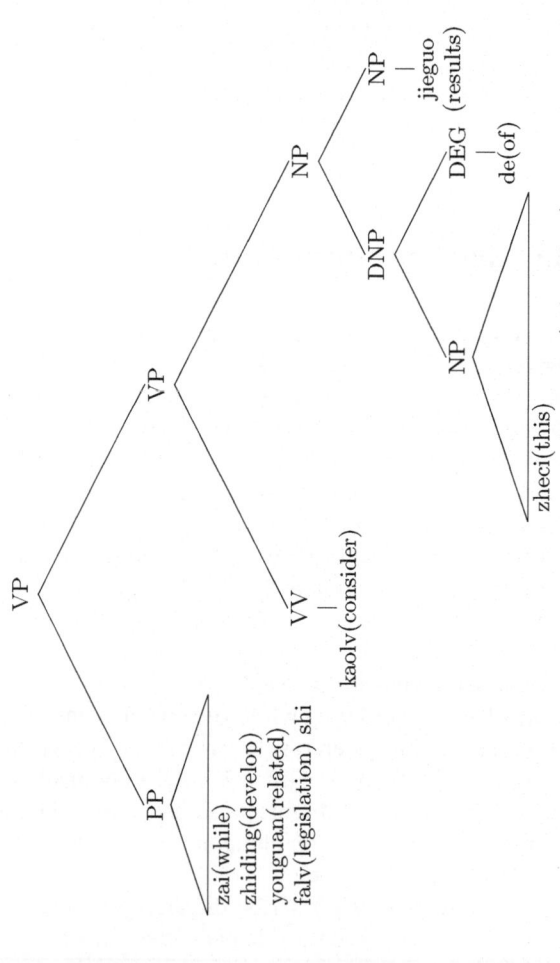

Fig. 3.6 A Chinese syntactic parse tree with its English translation. (*Reference* Consider the results of this referendum while developing related legislation)

node, then (2) annotating the sequence according to the source-side parse tree. If the sequence is exactly covered by a single subtree in the source-side parse tree, it is called *syntactic sequence*, otherwise it is *nonsyntactic sequence*. One of the challenges in this annotation is that phrases (BTG nodes) are not always covering syntactic sequence, in other words, they are not always aligned to constituent nodes in the source-side tree. To solve this problem, we generate pseudo head word and *composite category* which consists of syntactic categories of three relevant constituents for the nonsyntactic sequence. In this way, our annotation is capable of labeling both syntactic and nonsyntactic phrases and therefore providing linguistic information for any phrase reordering.

The annotation algorithm is shown in Fig. 3.7. For a syntactic sequence, the annotation is trivial. Annotation elements directly come from the subtree that covers the sequence exactly. For a nonsyntactic sequence, the process is more complicated. Firstly, we need to locate the smallest subtree c^* covering the sequence (line 6). Secondly, we try to identify the head word/tag of the sequence (line 7–12) by using its head word directly if it is within the sequence. Otherwise, the word within the sequence which is nearest to hw will be assigned as the head word of the sequence. Finally, we determine the composite category of the sequence (line 13–15), which is formulated as L-C-R. L/R refers to the syntactic category of the left/right *boundary node* of s, which is the highest leftmost/rightmost subnode of c^* not overlapping the sequence. If there is no such boundary node (the sequence s is exactly aligned to the left/right boundary of c^*), L/R will be set to NULL. C is the syntactic category of c^*. L, R, and C together describe the external syntactic context of s. The composite category we define for nonsyntactic phrases is similar to the CCG style category defined by Zollmann et al. (2008).

1: Annotator (sequence $s = \langle i, j \rangle$, source-side parse tree t)
2: **if** s is a syntactic sequence **then**
3:    Find the subtree c in t which exactly covers s
4:    $s.\{\ \} := \{c.hw, c.ht, c.sc\}$
5: **else**
6:    Find the smallest subtree c^* covering s in t
7:    **if** $c^*.hw \in s$ **then**
8:       $s.hw := c^*.hw$ and $s.ht := c^*.ht$
9:    **else**
10:       Find the word $w \in s$ which is nearest to $c^*.hw$
11:       $s.hw := w$ and $s.ht := w.t$ {$w.t$ is the POS tag of w}
12:    **end if**
13:    Find the left boundary node ln of s in c^*
14:    Find the right boundary node rn of s in c^*
15:    $s.sc := ln.sc\text{-}c^*.sc\text{-}rn.sc$
16: **end if**

Fig. 3.7 The annotation algorithm

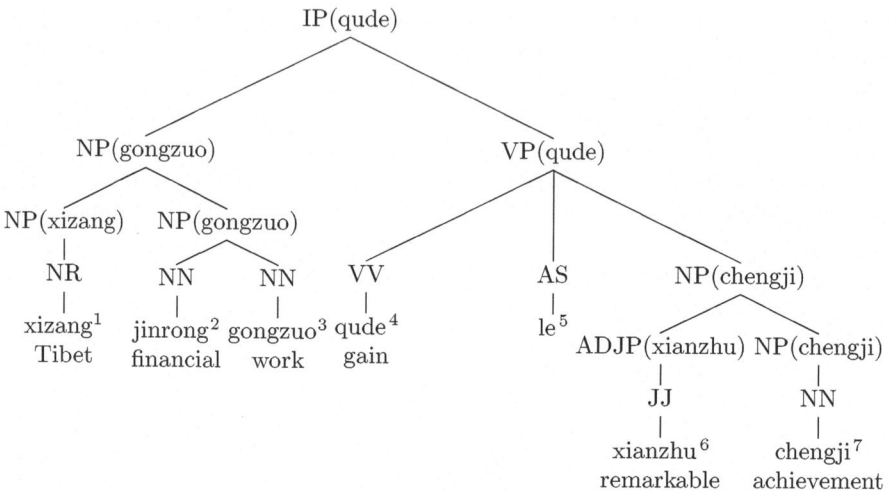

Fig. 3.8 A syntactic parse tree with head word annotated for each internal node. The superscripts of leaf nodes denote their surface positions from *left* to *right*

Table 3.2 Annotation samples according to the tree shown in Fig. 3.8

Sequence	hw	ht	sc
$\langle 1, 2 \rangle$	jinrong	NN	NULL-NP-NN
$\langle 2, 3 \rangle$	gongzuo	NN	NP
$\langle 2, 4 \rangle$	qude	VV	NP-IP-NP
$\langle 3, 4 \rangle$	qude	VV	NP-IP-NP

hw/ht represents the head word/tag, respectively. sc means the syntactic category

Figure 3.8 shows a syntactic parse tree for a Chinese sentence, with head word annotated for each internal node. Some sample annotations are given in Table 3.2.

3.4.2 Syntactically Annotated Reordering Model

The syntactically annotated reordering model P_{R_a} is also a MaxEnt-based classification model, which can be formulated as

$$P_{R_a}(r^b) = P_\theta(o|X_p^{a_p}, X_l^{a_l}, X_r^{a_r}) = \frac{\exp(\sum_i \theta_i f_i(o, X_p^{a_p}, X_l^{a_l}, X_r^{a_r}))}{\sum_{o'} \exp(\sum_i \theta_i f_i(o', X_p^{a_p}, X_l^{a_l}, X_r^{a_r}))} \quad (3.4)$$

where the feature functions $f_i \in \{0, 1\}$ are defined using annotated linguistic elements of each BTG node. Here, we use the superscripts a_l, a_r and a_p to stress that the BTG nodes are syntactically annotated.

Each bracketing rule involves 3 nodes $(X_p^{a_p}, X_l^{a_l}, X_r^{a_r})$ and each node has 3 linguistic elements (hw, ht, sc). Therefore, the model has 9 feature templates in total,

Table 3.3 Feature templates for the syntactically annotated reordering model

Template	$f(o, X_p^{a_p}, X_l^{a_l}, X_r^{a_r}) = 1$ if and only if
1	$o = \mathcal{O}$ and $X_p^{a_p}.hw = \beta$
2	$o = \mathcal{O}$ and $X_p^{a_p}.ht = \beta$
3	$o = \mathcal{O}$ and $X_p^{a_p}.sc = \beta$
4	$o = \mathcal{O}$ and $X_l^{a_l}.hw = \beta$
5	$o = \mathcal{O}$ and $X_l^{a_l}.ht = \beta$
6	$o = \mathcal{O}$ and $X_l^{a_l}.sc = \beta$
7	$o = \mathcal{O}$ and $X_r^{a_r}.hw = \beta$
8	$o = \mathcal{O}$ and $X_r^{a_r}.ht = \beta$
9	$o = \mathcal{O}$ and $X_r^{a_r}.sc = \beta$

$\mathcal{O} \in \{straight, inverted\}$

which are shown in Table 3.3. Taking the left node $X_l^{a_l}$ as an example, the model could use its head word *hw* as a feature as follows:

$$f_i(o, X_p^{a_p}, X_l^{a_l}, X_r^{a_r}) = \begin{cases} 1, & X_l^{a_l}.hw = w, o = straight \\ 0, & \text{otherwise} \end{cases}$$

Training an SAR model also takes 3 steps. Firstly, we extract annotated reordering examples from source-side parsed, word-aligned bilingual data using the reordering example extraction algorithm and the annotation algorithm. We then generate features using linguistic elements of these examples. Finally, we tune feature weights to build the MaxEnt model.

3.4.3 Combining SAR and BWR

SAR and BWR can be combined at two different levels.

1. *Feature level.* Since both SAR and BWR are trained under the maximum entropy principle, we can combine syntactically annotated features from SAR and boundary word features from BWR together and train a single MaxEnt model. We call this method *All-in-One* combination.
2. *Model level.* We can also train two reordering models separately and integrate them into BTG-based SMT. The model of BTG-based SMT shown in the Eq. (2.3) in Chap. 2 is therefore reformulated as follows.

$$M(D) = M_T(r_{1..n_l}^l) \cdot P_{R_b}(r_{1..n_b}^b)^{\lambda_{R_b}}$$
$$\cdot P_{R_a}(r_{1..n_b}^b)^{\lambda_{R_a}} \cdot P_L(e)^{\lambda_L} \cdot \exp(|e|)^{\lambda_w} \tag{3.5}$$

where P_{R_b} is the BWR reordering model and P_{R_a} is the SAR reordering model. We call this combination BWR + SAR.

Our experiment results (Xiong et al. 2010a, p. 554) show that the combination of BWR and SAR significantly outperforms a single reordering model BWR or SAR. Additionally, the model level combination is marginally better than the feature level combination.

3.5 Syntax-Based Reordering Analysis: Method

In this section, we introduce a syntax-based reordering analysis method that will help us understand the influence mechanism of syntactic knowledge on phrase reordering. We leverage the alignments between source-side parse trees and reference/system translations to summarize syntactic reordering patterns and calculate syntax-based measures of precision and recall for each syntactic constituent.

3.5.1 Overview

The alignment between a source parse tree and a target string is a collection of relationships between parse tree nodes and their corresponding target spans.[2] A *syntactic reordering pattern (SRP)* is defined as

$$\langle \alpha \rightarrow \beta_1 \ldots \beta_n \propto [i_1] \ldots [i_n] \rangle$$

The first part of an SRP is a CFG structure on the source side, while the second part $[i_1] \ldots [i_n]$ indicates the order of target spans $\beta_1^T \ldots \beta_n^T$ of nonterminals $\beta_1 \ldots \beta_n$ on the target side.[3]

Let us take the VP structure VP $\rightarrow$ PP$_1$VP$_2$ as an example to explain how the precision and recall can be obtained. On the target side, the order of PP$_1^T$ and VP$_2^T$ might be [1][2] or [2][1]. Therefore, we have two syntactic reordering patterns for this structure:

$$\langle VP \rightarrow PP_1 VP_2 \propto [1][2] \rangle \quad \text{and} \quad \langle VP \rightarrow PP_1 VP_2 \propto [2][1] \rangle$$

Suppose that the two reordering patterns occur a times in the alignments between source parse trees and reference translations, b times in the alignments between source parse trees and system translations, and c times in both alignments. Then, the reordering precision/recall for this structure is c/b and c/a, respectively. We can

---

[2] We adopt the definition of *span* from Fox (2002): given a node n that covers a word sequence $s_p \ldots s_i \ldots s_q$ and a word alignment matrix M, the target words aligned to n are $\{t_i : t_i \in M(s_i)\}$. We define the target span of node n as $n^T = (\min(\{t_i\}), \max(\{t_i\}))$. Note that n^T may contain words that are not in $\{t_i\}$.

[3] Please note that the order of structures may not be defined in some cases (see Sect. 3.5.3).

further calculate the F_1-score as $2 * c/(a + b)$. These syntax-based metrics intuitively show how well reordering model can reorder this structure. By summarizing all reordering patterns of all constituents, we can obtain an overall precision, recall and F_1-score for the tested reordering model.

This syntax-based analysis for reordering is motivated in part by the recent work which transforms the order of nodes in the source-side parse tree before translation (Xia and McCord 2004; Collins et al. 2005; Li et al. 2007; Wang et al. 2007). Here, we focus on the order transformation of syntactic constituents performed by reordering models during translation. In addition to aligning parse trees with reference translations, we also align parse trees with system translations, so that we can learn the movement of syntactic constituents done by the reordering models and investigate the performance of reordering models by comparing both alignments.

For notation convenience, we denote syntactic reordering patterns that are extracted from the alignments between source parse trees and reference translations as REF-SRP and those from the alignments between source parse trees and system translations as SYS-SRP. We refer those present in both alignments under some conditions that will be described in Sect. 3.5.4 MATCH-SRP. To conduct a thorough analysis on the reorderings, we run the following steps on the test corpus (source sentences + reference translations):

1. Parse source sentences.
2. Generate word alignments between source sentences and reference translations as well as word alignments between source sentences and system translations.
3. According to the word alignments of the step 2, for each multibranching node $\alpha \rightarrow \beta_1 \ldots \beta_n$ in the source parse tree generated in the step 1, find the target spans $\beta_1^T \ldots \beta_n^T$ and their order $[i_1] \ldots [i_n]$ in reference and system translations, respectively.
4. Generate REF-SRPs, SYS-SRPs, and MATCH-SRPs according to the target orders generated in the step 3 for each multibranching node.
5. Summarize all SRPs and calculate the precision and recall as described above.

We further elaborate step 2–4 in the following Sects. 3.5.2–3.5.4.

3.5.2 Generating Word Alignments

To obtain word alignments between source sentences and multiple reference translations, we pair the source sentences with each of the reference translations and include the created sentence pairs in our bilingual training corpus. Then, we run GIZA++ on the new corpus in both directions, and apply the "grow-diag-final" refinement rule (Koehn et al. 2005) to produce the final word alignments.

To obtain word alignments between source sentences and system translations, we store word alignments within each phrase pair in our phrase table. When we output the system translation for a source sentence, we trace back the original source phrase for each target phrase in the system translation. This will generate a phrase alignment between the source sentence and system translation. Given the phrase alignment and word alignments within phrase stored in the phrase table, we can easily obtain word alignments between the whole source sentence and system translation.

3.5.3 Generating Target Spans and Orders

Given the source parse tree and the word alignment between a source sentence and a reference/system translation, for each multibranching node $\alpha \rightarrow \beta_1 \ldots \beta_n$, we firstly determine the target span β_i^T for each child node β_i following Fox (2002). If one child node is aligned to NULL, we define a special target span for it. The order for this special target span will remain the same as the child node occurs in $\beta_1 \ldots \beta_n$.

Two target spans may overlap with each other because of inherent divergences between two languages or noises included in the word alignment. When this happens on two neighboring nodes β_i and β_{i+1}, we combine these two nodes together and redefine a target span $\beta_{i\&i+1}^T$ for the combined node. This process will be repeated until no more neighboring nodes can be combined. For example, the target span of node a and b in Fig. 3.9 overlaps ((1, 3) vs. (2, 2)). Therefore, these two nodes are to be combined into a new node, whose target span is (1, 3).

After performing all necessary node combinations, if there are no longer overlappings, we call the multibranching node *reorderable*, otherwise *nonreorderable*. To get a clearer picture of reorderable nodes, we divided them into 2 categories:

- *fully reorderable* if all target spans of child nodes do not overlap;
- *partially reorderable* if some child nodes are combined due to overlapping;

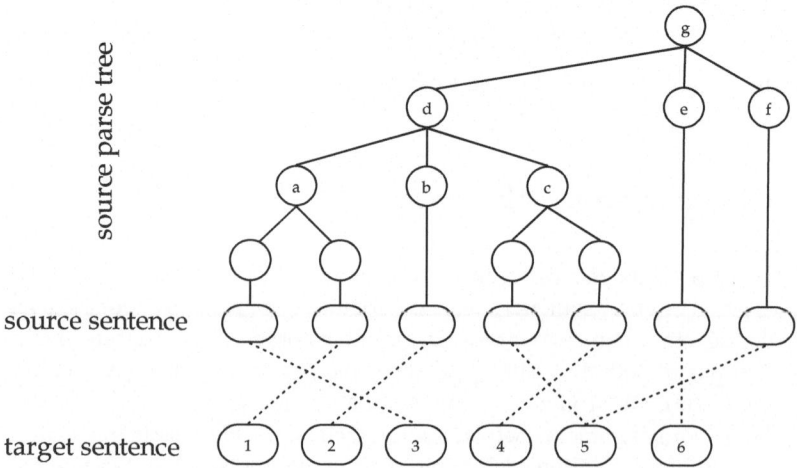

Fig. 3.9 An example source parse tree with the word alignment between the source sentence and the target translation. *Dotted lines* show the word alignment

In Fig. 3.9, both node a and c are fully reorderable nodes.[4] Node d is a partially reorderable node. Node g is a nonreorderable node because (1) target spans of its child node d and f overlaps and (2) child node d and f cannot be combined since they are not neighboring to each other.

Since we have multiple reference translations for each source sentence, we can define multiple orders for $\{\beta_i^T\}_1^n$. If one node is nonreorderable in all reference translations, we call it *REF-nonreorderable*, otherwise *REF-reorderable*. To specify the reorderable attribute of a node in the system translation, we prefix "SYS-" to { nonreorderable, reorderable, fully reorderable, partially reorderable}.

3.5.4 Generating Syntactic Reordering Patterns

After we obtain the orders of child nodes for each multibranching node, we generate REF-SRPs and SYS-SRPs from fully/partially reorderable nodes. We obtain the MATCH-SRP for each multibranching node by comparing the obtained SYS-SRP with REF-SRPs for this node under the following conditions:

1. Since we have multiple reference translations, we may have different REF-SRPs. We compare the SYS-SRP with the REF-SRP where the reference translation for this node (the sequence within the target span of the node defined by the REF-SRP) has the shortest Levenshtein distance (Navarro 2001) to that of the system translation.
2. If there are combined nodes in SYS/REF-SRPs, they are treated as a unit when comparing, without considering the order within each combined node. If the order of the SYS-SRP and the selected REF-SRP matches, we have one MATCH-SRP for the node.

Let us give an example to explain these conditions. Supposing that we are processing the structure VP $\rightarrow$ PP$_1$ADVP$_2$VP$_3$, we obtain four REF-SRPs from four different reference translations and one SYS-SRP from the system output. Here, we only show the orders:

$$\text{Ref.a} : [3][1][2]$$
$$\text{Ref.b} : [3][2][1]$$
$$\text{Ref.c\&d} : [2][3][1]$$
$$\text{SYS} : [3][1\&2]$$

Reference c and d have the same order. Therefore, we have 3 different REF-SRPs for this structure. In the SYS-SRP, PP$_1$ and ADVP$_2$ are combined and moved to the right side of VP$_3$. Supposing that the system translation for this structure has the shortest

---

[4] Their target translations are interrupted by other node's translation. We will discuss this situation in Sect. 3.6.4.

edit distance to that of Ref.b, we use the order of Ref.b to compare the system order. In the Ref.b order, both PP_1 and $ADVP_2$ are also moved to the right side of VP_3. Therefore, the two orders of Ref.b and SYS match. We have one matched SRP for this structure.

3.6 Syntax-Based Reordering Analysis: Results

We use the syntax-based reordering analysis method described in the last section to conduct an empirical investigation of syntactic constituent movement in reference translations and system translations. The system translations are generated by the BTG-based SMT system with two different reordering configurations: $BWR + SAR$ versus BWR on a test corpus. The BWR configuration only uses the boundary word reordering model while the $BWR + SAR$ configuration uses two reordering models BWR and SAR, which are combined in the way formulated in the Eq. (3.5). For more details about the experimental setup, such as the SMT system training data, the parser that we use and so on, readers can refer to (Xiong et al. 2010a). Throughout this section, the test corpus refers to the NIST MT-05.

There are essentially three issues that are addressed in this syntax-based comparative analysis.

1. The first issue is on syntactic constituent movement in human/machine translations. Fox (2002) investigates syntactic constituent movement in human translations. We study syntactic constituent movement in both human translations and machine translations that are generated by an actual SMT system and compare them.
2. The second issue concerns the change of phrase movement after rich syntactic knowledge is integrated into phrase reordering. To gain a better insight into this issue, we study phrase movement patterns for 13 specific syntactic constituents.
3. The last issue concerns which constituents remain difficult to reorder, even though rich syntactic knowledge is employed.

3.6.1 Syntactic Constituent Movement: Overview

If a syntactic constituent is fully reorderable or partially reorderable, it is considered to be moved as a unit. To denote the proportion of syntactic constituents to be moved as a unit, we introduce two variables REF-R-rate and SYS-R-rate, which are defined as

$$\text{SYS-R-rate} = \frac{\text{count(SYS-reorderable nodes)}}{\text{count(multibranching nodes)}} \tag{3.6}$$

$$\text{REF-R-rate} = \frac{\text{count(REF-reorderable nodes)}}{\text{count(multibranching nodes)}} \tag{3.7}$$

Table 3.4 Statistics of multibranching and REF/SYS-reorderable nodes per sentence

	BWR	BWR + SAR
Multibranching node	18.68	
REF-reorderable node	14.91	
REF-R-rate	79.82%	
SYS-fully reorderable node	13.16	14.01
SYS-partially reorderable node	1.31	1.26
SYS-R-rate	77.46%	81.79%

Table 3.4 shows the statistics of REF/SYS-reorderable nodes on the test corpus. From this table, we have the following observations:

1. A large amount of nodes are REF-reorderable, accounting for 79.82 % of all multi-branching nodes. This number shows that, in reference translations, a majority of syntactic constituent movement across Chinese-English can be performed by directly permuting constituents in a subtree.
2. The R-rates of BWR and BWR + SAR are 77.46 % and 81.79 %, respectively. The R-rate of BWR + SAR is obviously higher than that of BWR, which suggests that BWR + SAR tends toward moving more syntactic constituents together than BWR does. We will discuss this further later.

3.6.2 Syntactic Constituent Movement in Reference Translations

In this section, we study how syntactic constituents move in reference translations. Specially, we investigate (1) differences of constituent movement in difference reference translations and (2) REF-nonreorderable constituents as well as reasons why these constituents are nonreorderable in reference translations.

3.6.2.1 Differences in Movement Orientation

Since reference translations of each source sentence in the test corpus are generated by different human experts, we would like to analyze the differences among these multiple reference translations, especially on the orders of constituents being translated. Table 3.5 shows the overall distribution on the number of different orders for each multibranching constituent among the reference translations.

Table 3.5 Distribution of different number of orders by which syntactic constituents are translated in references

Number of different orders	1	2	3	4
Percentage (%)	75.40	22	2.33	0.33

Table 3.6 Two-order
translation distribution of four
NP-related constituents

Constituent	2-order translation percentage (%)
NP → DNP NP	16.93
NP → CP NP	9.43
CP → IP DEC	24.79
DNP → NP DEG	34.58

In most cases (75.4 %), four reference translations completely have the same order for syntactic constituents. This makes it easier for our analysis to compare the system order with the reference order. However, there are 22 % cases where two different orders are provided, which shows the flexibility of translation. According to our study, noun phrases taking DNP or CP modifiers, as well as DNPs and CPs themselves are more likely to be translated in two different orders. Table 3.6 shows the percentages in which two different orders in these constituents are observed in the reference corpus.

DNP and CP are always used as premodifiers of noun phrases in Chinese. They often include the particle word *de* (of) at the ending position. The difference is that DNP constructs a phrasal modifier, while CP a relative-clause modifier. There is no fixed reordering pattern for DNP and CP and therefore for NP which takes DNP/CP as a premodifier. In the DNP → NP DEG structure, the DEG (*de*) can be translated into *'s* or *of*, which are both appropriate in most cases, depending on the translator's preference. If the former is chosen, the order of DNP and therefore the order for NP → DNP NP will be both straight: [1][2]. Otherwise, the two orders will be inverted: [2][1]. Similarly, there are also different translation patterns for CP → IP DEC and NP → CP NP. CP can be translated into "that + clause" or adjective-like phrases in English. Figure 3.10 shows an example where the CP constituent is translated into an adjective-like phrase. Although the "that + clause" must be placed behind the noun phrase which it modifies, the order for adjective-like phrases is flexible (see Fig. 3.10).

For these constituents with different reference orders, we compare the order of system translation to that of the reference translation which has the shortest edit distance to the system translation as described above, so that we can take into account the potential influence of different translations on the order of syntactic constituents.

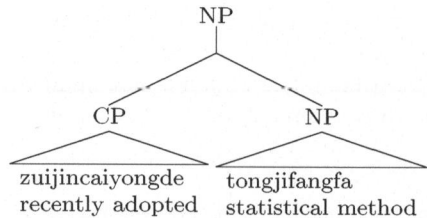

Fig. 3.10 An example for the translation of NP → CP NP. This constituent can be translated in two different orders: (1) the recently adopted statistical method (straight order); (2) the statistical method recently adopted (inverted order)

3.6.2.2 REF-Nonreorderable Constituents

We also study REF-R-rates for the 13 most frequent constituents listed in Table 3.8. We find that two constituents $VP_1 \to PP\ VP_2$ and $NP_1 \to CP\ NP_2$ have the lowest REF-R-rates, 58.20 and 61.77 %, respectively. This means that about 40 % of them are REF-nonreorderable. In order to understand the reasons why they are nonreorderable in reference translations, we further investigate REF-nonreorderable cases for the constituent type $VP_1 \to PP\ VP_2$ and roughly classify the reasons into three categories as follows.

1. *Outside interruption*. The reordering of PP and VP_2 is interrupted by other constituents outside VP_1. For example, the Chinese sentence [NP *mouren/somebody*] [VP_1 [PP *zai...shi/when...*] [VP_2 [*shuo/say* NP[...]]]]] is translated into *when..., somebody said ...*. Here, the translation of the first NP which is outside VP_1 is inserted between the translations of PP and VP_2 and therefore interrupts their reordering. Outside interruption accounts for 21.65 % of REF-nonreorderable cases.
2. *Inside interruption*. The reordering of PP and VP_2 is interrupted by the combination of PP's subnodes with VP_2's subnodes. Inside interruption accounts for 48.45 % REF-nonreorderable cases, suggesting that it is the major factor which decreases the reorderability of $VP \to PP\ VP$. Since both PP and VP have their own complex substructures, the inside interruption is very complicated, including various cases, some of which are even beyond our expectation. Here, we show two frequent examples of inside interruption

   a. The preposition word of PP and verb word/phrase of VP_2 are aligned to only one target word or one continuous phrase. For example, (*xiang...shiya, pressure*), (*dui...youxinxin, be confident of*), (*yin...ershouku, suffer from*), and so on. This is caused by the lexical divergence problem.
   b. PP is first combined with the verb word of VP_2 in an inverted order, then combined with the remaining of VP_2 in a straight order. For example, [PP [P *cong*] [*omission$_1$*]] [VP [VV *liaojiedao*] [*omission$_2$*]] might be translated into *learned from omission$_1$ that omission$_2$*.
3. *Parse error*. This accounts for 29.90 % of REF-nonreorderable cases.

Although the reasons listed above are summarized from our analysis on the constituent type $VP \to PP\ VP$, they can be used to explain other REF-nonreorderable constituents, such as $NP \to CP\ NP$.

3.6.3 Syntactic Constituent Movement in System Translations

Now, we investigate syntactic constituent movement in system translations. We report overall reordering precision and recall of syntactic constituents by comparing reorder-

Table 3.7 Syntactic reordering precision and recall of BWR + SAR versus BWR on the test corpus

	Precision (%)	Recall (%)	F_1 (%)
BWR	70.89	68.79	69.83
BWR + SAR	71.32	73.08	72.19

ing patterns in system translations and those in reference translations. We further study the effect of syntactic knowledge on phrase movement.

3.6.3.1 Overall Reordering Precision and Recall of Syntactic Constituents

By summarizing all syntactic reordering patterns (REF-SRP, SYS-SRP, and Match-SRP) for all constituents, we can calculate the overall reordering precision and recall of syntactic constituents. Table 3.7 shows the results for both BWR + SAR and BWR, where BWR + SAR clearly outperforms BWR.

3.6.3.2 The Effect of Syntactic Knowledge on Phrase Movement

To understand the effects of syntactic knowledge on phrase movement, we further investigate how well BWR and BWR + SAR reorder certain constituents, especially those with high distribution probability. Table 3.8 lists the 13 most frequent

Table 3.8 F_1-scores (BWR + SAR vs. BWR) for the 13 most frequent constituents on the test corpus

Type	Constituent	Percent. (%)	SYS-R-rate (%)		F_1-score (%)	
			BWR	B + S	BWR	B + S
VP	VP → VV NP	8.12	79.22	84.10	76.97	80.53
	VP → ADVP VP	4.30	63.45	65.86	70.83	73.67
	VP → PP VP	**1.87**	**60.32**	**70.37**	**39.29**	**40.33**
	VP → VV IP	1.82	79.35	86.14	77.16	82.26
NP	NP → NN NN	6.88	84.68	85.18	76.17	79.10
	NP → NP NP	5.12	82.13	84.93	69.25	72.17
	NP → DNP NP	**2.14**	**69.75**	**74.83**	**56.68**	**56.61**
	NP → CP NP	**2.12**	**59.67**	**73.43**	**48.75**	**54.48**
Misc.	IP → NP VP	6.78	71.99	79.80	63.22	65.79
	PP → P NP	3.63	80.63	85.95	82.75	84.93
	CP → IP DEC	3.51	83.94	87.89	69.91	72.24
	QP → CD CLP	2.74	66	65	67.52	68.47
	DNP → NP DEG	2.43	85.98	89.84	67.5	68.75

Constituents indicated in bold have relatively lower F_1 score of reordering. B + S denotes BWR + SAR constituents, which jointly account for 51.46 % of all multibranching constituents. Except for the NP → DNP NP, the reordering F_1 score of all these constituents in BWR + SAR is better than that in BWR. This indicates that one effect of syntactic knowledge on constituent movement is that syntactic knowledge is indeed able to improve constituent reordering.

Yet another effect on phrase movement is that the integrated syntactic knowledge makes phrase movement in BWR + SAR pay more respect to syntactic constituent boundaries. The overall R-rates of BWR + SAR versus BWR described in Sect. 3.6.1 indicate that BWR + SAR tends toward moving more syntactic constituents together than BWR does. We want to know whether this is also true for a specific constituent type. The 4th and 5th columns in Table 3.8 present the R-rate for each individual constituent type that we have analyzed. It is obvious that the R-rate of BWR + SAR is much higher than that of BWR for almost all constituents. This indicates that higher R-rate is one of the reasons for the higher performance of BWR + SAR.

To have a more concrete understanding of this effect, we show two examples for the reordering of VP → PP VP in Table 3.9. In both examples, BWR fails to move the PP constituent to the right of the VP constituent while BWR + SAR does it successfully. By tracing the binary BTG trees generated by the decoder, we find that BWR generates a very different BTG tree from the source parse tree, while the BTG tree in BWR + SAR almost matches the source parse tree. In the first example, BWR combines the VP phrase *ditou* with *yali* and then combine *zhengzhi*. The preposition word *xiang* is combined with the NP phrase *NHK*, which makes the translation of *NHK* interrupt the reordering of VP → PP VP in this example. The BWR tree in the second example is even worse. The nonsyntactic phrase *zhankai kongqian* in the VP phrase is first combined with *haixiao zaimin* which is a subphrase of PP preceding VP in an inverted order. The remaining part of the VP phrase is then merged. This merging process continues regardless of the source parse tree. The comparison of BTG trees of

Table 3.9 Two examples for the translation of VP → PP VP. Square brackets indicate combinations in a straight order, while angular brackets represent combinations in an inverted order

Input:	[**NP** NHK] [**VP** [**PP** xiang zhengzhi yali] [**VP** ditou]]
Ref:	[**NP** NHK] [**VP** [**VP** bowed] [**PP** to political pressure]]
BWR:	[[⟨the/xiang NHK/NHK⟩ political/zhengzhi] pressure/yaliditou]
BWR + SAR:	[NHK/NHK ⟨bow/ditou [to political/xiangzhengzhi pressure/yali]⟩]
Input:	[**NP** wu jiao dasha] [**VP** [**PP** wei yazhou haixiao zaimin] [**VP** zhankai kongqian jiuyuan xingdong]]
Ref:	[**NP** Pentagon] [**VP** [**VP** launches unprecedented relief operations] [**PP** for Asian tsunami victims]]
BWR:	[Pentagon/wu jiao dasha [is/wei ⟨[⟨[an/zhankai unprecedented/kongqian] [tsunami/haixiao disaster/zaimin]⟩ relief operations/jiuyuan xingdong] in Asia/yazhou⟩
BWR + SAR:	[Pentagon/wu jiao dasha ⟨[[launched/zhankai an unprecedented/kongqian] rescue operations/jiuyuan xingdong] [[for Asian/yazhou tsunami/haixiao] victims/zaimin]⟩]

BWR + SAR and BWR on the two examples suggests that reordering models should respect syntactic structures in order to capture reorderings under these structures.

This observation on phrase movement resonates with the recent efforts in phrasal SMT which allow the decoder to prefer translations which show more respect to syntactic constituent boundaries (Marton and Resnik 2008; Cherry 2008; Yamamoto et al. 2008). Mapping to syntactic constituent boundaries, or in other words, syntactic cohesion (Cherry 2008; Fox 2002), has been studied and used in early syntax-based SMT models (Wu 1997; Yamada and Knight 2001). But its value has receded in more powerful syntax-based models (Chiang 2005; Galley et al. 2004) and nonsyntactic phrasal models (Koehn et al. 2003). Marton and Resnik (2008) and Cherry (2008) use syntactic cohesion as soft constraint by penalizing hypotheses which violate constituent boundaries. Yamamoto et al. (2008) impose this as hard constraint on the ITG constraint to allow reorderings which respect the source parse tree. They all report significant improvements on different language pairs, which indicate that syntactic cohesion is very useful for phrasal SMT. Our analysis demonstrates that syntactically annotated reordering provides an alternative way to incorporate syntactic cohesion into phrasal SMT.

3.6.4 Syntactic Reordering Patterns with Gaps

In the definition of syntactic reordering patterns, we only consider the relative order of individual constituents on the target side. We do not consider whether or not they remain contiguous on the target side. It is possible that other words are inserted between spans of two contiguous constituents. We call it *gap* when this happens. The absence of gap in the definition of syntactic reordering patterns may produce more matched SRPs and therefore lead to higher precision and recall. Table 3.10 shows the revised overall precision and recall of syntactic reordering patterns when we also compare gaps. The revised results still show that BWR + SAR significantly outperforms BWR. This also applies to the 13 constituents identified in Table 3.8. The analysis results obtained before are still valid when we consider gaps.

3.6.5 Challenges in Phrase Reordering and Suggestions

We highlight three constituent types in Table 3.8 (indicated in bold) which are much more difficult to be reordered according to their relatively lower F_1 scores. The

Table 3.10 Revised overall precision and recall of BWR + SAR versus BWR on the test corpus when we consider the gap in syntactic reordering patterns

	Precision (%)	Recall (%)	F_1 (%)
BWR (gap)	46.28	44.91	45.58
BWR + SAR (gap)	48.80	50	49.39

lower F_1 scores indicate that BWR+LAR is not fully sufficient for reorderings of these constituents, although it performs much better than BWR. We find two main reasons for the lower F_1 scores and provide suggestions accordingly as follows.

1. *Integrating bracketing models.* We observe that in reorderable constituents which involve long-distance reorderings, their boundaries are easy to be violated by phrases outside them. In order to avoid such boundary violations, we should encourage the decoder to select hypotheses that bracket reorderable constituents together and translate them as a unit. This is a bracketing problem. Although we find that the syntactically annotated reordering model is able to improve bracketing as discussed in the last section, such an improvement is a by-product as SAR is dedicated to reordering. In Chaps. 5 and 6, we will introduce various bracketing models that directly deal with the bracketing issue for SMT.
2. *Integrating special reordering rules.* Some constituents are indeed nonreorderable as we discussed in Sect. 3.6.2. Inside or outside interruptions have to be allowed to obtain fluent translations for these constituents. However, the allowance of interruptions, sometimes, is beyond the representability of BTG rules. For example, to solve the lexical divergence problem, bilingual rules with aligned lexicons have to be introduced. To capture reorderings of these constituents, we propose to integrate special reordering rules with richer contextual information into BTG to extend BTG's ability of dealing with interruptions.

3.7 Summary and Additional Readings

This chapter introduces two linguistically motivated reordering models for SMT. In particular, the chapter provides the following techniques for the ITG reordering.

- *Boundary word reordering model* which exploits lexical information to predict the ITG orientation $o \in$ *straight, inverted*.
- *Syntactically annotated reordering model* that integrates annotated syntactic elements into the BTG reordering. The two reordering models adopt the maximum entropy classifier to estimate the order probability.
- *Reordering example extraction algorithms* that extract reordering information from word-aligned bilingual data. We also use the boundary word reordering model to compare the two reordering example extraction algorithms and the four heuristic extraction strategies adopted in AExtractor.
- *Annotation algorithm* that annotates any phrases with syntactic elements from source-side parse trees.
- *Reordering model combination* that combines the two reordering models at the feature/model level.

The empirical evaluation of these two models and their combination is given in "Linguistically Annotated Reordering: Evaluation and Analysis" (Xiong et al., *Computational Linguistics*, 36(3):535–568, 2010).

This chapter also presents a syntax-based reordering analysis method that automatically detects constituent movement in system and reference translations. With this method, we conduct an in-depth analysis on the phrase movement changes after the syntactically annotated reordering model is integrated. The analysis results reveal that the syntactically annotated reordering model is able to improve phrase reordering, especially syntactic constituent reordering. Additionally, it makes the decoder show more respect to constituent boundaries. Finally, the analysis results also suggest that bracketing models should be integrated into the decoder to improve bracketing in SMT.

Additional Readings. Zens and Ney (2006) also propose a maximum entropy based model for phrase reordering. The biggest difference is that their model predicts phrase orientations under the IBM constraint rather than the ITG constraint. Hence distance-based orientation classes are designed to capture the start position for the next phrase. Zhang et al. (2007) integrate source-side syntactic knowledge into a phrase reordering model based on BTG-style rules. However, one limitation of their method is that it only reorders syntactic phrases. Nonsyntactic phrases are combined monotonously with a flat reordering score in their model. He et al. (2010b) incorporate the boundary word reordering model into hierarchical phrase-based SMT. Li et al. (2013) propose a new reordering model for BTG-based SMT that conditions on entire neighboring blocks with recursive autoencoders. Hassan et al. (2007) integrate linguistic knowledge into SMT by supertagging plain phrases on the target side. Mylonakis and Sima'an (2011) introduce a method to annotate each phrase-pair span with multiple linguistically motivated categories from the source language.

Although there are various work on phrase reordering, automatic analysis of phrase reordering is not widely explored in the SMT literature. Chiang et al. (2005) propose an automatic method to compare different system outputs based on part-of-speech (POS) tag sequences. A recall is calculated for each certain POS tag sequence to indicate the ability of reordering models to capture such tag sequence. Popovic et al. (2006) use the relative difference between WER (word error rate) and PER (position independent word error rate) to indicate reordering errors. The larger the difference, the more reordering errors there are. Callison-Burch et al. (2007) propose a constituent-based evaluation that is very similar to the step (1)–(3) of the syntax-based analysis method described in Sect. 3.5. They also parse the source sentence and automatically align the parse tree with the reference/system translations. The difference is that they highlight constituents from the parse tree to have human evaluate the translations of these constituents, rather than automatically analyze constituent movement.

Chapter 4
Semantically Informed Reordering

Abstract This chapter elaborates yet another reordering approach: *semantically informed reordering* that incorporates semantic knowledge from predicate-argument structures into reordering. Predicate-argument structure contains rich semantic information of which current statistical machine translation has not taken full advantage. Due to this semantic insensitiveness, one common error in statistical machine translation is about argument reordering: arguments are placed at incorrect positions after translation. In order to reduce such errors, we introduce a semantically informed reordering model that uses the position of a predicate as the reference axis to estimate positions of its associated arguments on the target side. In this way, the model predicts moving directions of arguments relative to their predicates with semantic features.

In the last section, we have discussed the integration of syntactic information into reordering under the ITG constraint and its effects on target translations. Similarly, semantic knowledge is also very useful for phrase reordering. This chapter will describe a semantically informed reordering model, which integrates shallow semantic knowledge encoded in predicate-argument structures into SMT. We still model phrase reordering as a classification problem so that we can resort to the maximum entropy classifier for estimating reordering probabilities. We predict the motion direction of source-side arguments relative to their predicates with annotated semantic knowledge from predicate-argument structures. In doing so, we want to directly reduce argument reordering errors as they commonly occur in SMT systems (Wu and Fung 2009a). This brings the following two challenges.

1. We have to design appropriate orientations for argument movement. In the ITG reordering, we have well-defined orientations $o \in \{straight, inverted\}$. However, we need to define new orientations with regard to argument reordering in order to detect positions of arguments after translation.
2. We have to align source-side predicate-argument structures with trees built by the SMT decoder when we integrate the argument reordering model into SMT.

We will introduce the model and integration algorithm to address the two challenges in the reminder of this chapter. Section 4.1 elaborates the semantically informed argument reordering model. We start with a brief introduction of predicate-argument structures. Then we define motion orientations of arguments relative to their predicates and develop a maximum entropy classifier to predict such relative

© Springer Science+Business Media Singapore 2015
D. Xiong and M. Zhang, *Linguistically Motivated Statistical Machine Translation*, DOI 10.1007/978-981-287-356-9_4

orientations. The classifier is trained with various semantic features from both the source and target side.

Section 4.2 presents the integration algorithm that addresses the second challenge. As a special case, we integrate the semantically informed argument reordering model into BTG-based SMT. We define functions to project source-side arguments onto BTG trees and then adopt a dynamic programming algorithm to recursively update the semantically informed argument reordering score on projected arguments.

Section 4.3 provides an analysis on a concrete translation example to demonstrate how the semantically informed argument reordering model improve phrase reordering. Section 4.4 summarizes and gives additional readings.

4.1 Semantically Informed Argument Reordering

Before we present the semantically informed argument reordering model, we briefly introduce predicate-argument structures. A *predicate-argument structure* can be roughly defined as a representation of the relationships between predicates (generally verbal) and their associated arguments as well as semantic and syntactic properties of a sentence. In a predicate-argument structure, predicates are the completers of the structure. Arguments in the structure are linguistic expressions that complete the meaning of predicates by containing information for questions of *who, what, when, where, why,* and *how* (Xue 2008). Most predicates take 1–3 arguments.[1]

The relation of a predicate and one of its arguments is called a *semantic role.* Figure 4.1 shows a Chinese predicate-argument structure example with its English translation. The verbal predicate "xiuhui/adjourn" (in bold) has four arguments: one in an ARG0 agent role, one in an ARGM-ADV adverbial modifier role, one in an ARGM-TMP temporal modifier role, and the last one in an ARG1 patient role.

4.1.1 Model

As arguments tend to move together with their predicates across languages (Fung et al. 2006), the movement of a predicate and its arguments across translations is like the motion of a planet and its satellites. Therefore, we consider the reordering of an argument as the motion of the argument relative to its predicate. In particular, we use the position of the predicate as the reference axis. The motion of associated arguments relative to the reference axis can be roughly divided into three categories[2]:

---

[1] According to our study on Chinese sentences (Xiong et al. 2012), the number of arguments for 96.5 % verbal predicates on each side (left/right) is not larger than 3.

[2] Here, we assume that the translations of arguments are not interrupted by their predicates, other arguments, or any words outside the arguments in question. We will discuss how to determine whether arguments should be translated as a unit or not in Chap. 6.

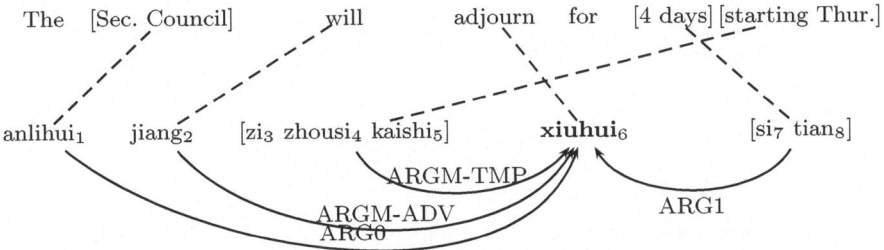

Fig. 4.1 An example of predicate-argument structure in Chinese and its aligned English translation. The *bold word* in Chinese is the verbal predicate. The *subscripts* on the Chinese sentence show the indexes of words from *left* to *right*

- No change across languages (NC);
- Moving from the left side of its predicate to the right side of the predicate after translation (L2R);
- Moving from the right side of its predicate to the left side of the predicate after translation (R2L).

These three categories NC, L2R, and R2L (visualized in Fig. 4.2) describe *argument motion orientations* relative to corresponding predicates.

Let us revisit Fig. 4.1. The ARG0, ARGM-ADV, and ARG1 arguments are located at the same side of their predicate after being translated into English. Therefore, the motion orientation of these three arguments is assigned as "NC". The argument ARGM-TMP is moved from the left side of "xiuhui/adjourn" to the right side of "adjourn" after translation, thus its motion orientation is L2R.

We use the maximum entropy classifier to predict the potential motion orientation $o \in \{NC, L2R, R2L\}$ of an argument A relative to its predicate as follows:

$$P(o|\mathcal{C}(A)) = \frac{\exp(\sum_i \theta_i f_i(o, \mathcal{C}(A)))}{\sum_{o'} \exp(\sum_i \theta_i f_i(o', \mathcal{C}(A)))} \quad (4.1)$$

where $\mathcal{C}(A)$ indicates the surrounding context of A. The features f_i will be introduced in the next section. We assume that motions of arguments are independent on

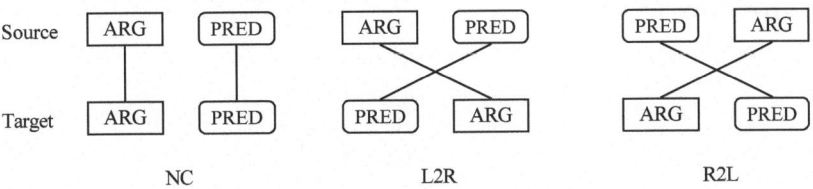

Fig. 4.2 Three categories of argument reorderings. "ARG" represents arguments and "PRED" denotes predicates

each other. Given a source sentence with labeled arguments $\{A_i\}_1^N$, the semantically informed argument reordering model P_{R_s} is formulated as

$$P_{R_s} = \prod_{i=1}^{N} P(o_{A_i} | \mathcal{C}(A_i)) \tag{4.2}$$

where o_{A_i} is the motion orientation of argument A_i.

4.1.2 Features

The feature f_i used in the semantically informed argument reordering model takes the following binary form.

$$f(o, \mathcal{C}(A)) = \begin{cases} 1, & \text{if } o = \clubsuit \text{ and } \mathcal{C}(A).\heartsuit = \spadesuit \\ 0, & \text{else} \end{cases} \tag{4.3}$$

where the symbol $\clubsuit$ represents a possible argument motion orientation ($\{NC, L2R, R2L\}$), the symbol $\heartsuit$ indicates a contextual element for the argument A, and the symbol $\spadesuit$ represents the value of $\heartsuit$. We extract contextual elements from both the source and target side and use them as features for argument reordering.

- *Source-side features.* On the source side, the features include the verbal predicate, the semantic role of the argument, the head word and the boundary words of the argument.
- *Target-side features.* On the target side, the translation of the verbal predicate, the translation of the head word of the argument, as well as the boundary words of the translation of the argument are used as features.

Table 4.1 shows all the features that are used in the semantically informed argument reordering model, including five features extracted from the source side and four features from the target side.

Table 4.1 Features adopted in the argument reordering model

	Features of an argument A for reordering
src	Its predicate A^p
	Its semantic role A^r
	Its head word A^h
	The leftmost word of A
	The rightmost word of A
tgt	The translation of A^p
	The translation of A^h
	The leftmost word of the translation of A
	The rightmost word of the translation of A

Table 4.2 Semantic feature examples. T_{A^h} denotes the translation of A^h

$f(o, C(A)) = 1$ if and only if
o = L2R and $C(A).A^p$ = xiuhui
o = L2R and $C(A).A^r$ = ARGM-TMP
o = L2R and $C(A).A^h$ = zi
o = L2R and $C(A).T_{A^h}$ = starting

Table 4.2 shows some feature examples for the argument "ARGM-TMP" in Fig. 4.1. For example, the feature shown in the second row denotes that the argument "ARGM-TMP" will be moved from the left side of its predicate to the right side of the predicate after translation (L2R), if the predicate is "xiuhui".

4.1.3 Training

In order to train the semantically informed argument reordering model, we take the following three steps.

1. In the first step, we annotate semantic roles for all predicates in source sentences. For instance, if the source language is Chinese, we can first parse all source sentences using a Chinese parser, such as the Berkeley Chinese parser (Petrov et al. 2006), and then run off-the-shelf Chinese semantic role labeler[3] (Li et al. 2010) on all source parse trees to annotate semantic roles for predicates.
2. Second, from such a bilingual training corpus that is annotated with semantic roles on the source side, we extract features defined in the last section.
3. Finally, after all features are extracted, we use a maximum entropy toolkit to train the maximum entropy classifier as formulated in Eq. (4.1).

We show this training process in Fig. 4.3.

According to our study of the distribution of argument reordering categories (i.e., NC, L2R, and R2L) in a Chinese training corpus (Xiong et al. 2012), most arguments, accounting for 82.43 %, are on the same side of their verbal predicates after translation. The remaining arguments (17.57 %) are moved either from the left side of their predicates to the right side after translation (accounting for 11.19 %) or from the right side to the left side of their translated predicates (accounting for 6.38 %). These percentages are shown in Table 4.3.

---

[3] Available at: http://nlp.suda.edu.cn/~jhli/.

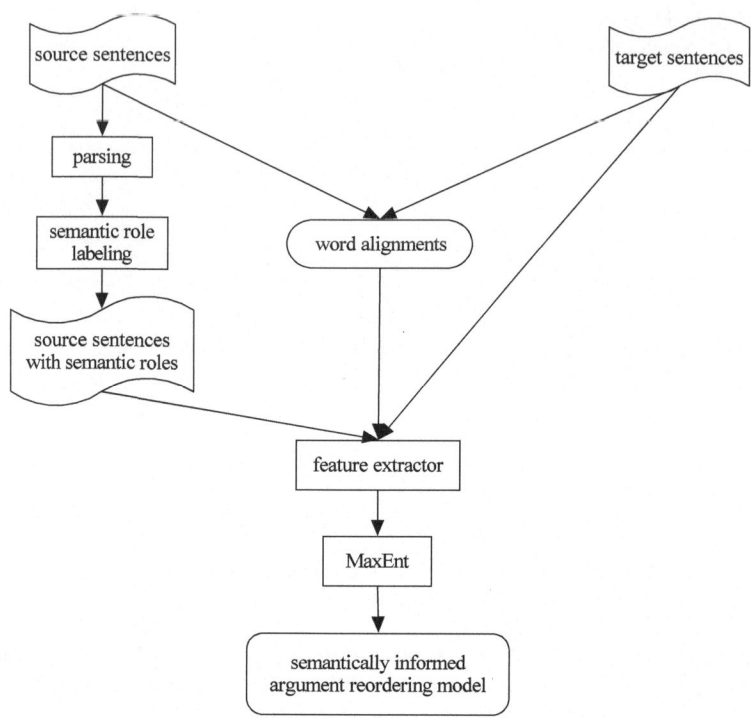

Fig. 4.3 The training process of the semantically informed argument reordering model

Table 4.3 Distribution of
argument reordering
categories in the training data

Reordering category	Percent (%)
NC	82.43
L2R	11.19
R2L	6.38

4.2 Integration

The challenge that we face when integrating the semantically informed argument
reordering model into BTG-based SMT is that arguments are not necessarily aligned
with BTG notes. We have a similar challenge in the last chapter: aligning syntactic
parse trees with BTG trees. In order to address such a challenge, we project BTG
nodes onto source-side parse trees and then annotate projections with source-side
syntactic elements. The whole procedure is visualized in Fig. 4.4a. In this chapter, in
order to address the challenge of aligning predicate-argument structures with BTG
trees, we take a similar projection but with an inverse projection direction. Instead
of projecting BTG nodes onto source-side predicate-argument structures, we project
source-side arguments onto BTG trees, which is shown in Fig. 4.4b.

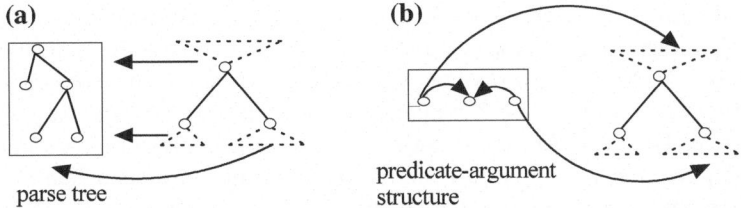

(a)

parse tree

(b)

predicate-argument
structure

Fig. 4.4 Tree Projection in the syntactically annotated reordering (**a**) and the semantically informed argument reordering (**b**). The *dotted triangle* represents a source-side span covered by a corresponding BTG node

In particular, we define two functions $\mathcal{A}$ and $\mathcal{N}$ to project a predicate-argument structure τ onto a BTG tree as follows.

- $\mathcal{A}(i, j, \tau)$. This function projects the predicate-argument structure τ onto a span (i, j) covered by a BTG node. It finds all predicate-argument pairs which are completely located within the span from source word i to j. For example, in Fig. 4.1, $\mathcal{A}(3, 6, \tau) = \{(\text{xiuhui, ARGM-TMP})\}$ while $\mathcal{A}(2, 3, \tau) = \{\}$, $\mathcal{A}(1, 5, \tau) = \{\}$ because the verbal predicate "xiuhui" is located outside the span $(2, 3)$ and $(1, 5)$.
- $\mathcal{N}(i, k, j, \tau)$. the function projects τ onto two neighboring spans (i, k) and $(k+1, j)$ and finds all predicate-argument pairs that cross these two spans. It can be formulated as $\mathcal{A}(i, j, \tau) - (\mathcal{A}(i, k, \tau) \bigcup \mathcal{A}(k + 1, j, \tau))$.

We then define another function $\mathcal{P}_r$ to calculate the argument reordering probability on all arguments which are found by the previous two functions $\mathcal{A}$ and $\mathcal{N}$ as follows.

$$\mathcal{P}_r(\mathcal{B}) = \prod_{A \in \mathcal{B}} P(o_A | \mathcal{C}(A)) \tag{4.4}$$

where $\mathcal{B}$ denotes either $\mathcal{A}$ or $\mathcal{N}$.

Similar to the $-$LM decoding algorithm discussed in Chap. 2, we describe the algorithm in a deductive system. It is shown in Fig. 4.5. The algorithm integrates the semantically informed argument reordering model into BTG-based SMT. For

$$\frac{X \to e/f}{[X, i, j] : \mathcal{P}_r(\mathcal{A}(i, j, \tau))} \tag{4.5}$$

$$\frac{\begin{array}{c} X \to [X_1, X_2] \text{ or } \langle X_1, X_2 \rangle \\ [X_1, i, k] : \mathcal{P}_r(\mathcal{A}(i, k, \tau)) \\ [X_2, k + 1, j] : \mathcal{P}_r(\mathcal{A}(k + 1, j, \tau)) \end{array}}{[X, i, j] : \mathcal{P}_r(\mathcal{A}(i, k, \tau)) \cdot \mathcal{P}_r(\mathcal{A}(k + 1, j, \tau)) \cdot \mathcal{P}_r(\mathcal{N}(i, k, j, \tau))} \tag{4.6}$$

Fig. 4.5 Integrating the semantically informed argument reordering model into BTG-based SMT

notational convenience, we only show the argument reordering model probability for each item, ignoring all other submodel probabilities such as the language model probability. The Eq. (4.5) shows how we calculate the argument reordering model probability when a lexical rule is applied to translate a source phrase f to a target phrase e. The Eq. (4.6) shows how we compute the argument reordering model probability for a span (i, j) in a dynamic programming manner when a bracketing rule is applied to combine its two subspans in a straight $(X \rightarrow [X_1, X_2])$ or inverted order $(X \rightarrow \langle X_1, X_2 \rangle)$. We directly use the probabilities $\mathcal{P}_r(\mathcal{A}(i, k, \tau))$ and $\mathcal{P}_r(\mathcal{A}(k + 1, j, \tau))$ that have been already obtained for the two subspans (i, k) and $(k + 1, j)$. In this way, we only need to calculate the probability $\mathcal{P}_r(\mathcal{N}(i, k, j, \tau))$ for predicate-argument pairs that cross the two subspans.

4.3 Analysis

In this section, we demonstrate how the proposed semantically informed argument reordering model improves phrase reordering by looking into the differences that the model makes on a concrete translation example, which is shown in Fig. 4.6.

In this example, the verbal predicate "jinxing/carry out" has three arguments, ARG0, ARG-ADV, and ARG1. The ARG1 argument should be moved from the right side of the predicate to its left side after translation. The ARG0 argument can either stay on the left side or move to right side of the predicate. According to the phrase alignments of the baseline, we clearly observe three serious translation errors: (1) the ARG0 argument is translated into separate groups which are not adjacent on the target side; (2) the predicate is not translated at all; and (3) the ARG1 argument is not moved to the left side of the predicate after translation. All of these 3 errors are avoided in the Base + ARM system output as a result of the argument reordering model that correctly identifies arguments and moves them in the right directions.

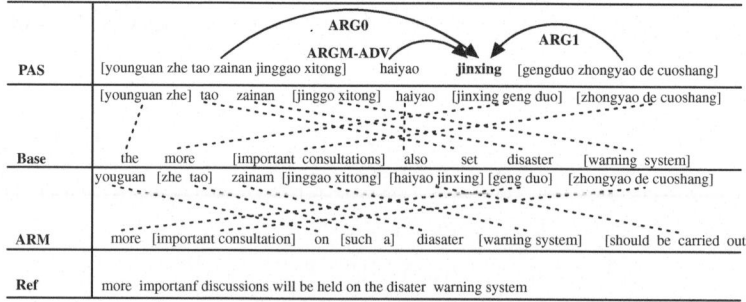

Fig. 4.6 A translation example showing the difference between the baseline and the system with the argument reordering model (ARM). The baseline is a BTG-based SMT system with the boundary word reordering model described in the last chapter. The predicate-argument structure (PAS) of the source sentence is also displayed in the first row

4.4 Summary and Additional Readings

This chapter describes a semantically informed argument reordering model that integrates shallow semantic knowledge represented in predicate-argument structures on the source side into argument reordering. We model the argument reordering as an argument motion orientation (relative to its predicate) prediction problem. We define three motion orientations and train a maximum entropy classifier to predict these orientations during decoding using semantic features. We also introduce an algorithm to integrate the model into the CKY-style decoder in a dynamic programming manner. The empirical evaluation of this model is given in "Modeling the Translation of Predicate-Argument Structure for SMT" (Xiong et al., *Proceedings of the 50th Annual Meeting of the Association for Computational Linguistics*, Jeju, Korea, July 8–14, 2012; pp. 1288–1297.).

Additional Readings. Predicate-argument structures (PAS) are explored for SMT on both the source and target side in other work. As PAS analysis widely employs global and sentence-wide features, it is computationally expensive to integrate target-side predicate-argument structures into the dynamic programming style of SMT decoding (Wu and Fung 2009b). Therefore, they either postpone the integration of target-side PASs until the whole decoding procedure is completed (Wu and Fung 2009b), or directly project semantic roles from the source side to the target side through word alignments during decoding (Liu and Gildea 2010).

The following studies explore only source-side predicate-argument structures. Komachi and Matsumoto (2006) reorder arguments in source language (Japanese) sentences using heuristic rules defined on source-side predicate-argument structures in a preprocessing step. Wu et al. (2011) automate this procedure by automatically extracting reordering rules from predicate-argument structures and applying these rules to reorder source language sentences. Aziz et al. (2011) incorporate source language semantic role labels into a tree-to-string SMT system. Zhai et al. (2012) propose a framework to translate source-side predicate-argument structures into target-side strings.

Chapter 5
Lexicalized Bracketing

Abstract This chapter describes a *lexicalized bracketing* approach to the bracketing issue. We automatically learn lexical features from word-aligned training data and use them to detect source segments that can be bracketed and translated as a unit. In particular, we build two classifiers to predict the beginning and ending positions for such source segments. In the penalty model, we output the best sequence of beginning and ending positions from the two classifiers and then build a penalty feature which penalizes translation hypotheses whenever they cross those source segment beginning and ending positions. In order to take full advantage of the classifiers learned from training data, we extend the penalty model to the lexicalized bracketing model that integrates the whole classifiers into the decoder rather than the best sequence of beginning and ending positions generated by the classifiers.

In the last two chapters, we discuss how linguistically motivated reordering models are developed for SMT in order to determine the order of general phrases (Chap. 3) or the order of arguments (Chap. 4) on the target side. Yet another important issue is about bracketing: which source segments should be bracketed together and translated as a unit. This time we focus on segments on the source side.

Figure 5.1 shows how we bracket a source sentence according to phrase alignments between the source sentence and its reference translation. If the translations of two neighboring source segments remain continuous, we can bracket them together. For example, phrase 4 and 5 in Fig. 5.1 can be bracketed together while phrase 3 and 4 cannot be. Such bracketings can be easily done because we have phrase alignments between the source sentence and its reference translation at hand. However, neither reference translations nor phrase alignments are available during decoding. The decoder may choose undesirable bracketings to produce the final translation. For example, the bracketing "[wancheng danren]" may be selected by the decoder if the phrase table includes a phrase entry "wancheng danren|completes solo". But in this sentence, the decoder shall not use this translation option because the two source phrases "wancheng" and "danren" are translated separately and their correspondences are NOT consecutive on the target side.[1]

---

[1] Just because a source phrase can be translated together in one sentence does not mean that it can be translated together in other sentences.

© Springer Science+Business Media Singapore 2015

D. Xiong and M. Zhang, *Linguistically Motivated Statistical Machine Translation*, DOI 10.1007/978-981-287-356-9_5

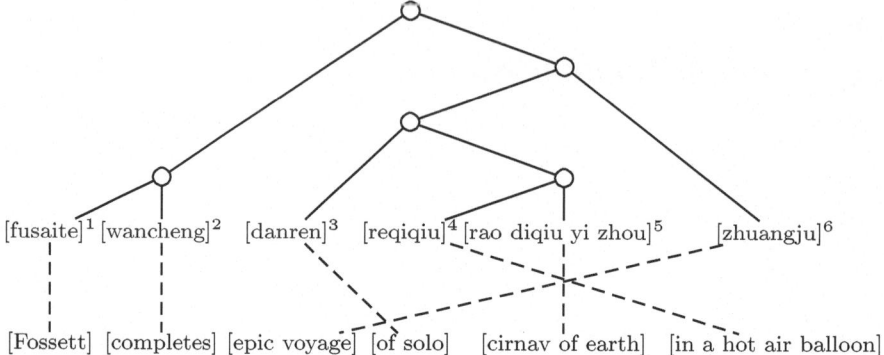

Fig. 5.1 An example of a bracketed source sentence (Chinese) and its reference translation (English). The hierarchical tree over the source sentence shows how the source sentence is bracketed according to the phrase alignments between the source sentence and reference translation. The *superscripts* on the source sentence show the indexes of phrases from *left* to *right*. "cirnav" = "circumnavigation"

We call a source segment that can be translated as a unit *bracketable segment* otherwise *unbracketable segment*.[2] In other words, target correspondences of source phrases in each bracketable segment are still continuous in the target language. Apparently, translations that are built on bracketable segments are preferable to those that are not.

So how do we make the decoder correctly find those bracketable segments? Since it is not practical to learn the distribution of all variable-length bracketable segments from training data, we learn the distributions of their boundaries. We define a bracketable segment within two *bracketable segment boundaries*: beginning and ending boundary. We extract these bracketable segment boundaries from word-aligned data without using any additional resources. Inspired by Roark and Hollingshead (2008) who introduce classifiers to decide if a word can begin/end a multiword constituent, we train two MaxEnt classifiers from the extracted boundaries. The first classifier decides if a word can begin a bracketable segment; the second classifier decides if a word can end a bracketable segment. The reason why we build two classifiers instead of one classifier is that the beginning and ending boundaries of bracketable segments have very different distributions according to our study (Xiong et al. 2011).

With these two classifiers, we develop two different lexicalized bracketing models for SMT as follows.

- *Penalty Model*. We first output the best sequence of bracketable segment boundaries from the trained two classifiers for each source sentence; We then integrate a penalty feature which penalizes hypotheses whenever they cross the output bracketable segment boundaries into the decoder.

---

[2] We will give a formal definition of bracketable segment in Sect. 5.1.

- *Bracketing Strength Model.* Instead of integrating the best bracketable segment boundary sequence, we integrate the whole segment boundary classifiers into the decoder. We use segment boundary probabilities estimated by the classifiers to build the bracketing model.

We call these two models as lexicalized bracketing models because we only use lexical features to detect desirable bracketings.

The remainder of this chapter is organized as follows. Section 5.1 formally defines bracketable segment and its beginning and ending boundary. Section 5.2 describes the algorithm that automatically learn bracketable segment boundaries from word-aligned training data. Section 5.3 introduces the maximum entropy based bracketable segment boundary classifiers and features that are used to train the classifiers. Sections 5.4 and 5.5 present the penalty model and bracketing strength model, respectively. Section 5.6 compares the two bracketing models and discusses how to integrate the two models into SMT. We summarize the chapter in Sect. 5.7 with additional readings.

5.1 Bracketable Segment and Its Boundaries

A bracketable segment is a consecutive source sequence f_i^j which is mapped to a consecutive target sequence e_p^q. The mapping between the two sequences must be consistent with the word alignment M

$$\forall (u, v) \in M, i \leq u \leq j \leftrightarrow p \leq v \leq q \tag{5.1}$$

In this way, it is required that no words inside the source sequence f_i^j are aligned to words outside the target sequence e_p^q and that no words outside the source sequence are aligned to words inside the target sequence. In other words, the source sequence f_i^j is mapped as a unit onto the target sequence e_p^q.

Each bracketable segment f_i^j have two boundaries: bracketable segment beginning boundary (word f_i) and bracketable segment ending boundary (word f_j). Without ambiguity, we sometimes refer to them just as beginning/ending boundaries hereafter. Given a source sentence $f_1 \ldots f_n$, we will say that a word f_i ($1 < i < n$) is in the class $\mathcal{Y}_b$ if there is a bracketable segment spanning $f_i \ldots f_j$ for some $j > i$; and $f_i \in \mathcal{Y}_{\bar{b}}$ otherwise. Similarly, we will say that a word f_j is in the class $\mathcal{Y}_e$ if there is a bracketable segment spanning $f_i \ldots f_j$ for some $j > i$; and $f_j \in \mathcal{Y}_{\bar{e}}$ otherwise.

When defining the $\mathcal{Y}_b$ and $\mathcal{Y}_e$ class, we require that the bracketable segment must contain multiple words ($j > i$) because we are interested in whether a sequence of consecutive source words can be a bracketable segment. Following the definition, a single-word source phrase is therefore always a bracketable segment since it is translated as a unit in the context of phrase-based decoding.

Note that the first word f_1 and the last word f_n in the given sentence $f_1 \ldots f_n$ are unambiguous bracketable segment beginning and ending boundaries. The first word f_1 must begin a bracketable segment spanning the whole source sentence. The last word f_n must end a bracketable segment spanning the whole source sentence. Therefore, we only need to predict for the other $n - 2$ words in a source sentence of length n whether they are bracketable segment beginning and ending boundaries.

5.2 Learning Bracketable Segment Boundaries

Given a source sentence and a target sentence together with word alignments between them, we can easily enumerate all bracketable segments and their boundaries using a phrase extraction algorithm according to the definitions in the last section. The problem here is that words in the same sentence may have different boundary categories. Let's look at the Fig. 5.2a, which shows an example of many-to-many alignment. The source language is Chinese and the target language is English. Each word is indexed with their occurring position from left to right. If we extract a bracketable segment covering source words 1–4, the source word 4 ("feixing") will be a bracketable segment ending boundary ($\in \mathcal{Y}_e$). If we have a bracketable segment beginning with the source word 4, the source word 4 will be nicely a bracketable segment beginning boundary ($\in \mathcal{Y}_b$). However, supposing we extract a bracketable segment spanning source words 2–5, the source word 4 will be neither beginning nor ending boundary ($\notin \mathcal{Y}_b$ or $\mathcal{Y}_e$).

(a)

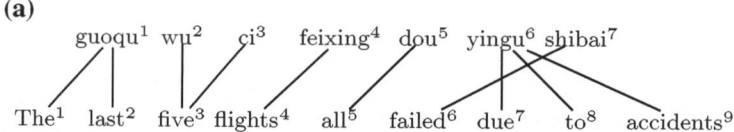

(b)

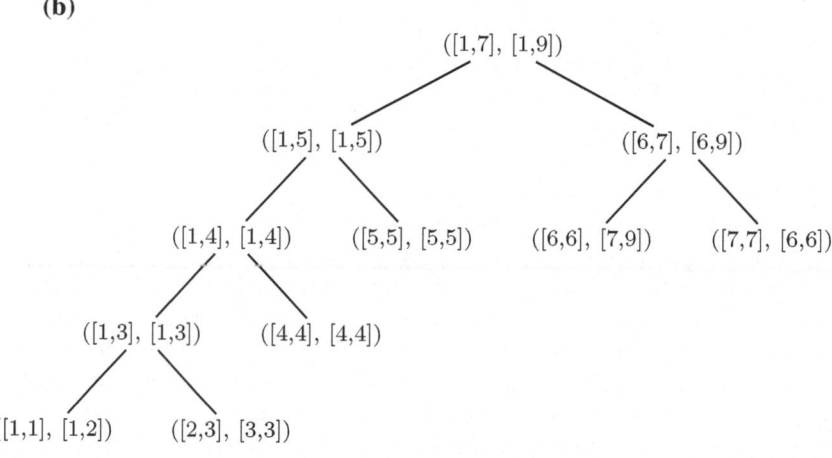

Fig. 5.2 An example of many-to-many word alignment (**a**) and its tree representation produced by SRA (**b**)

This inconsistency arises from the exploration of multiple segmentations in one sentence at the same time. In order to avoid the inconsistency, we explore only one segmentation per sentence. This allows a word to have only one boundary category in the same sentence. Even so, we are still able to obtain the diversity of boundary categories of a word in the training data by allowing multiple categories for this word in different sentences. We generate one segmentation for each aligned source sentence in our training data in a consistent manner by using the SRA (shift-reduce algorithm) (Zhang et al. 2008). For more details of this algorithm, readers can refer to Sect. 3.2.2 of Chap. 3. The algorithm transforms word alignments into hierarchical structures, which also enables our learning algorithm to capture hierarchical bracketings easily.

Given an arbitrary word-level alignment as an input, SRA is able to output a tree representation of the word alignment (a.k.a *decomposition tree*). Each node of the tree is a bracketable segment together with its translation. Therefore, the first word on the bracketable segment of each multisource-word node is a bracketable segment beginning boundary ($\in \mathcal{Y}_b$); the last word on the bracketable segment of each multisource-word node is a bracketable segment ending boundary ($\in \mathcal{Y}_e$).

Figure 5.2b shows the tree representation of the word alignment in Fig. 5.2a after hierarchical analysis using SRA. We use ($[i, j], [p, q]$) to denote a tree node, where i, j and p, q are the beginning and ending index in the source and target language, respectively. By visiting nodes in the decomposition tree, we can easily decide that the source words {*guoqu, wu, yingu*} are in the class $\mathcal{Y}_b$ and any other words are in the class $\mathcal{Y}_{\bar{b}}$ if we want to train a $\mathcal{Y}_b/\mathcal{Y}_{\bar{b}}$ classifier with class labels {$\mathcal{Y}_b, \mathcal{Y}_{\bar{b}}$}. Similarly, the source words {*ci, feixing, dou, shibai*} are in the class $\mathcal{Y}_e$ and any other words are in the class $\mathcal{Y}_{\bar{e}}$ when we train a $\mathcal{Y}_e/\mathcal{Y}_{\bar{e}}$ classifier with class labels {$\mathcal{Y}_e, \mathcal{Y}_{\bar{e}}$}.

The investigation (Xiong et al. 2010b) on a bilingual corpus that contains nearly 100 M Chinese words in approximately 4 M sentences shows that

- 23.4 % among these words can begin a bracketable segment which covers multiple source words.
- 41 M words can end a bracketable segment spanning multiple source words, which accounts for more than 42 % in all words.
- We still have more than 33 M words, accounting for 34.3 %, which neither begin nor end a multisource-word bracketable segment.

These statistic data are shown in Table 5.1.

Table 5.1 Statistics on bracketable segment boundaries from a Chinese–English bilingual corpus

Item	Count (M)	P (%)
Sentences	3.8	–
Words	96.9	–
Words $\in \mathcal{Y}_b$	22.7	23.4
Words $\in \mathcal{Y}_e$	41.0	42.3
Words $\notin \mathcal{Y}_b$ and $\notin \mathcal{Y}_e$	33.2	34.3

All numbers are calculated on the source side. P means the percentage

5.3 Building Bracketable Segment Boundary Classifiers

In this section, we discuss how to build the bracketable segment boundary detection classifiers and the features used in these classifiers.

5.3.1 Classifiers

We build two maximum entropy classifiers to automatically detect bracketable segment beginning and ending boundaries, respectively. In particular, the classifiers predict whether a source word w is in the class $y \in \{\mathcal{Y}_b, \mathcal{Y}_{\bar{b}}\}$ or $\in \{\mathcal{Y}_e, \mathcal{Y}_{\bar{e}}\}$ as follows:

$$P(y|x(w)) = \frac{\exp(\sum_i \theta_i f_i(y, x(w)))}{\sum_{y'} \exp(\sum_i \theta_i f_i(y', x(w)))} \quad (5.2)$$

where the functions $f_i \in \{0, 1\}$ are features which we will introduce in the next subsection, the θ_i are the weights of these features and $x(w)$ is the context of word w.

In order to train a beginning boundary classifier, we take the following steps:

1. We first run SRA on word-aligned bilingual sentences to obtain decomposition trees as described in the last section.
2. Visiting each node in decomposition trees, we tag the leftmost source word of each multisource-words node with the label $\mathcal{Y}_b$ and any other words in the node with the label $\mathcal{Y}_{\bar{b}}$.
3. We extract features (see the next subsection) for each labeled word and use these features to train the classifier with an off-the-shelf maximum entropy tool.

Similarly, we can also train an ending boundary classifier by annotating source words with class labels $\{\mathcal{Y}_e, \mathcal{Y}_{\bar{e}}\}$. Note that the two classifiers are separately trained.

5.3.2 Features

To predict whether a given source word w is a bracketable segment boundary, we define the features as binary indicator functions $f(x(w), y)$ that equal to one if y belongs to $\{\mathcal{Y}_b, \mathcal{Y}_{\bar{b}}\}$ or $\{\mathcal{Y}_e, \mathcal{Y}_{\bar{e}}\}$ and the context x contains a given source word, and equal to zero otherwise. The features can be represented using the following notation:

$$f_1(x(w), y) = \begin{cases} 1, & y = \mathcal{Y}_b \text{ and } w_{-1} = \text{``zai''} \\ 0, & \text{otherwise} \end{cases}$$

$$f_2(x(w), y) = \begin{cases} 1, & y = \mathcal{Y}_e \text{ and } w = \text{``.''} \\ 0, & \text{otherwise} \end{cases}$$

$$f_3(x(w), y) = \begin{cases} 1, & y = \mathcal{Y}_{\bar{e}} \text{ and } w_1 = \text{``de''} \\ 0, & \text{otherwise} \end{cases}$$

Table 5.2 Feature templates for bracketable segment boundary detection

Template	$f(x(w), y) = 1$ if and only if
1	$y = \alpha$ and $w_{-2} = \beta$
2	$y = \alpha$ and $w_{-1} = \beta$
3	$y = \alpha$ and $w = \beta$
4	$y = \alpha$ and $w_1 = \beta$
5	$y = \alpha$ and $w_2 = \beta$

Here, $f_1(x(w), y) = 1$ when the current word w is a bracketable segment beginning boundary and the pervious word w_{-1} is "zai"; $f_2(x(w), y) = 1$ when w is a bracketable segment ending boundary and it is a full stop in Chinese; $f_3(x(w), y) = 1$ when w is not a bracketable segment boundary and the next word w_1 is "de".

We define the context $x(w)$ to be a 5-word window centered at the current word w: $\{w_{-2}, w_{-1}, w, w_1, w_2\}$. All features are extracted from this window context. In Table 5.2, we summarize 5 feature templates, where $\alpha \in \{\mathcal{Y}_b, \mathcal{Y}_{\bar{b}}\}$ or $\{\mathcal{Y}_e, \mathcal{Y}_{\bar{e}}\}$ and β is a word from the source language vocabulary $\mathcal{V}_s$. The feature f_1 mentioned above is thus derived from feature template 2 with $\alpha = \mathcal{Y}_b$ and $\beta = $ "zai". Similarly, the feature f_2 is derived from template 3 and the feature f_3 is from template 4. In this way, if we build two classifiers to predict the beginning and ending boundary separately, we will extract $2 \times |\mathcal{V}_s|$ features from each template for each classifier.

5.4 Penalty Model

The first bracketing model that we build with the beginning and ending boundary classifiers is the *penalty model*. The core idea behind the model is that

- The boundary labels predicted by the two classifiers are used to form a *constraint*;
- Any hypotheses that violate the constraint will be penalized.

We run the two trained classifiers on source sentences separately to obtain two classified word sets: $\mathcal{Y}_b/\mathcal{Y}_{\bar{b}}$ words and $\mathcal{Y}_e/\mathcal{Y}_{\bar{e}}$ words. Table 5.3 shows a labeled example. With these output labels, we can define two kinds of constraints. The first constraint is a *hard constraint*. With the hard constraint, we prohibit any bracketings on source spans ranging from f_i to f_j ($j > i$) where $f_i \notin \mathcal{Y}_b$ or $f_j \notin \mathcal{Y}_e$.

Table 5.3 An example source sentence with labels predicted by the beginning and ending boundary classifier

Index	1	2	3	4	5	6	7
Word	guoqu	wu	ci	feixing	dou	yingu	shibai
BC	$\mathcal{Y}_b$	$\mathcal{Y}_b$	$\mathcal{Y}_{\bar{b}}$	$\mathcal{Y}_{\bar{b}}$	$\mathcal{Y}_{\bar{b}}$	$\mathcal{Y}_b$	$\mathcal{Y}_{\bar{b}}$
EC	$\mathcal{Y}_{\bar{e}}$	$\mathcal{Y}_{\bar{e}}$	$\mathcal{Y}_e$	$\mathcal{Y}_e$	$\mathcal{Y}_e$	$\mathcal{Y}_{\bar{e}}$	$\mathcal{Y}_e$

BC/EC represents the output labels from the beginning/end boundary classifier, respectively

In other words, bracketings on unbracketable segments that are predicted by the two classifiers are completely prohibited. Obviously, such a hard constraint is at the risk of producing no final translation that covers the whole source sentence.

Alternatively, we introduce a *soft constraint*. In the soft constraint, We add a new feature to the log-linear model: bracketable segment boundary violation counting feature. This counting feature accumulates whenever hypotheses violate bracketable segment boundaries, or formally have a partial translation spanning $f_i \ldots f_j$ $(j > i)$ where $f_i \notin \mathcal{Y}_b$ or $f_j \notin \mathcal{Y}_e$. For example, if we bracket the segment $(3, 4)$ shown in Table 5.3, the counting feature will accumulate because the segment $(3, 4)$ is not a bracketable segment according to the labels predicted by the two classifiers. The weight λ_v of this feature is tuned via minimal error rate training (Och 2003) with other feature weights.

Unlike the hard constraint, which simply prevent any hypotheses from violating bracketable segment boundaries, the soft constraint allows violations of such boundaries but with a penalty of $\exp(-\lambda_v C_v)$ where C_v is the violation count. With the soft constraint, we can enable the model to prefer hypotheses which are consistent with bracketable segment boundaries.

Theoretically, the accuracy of the two classifiers has an impact on the performance of the penalty model. In order to improve the accuracy of the classifiers, we can use the Maximum Entropy Markov Model (MEMM) (Mccallum and Freitag 2000) so that we can integrate class features, such as the class $\mathcal{Y}$ of previous word w_{-1}, into the classifier (Xiong et al. 2010b). A classifier trained in such a way is called MEMM classifier with Markov order 1. The classifiers trained in the last section can be considered as MEMM classifiers with Markov order 0.

5.5 Bracketing Strength Model

The penalty model only uses the best output from the two classifiers in a pipeline fashion, which may be prone to errors. In this section, we introduce yet another model to integrate bracketable segments into SMT. Instead of using the best output labels from the two classifiers to define a bracketable segment, we measure how likely a segment is bracketable with the probabilities estimated by the two classifiers.

We call such a bracketable likelihood as *bracketing strength (BS)*. A naive method to calculate the bracketing strength for a source segment s is using the maximum likelihood estimate by taking counts from training data as follows:

$$\text{BS}(s) = \frac{\text{Count}(s \text{ is a bracketable segment})}{\text{Count}(s)} \tag{5.3}$$

There is a serious data sparseness problem with the Eq. (5.3) because segment s may be very long and unseen in the training data.

We therefore calculate the bracketing strength of s by only looking at the first and last word of s. In our intuition, the more likely the first/last words of a segment are bracketable segment boundaries, the more likely the segment is a bracketable segment. In particular, given a segment s, its bracketing strength $BS(s)$ is measured by

$$BS(s) = P(\mathcal{Y}_b | x(s_f)) \times P(\mathcal{Y}_e | x(s_l)) \tag{5.4}$$

Here, the probability $P(\mathcal{Y}_b | \cdot)$ and $P(\mathcal{Y}_e | \cdot)$ are separately calculated by the two bracketable segment boundary classifiers. s_f and s_l are the first and last word in the segment s, respectively. $x(w)$ represents the context where the word w occurs. For example, in Fig. 5.1, phrases 3–6 form a segment "danren...zhuangju". Its bracketing strength is calculated as follows

$$BS(\text{danren...zhuangju}) = P(\mathcal{Y}_b | x(\text{danren})) \times P(\mathcal{Y}_e | x(\text{zhuangju}))$$

Given a derivation $\mathcal{D}$ with a sequence of applications of translation rules $\mathcal{D} = \langle r_1^n \rangle$, the bracketing strength model can be formulated as follows:

$$M_B(\mathcal{D}) = \prod_{i=1}^{n} BS(s_{r_i}) \tag{5.5}$$

where s_{r_i} represents the source segment covered by the translation rule r_i.

5.6 Integration

The integration of the two lexicalized bracketing models, i.e., the penalty model and the bracketing strength model, into SMT is straightforward. The integration is visualized in Fig. 5.3. The biggest difference between the integration of the penalty model and that of the bracketing strength model is that the latter uses probabilities estimated by the bracketable segment boundary classifiers rather than the best labels generated by the two classifiers.

For the penalty model, the integration procedure is as follows:

- We use the trained bracketable segment beginning boundary classifier to output the best beginning boundary sequence for each source sentence to be translated.
- Similarly, we annotate the best ending boundary sequence for each source sentence with the trained bracketable segment ending boundary classifier.
- During decoding, for each application of a translation rule,[3] we check whether the source span covered by the rule violates bracketable segment boundaries. If so, the violation count C_v will be accumulated.

For the bracketing strength model, we integrate the two classifiers into the decoder rather than the best bracketable segment boundaries. Whenever a translation rule is

---

[3] See Sect. 1.1 of Chap. 1 for the definition of translation rule.

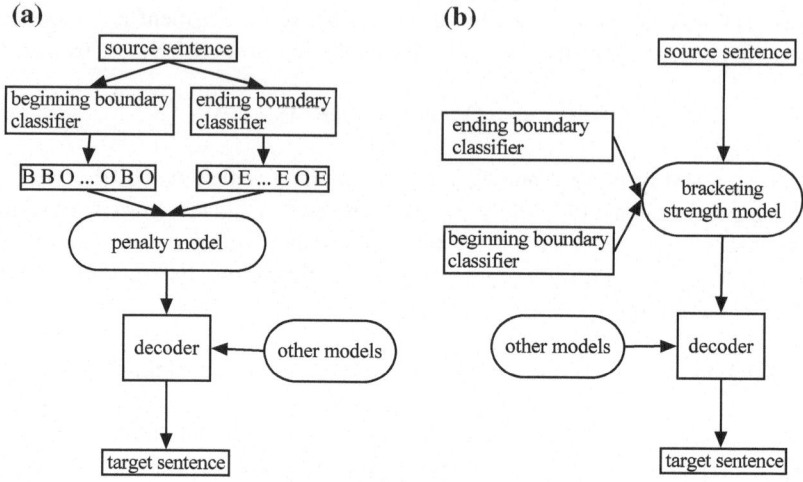

Fig. 5.3 The comparison between the penalty model and the bracketing strength model. B/E represent $\mathcal{Y}_b/\mathcal{Y}_e$, respectively and O represents $\mathcal{Y}_{\bar{b}}$ or $\mathcal{Y}_{\bar{e}}$

applied, we first determine the source segment that is covered by the translation rule and then calculate the bracketing strength according to the Eq. (5.4) for the segment.

Here, we give more details about integrating the bracketing strength model into BTG-based SMT. Given a BTG derivation D which includes applied lexical and bracketing rules $r^l_{1..n_l}$ and $r^b_{1..n_b}$, the bracketing strength model $M_B(D)$ is formulated as

$$M_B(D) = \prod_1^{n_l} BS(s_{r^l}) \times \prod_1^{n_b} BS(s_{r^b}), \quad |s_i| > 1 \tag{5.6}$$

where s_{r^l} are segments covered by lexical rules (e.g., segments s_1–s_5 in Fig. 5.4) and s_{r^b} by bracketing rules (e.g., segments s_6–s_9 in Fig. 5.4). $|s|$ is the length of s.[4]

Fig. 5.4 A BTG derivation. *Diamonds* are segments covered by lexical rules while *circles* are segments covered by bracketing rules

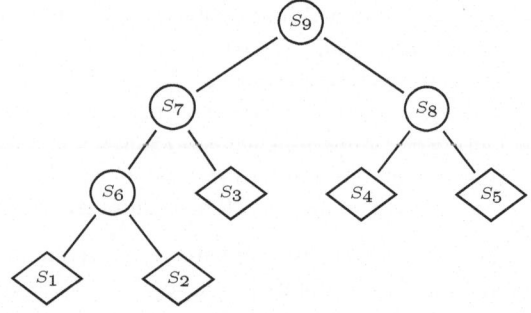

---

[4] As mentioned in Sect. 5.1, single-word segments are always bracketable in phrase-based decoding. Therefore, we are only interested in multiword segments.

We can also only monitor segments covered by lexical rules by a variant model which we call phrasal segmentation model (Xiong et al. 2011). In this model, we require that segments in the Eq. (5.6) are only from those covered by lexical rules, ignoring all segments covered by bracketing rules. For example, the phrasal segmentation model only calculates the bracketing strength for segments s_1–s_5 in Fig. 5.4.

We can easily integrate the bracketing strength model into BTG-based SMT as follows:

$$M(D) = M_T(r^l_{1..n_l}) \cdot P_R(r^b_{1..n_b})^{\lambda_R} \cdot M_B(D)^{\lambda_B} \cdot P_L(e)^{\lambda_L} \cdot \exp(|e|)^{\lambda_w} \qquad (5.7)$$

where $M_B(D)$ is defined in the Eq. (5.6), λ_B is the weight of the bracketing strength model.

5.7 Summary and Additional Readings

This chapter presents two different lexicalized bracketing models: the penalty model and the bracketing strength model. Both models integrate bracketable segment boundaries into SMT. We automatically learn such boundaries from word-aligned training data. The learned boundaries and their lexical contexts are then used to train two maximum entropy classifiers that detect bracketable segment beginning boundaries and ending boundaries, respectively. The penalty model uses the best output boundaries from the two classifiers to define bracketable segments while the bracketing strength model uses the boundary probabilities estimated by the classifiers to measure how likely a segment is bracketable.

We empirically evaluate and compare these two models. Experiment results show that the two models are both able to significantly improve the performance over the baseline which does not use any bracketing models. Furthermore, the bracketing strength model is better than the penalty model. The empirical evaluation of the two models is reported in "Learning Translation Boundaries for Phrase-Based Decoding" (Xiong et al., *Proceedings of Human Language Technologies: The 2010 Annual Conference of the North American Chapter of the ACL*, Los Angeles, California, June 2010; pp. 136–144) and "A Maximum Entropy Segmentation Model for Statistical Machine Translation" (Xiong et al., *IEEE Transactions on Audio, Speech and Language Processing*, 19(8):2494–2505).

Additional Readings. Zhao et al. (2011) also use a MaxEnt-based classifier to predict bracketable constituent boundaries and then integrate the output probabilities into a syntax-based decoder. Experiment results show that such a bracketing model can improve their syntax-based SMT system. As hierarchical phrase-based SMT also faces the challenge to find source fragments that can be bracketed together and translated as a cohesive unit, He et al. (2010a) successfully adapt the bracketing approach discussed in this chapter to Hierarchical phrase-based SMT. Xiao et al. (2012); Xiao and Xiong (2013); Huang et al. (2012) incorporate bracketing boundaries as features into synchronous and monolingual grammar induction. Mylonakis and Sima'an (2008) also study the issue of phrase segmentation and propose an ITG-based prior over segmentations to learn phrase translation probabilities.

Various approaches incorporate constraints into phrase-based decoding in a soft or hard manner. Cherry (2008) and Marton and Resnik (2008) utilize source-side parse tree boundary violation counting feature to build soft constraints for phrase-based decoding. More previously, Chiang (2005) rewards hypotheses whenever they exactly match constituent boundaries of parse trees on the source side.

In addition, hard linguistic constraints are also explored. Wu and Ng (1995) employ syntactic bracketing information to constrain search in order to improve speed and accuracy. Collins et al. (2005) and Wang et al. (2007) use hard syntactic constraints to perform reorderings according to source-side parse trees. Xiong et al. (2008) prohibit any swappings which violate punctuation based constraints.

Berger et al. (1996) introduce the concept of *rift* into a machine translation system, which is similar to our definition of bracketable segment boundary. They also use a maximum entropy model to predict whether a source position is a rift based on features only from source sentences. Our work differs from the method of Berger et al. (1996) in three major respects.

- We distinguish a bracketable segment boundary into two categories: beginning and ending boundary due to their different distributions (Xiong et al. 2010b). However, Berger et al. ignore this difference.
- We train two classifiers to predict beginning and ending boundary, respectively, while Berger et al. build only one classifier. Experiments show that two separate classifiers outperform one classifier (Xiong et al. 2010b).
- The last difference is how segment boundaries are integrated into a machine translation system. Berger et al. use predicted rifts to divide a long source sentence into a series of smaller segments, which are then translated sequentially in order to increase decoding speed. This can be considered as a hard integration, which may undermine translation accuracy given wrongly predicted rifts. We integrate predicted translation boundaries into phrase-based decoding in a soft manner, which improves translation accuracy in terms of BLEU score.

Chapter 6
Linguistically Motivated Bracketing

Abstract Instead of using two classifiers to detect the beginning and ending positions for a source segment that can be bracketed and translated together, we introduce a *linguistically motivated bracketing* approach in this chapter that directly determines whether a source segment can be bracketed and translated as a unit or not. We achieve this by using high-level information: syntactic and semantic structure knowledge. In the syntax-driven bracketing model, we employ syntactic knowledge from source-side parse trees to determine whether a source segment is bracketable. In the semantically informed argument bracketing model, we focus on argument translations and use semantic features from predicate-argument structures to predict whether an argument can be translated as a unit.

The bracketing strength model in the last chapter measures how likely a segment is bracketable with probabilities estimated from two boundary classifiers that are trained with lexical features. In this chapter we introduce two linguistically motivated bracketing models that also measure how likely a segment is bracketable. The differences between the two linguistically motivated bracketing models and the bracketing strength model are twofold. In the two linguistically motivated bracketing models,

1. We build classifiers to directly detect whether a segment is bracketable rather than resort to the beginning/ending boundary classifiers. Given an arbitrary segment s, the probability $P(bracketable|s)$ that s is bracketable is directly estimated by classifiers. We do NOT calculate $P(bracketable|s)$ as follows:

$$P(bracketable|s) = P(\mathcal{Y}_b|s_f) \times P(\mathcal{Y}_e|s_l)$$

where s_f/s_l is the first/last word of s.
2. We explore high-level syntactic and semantic knowledge in the new classifiers. As we mentioned in the previous chapter, it is not practical to calculate the bracketable probability of a segment by the maximum likelihood estimate with counts that the segment occurs as a bracketable or unbracketable segment in the training data. We therefore incorporate high-level features into discriminative classifiers to estimate the probability.

The first linguistically motivated bracketing model is *Syntax-Driven Bracketing Model* (SDB) that predicts whether a phrase is bracketable using rich syntactic

© Springer Science+Business Media Singapore 2015
D. Xiong and M. Zhang, *Linguistically Motivated Statistical Machine Translation*, DOI 10.1007/978-981-287-356-9_6

features. In this model, we parse the source language sentences in a word-aligned training corpus. Based on these word alignments, we define bracketable and unbracketable instances. For each of these instances, we automatically extract relevant syntactic features from source parse trees as bracketing evidences. Then we tune the weights of these features using a maximum entropy trainer. In this way, we build two syntax-driven bracketing models: (1) a unary SDB model (UniSDB) that predicts whether an independent phrase is bracketable or not; and (2) a binary SDB model (BiSDB) that predicts whether two neighboring phrases can be bracketed together.

The second bracketing model is *Semantically Informed Argument Bracketing Model* (SIAB) that predicts whether an argument from source-side predicate-argument structures is bracketable. In order to collect training instances for the model, we first generate predicate-argument structures for source sentences in the training data as we do in Sect. 4.1.3 of Chap. 4. With word alignments and source-side arguments, we can easily learn argument bracketing instances. From these instances, we extract semantic features, which are tuned in a maximum entropy classifier. The tuned classifier is then used to estimate how likely an argument is bracktable during decoding.

The chapter proceeds as follows. Section 6.1 presents the syntax-driven bracketing model. We introduce the algorithm that automatically learns bracketing instances from word-aligned training data, the discriminative model with various syntactic features, and the integration of the model into SMT. Section 6.2 describes the semantically informed argument bracketing model. We discuss the model, semantic features that are used in the model as well as the algorithm that integrates the model into SMT. Finally, we summarize the whole chapter in Sect. 6.3.

6.1 Syntax-Driven Bracketing

As we mentioned in Chap. 3, the integration of syntactic knowledge into reordering not only improves reordering itself but also makes hypotheses more consistent with syntactic structures. This suggests that syntactic constraints are useful in phrase-based translation. If we only allow syntactic translations in order to make final translations fully consistent with syntactic constraints, this will jeopardize the performance of phrasal translation (Koehn et al. 2003). To better leverage syntactic constraints yet still allow non-syntactic translations, Chiang (2005) introduced a count for each hypothesis and accumulated it whenever the hypothesis exactly matched syntactic boundaries on the source side. On the contrary, Marton and Resnik (2008) accumulated a count whenever hypotheses violated constituent boundaries. These constituent matching/violation counts are used as a feature in the log-linear model of SMT and their weights are tuned via minimal error rate training (Och 2003). In this way, syntactic constraint is integrated into decoding as a soft constraint to enable the decoder to reward hypotheses that respect syntactic parse trees or to penalize hypotheses that violate syntactic structures on the source side.

There are two disadvantages in the above method that uses constituent matching/violation counts as features, which are listed as follows.

1. The best combination of syntactic categories (e.g., NP, VP, and so on) that are used to count matchings or violations is usually language-dependent and has to be found manually. For example, through a lot of experiments, Marton and Resnik (2008) found that the best combination for Chinese-to-English translation is called XP+ including {NP, VP, CP, IP, PP, ADVP, QP, LCP, DNP} while in Arabic-to-English translation this combination works even worse than their baseline.
2. The method only explores syntactic categories. Actually, in addition to syntactic categories, we have other rich syntactic contexts that can also be used as syntactic constraints.

This section provides a syntax-driven bracketing model that automatically learns rich syntactic constraints from training data. With this model, we shift our attention from syntactic/non-syntactic translations to the nature of such translations: phrase bracketability (i.e., whether a phrase can be bracketed together and translated as a whole unit). We first introduce the algorithm that automatically learns syntax-driven bracketing instances from word-aligned source-side-parsed training data. We then describe the model and features based on learned bracketing instances. Additionally, we also discuss how we integrate the syntax-driven bracketing model into SMT. Finally, we visually compare the syntax-driven bracketing model against Marton and Resnik's (2008) best syntactic constraint XP+ on Chinese-to-English translation with several translation examples.

6.1.1 Learning Syntax-Driven Bracketing Instances

At first, we formally define the syntax-driven bracketing instance, which comprises two types, namely *binary bracketing instance* and *unary bracketing instance*. We then present the algorithm to automatically extract these bracketing instances from word-aligned bilingual corpus where the source language sentences are parsed.

Let f and e be a source sentence and a target sentence, M be the word alignment between them, and T be the parse tree of f. We define a *binary bracketing instance* as a tuple $\langle b, \tau(f_{i..j}), \tau(f_{j+1..k}), \tau(f_{i..k}) \rangle$ where $b \in \{bracketable, unbracketable\}$, $f_{i..j}$ and $f_{j+1..k}$ are two neighboring source phrases and $\tau(T, s)$ ($\tau(s)$ for short) is a subtree function, which returns the minimal subtree subsuming the source sequence s from the source parse tree T. For the two neighboring source phrases, the following conditions are satisfied:

$$\exists e_{u..v}, e_{p..q} \in e \; s.t.$$

$$\forall (m, n) \in M, i \leq m \leq j \leftrightarrow u \leq n \leq v \tag{6.1}$$

$$\forall (m, n) \in M, j + 1 \leq m \leq k \leftrightarrow p \leq n \leq q \tag{6.2}$$

The above Eq. (6.1) means that there exists a target phrase $e_{u..v}$ aligned to $f_{i..j}$ and (6.2) denotes a target phrase $e_{p..q}$ aligned to $f_{j+1..k}$. If $e_{u..v}$ and $e_{p..q}$ are neighboring to each other or all words between the two phrases are aligned to null, we set $b = $ *bracketable*, otherwise $b = $ *unbracketable*. From a binary bracketing instance, we derive a *unary bracketing instance* $\langle b, \tau(c_{i..k}) \rangle$, ignoring inner subtrees $\tau(f_{i..j})$ and $\tau(f_{j+1..k})$.

Let n be the number of words of f. If we extract all potential bracketing instances, there will be $o(n^2)$ unary instances and $o(n^3)$ binary instances. In order to keep the number of bracketing instances tractable, we follow the heuristic strategies adopted in the reordering example extraction algorithm as shown in Sect. 3.2.1 of Chap. 3. We record only four representative bracketing instances for each index j: (1) the bracketable instance with the minimal $\tau(f_{i..k})$, (2) the bracketable instance with the maximal $\tau(f_{i..k})$, (3) the unbracketable instance with the minimal $\tau(f_{i..k})$, and (4) the unbracketable instance with the maximal $\tau(f_{i..k})$.

Figure 6.1 shows the algorithm to extract bracketing instances. Lines 3–11 find all potential bracketing instances for each $(i, j, k) \in f$ but only keep four bracketing instances for each index j: two minimal and two maximal instances. Although this algorithm learns binary bracketing instances, we can easily derive unary bracketing instances from binary instances according to their definitions.

6.1.2 Model

Our interest is to automatically detect phrase bracketing using rich syntactic information. We consider this task as a binary-class classification problem: whether the current source phrase s is bracketable (b) within particular syntactic contexts ($\tau(s)$).

1: **Input**: sentence pair (f, e), the pase tree T of f and the word alignment M between f and e
2: $\Re := \emptyset$
3: **for** each $(i, j, k) \in f$ **do**
4:      **if** there exists a target phrase $e_{u..v}$ aligned to $f_{i..j}$ and $e_{p..q}$ aligned to $f_{j+1..k}$ **then**
5:          Get $\tau(f_{i..j})$, $\tau(f_{j+1..k})$, and $\tau(f_{i..k})$
6:          Determine b according to the relationship between $e_{u..v}$ and $e_{p..q}$
7:          **if** $\tau(f_{i..k})$ is currently maximal or minimal **then**
8:              Update bracketing instances for index j
9:          **end if**
10:     **end if**
11: **end for**
12: **for** each $j \in f$ **do**
13:     $\Re := \Re \cup \{$bracketing instances from $j\}$
14: **end for**
15: **Output**: bracketing instances $\Re$

Fig. 6.1 Syntax-driven bracketing instances extraction algorithm

If two neighboring sub-phrases s_1 and s_2 are given, we can use more inner syntactic contexts to complete this binary classification task.

We construct the syntax-driven bracketing model within the maximum entropy framework. A unary SDB model is defined as

$$P_{\text{UniSDB}}(b|\tau(s), T) = \frac{\exp(\sum_i \theta_i f_i(b, \tau(s), T)}{\sum_{b'} \exp(\sum_i \theta_i f_i(b', \tau(s), T)} \tag{6.3}$$

where $f_i \in \{0, 1\}$ is a binary feature function which we will describe in the next subsection, and θ_i is the weight of f_i. Similarly, a binary SDB model is defined as

$$P_{\text{BiSDB}}(b|\tau(s_1), \tau(s_2), \tau(s), T) = \frac{\exp(\sum_i \theta_i f_i(b, \tau(s_1), \tau(s_2), \tau(s), T)}{\sum_{b'} \exp(\sum_i \theta_i f_i(b', \tau(s_1), \tau(s_2), \tau(s), T)} \tag{6.4}$$

The most important advantage of syntax-driven bracketing model is its capacity of incorporating more fine-grained contextual features, besides the binary feature that detects constituent boundary violation or matching. Employing these features, we can investigate the value of various syntactic constraints in phrase translation.

6.1.3 Syntax-Driven Features

Let s be the source phrase in question, s_1 and s_2 be the two neighboring sub-phrases in s. $\sigma(.)$ is the root node of $\tau(.)$. The SDB model exploits various syntactic features as listed below.

- *Rule Features* (RF). We use the CFG rules of $\sigma(s)$, $\sigma(s_1)$ and $\sigma(s_2)$ as features. These features capture syntactic "horizontal context" which demonstrates the expansion trend of the source phrase s, s_1 and s_2 on the parse tree. In Fig. 6.2,

Fig. 6.2 Illustration of syntax-driven features used in SDB. Here we only show the features for the source phrase s. The *triangle*, *rounded rectangle*, and *rectangle* denote the rule feature, path feature, and constituent boundary matching feature respectively

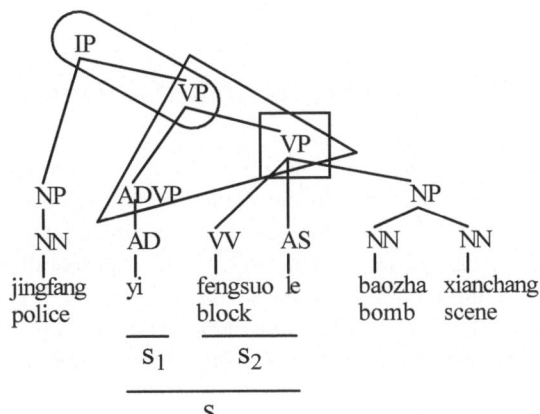

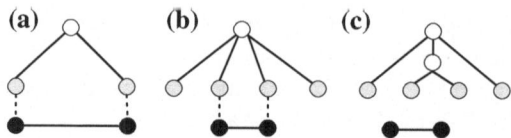

Fig. 6.3 Three scenarios of the relationship between phrase boundaries and constituent boundaries. The *gray circles* are constituent boundaries while the *black circles* are phrase boundaries

the CFG rule "ADVP→AD," "VP→VV AS NP," and "VP→ADVP VP" are used as features for s_1, s_2 and s respectively.

- *Path Features* (PF). The tree path $\sigma(s_1)..\sigma(s)$ connecting $\sigma(s_1)$ and $\sigma(s)$, $\sigma(s_2)..$ $\sigma(s)$ connecting $\sigma(s_2)$ and $\sigma(s)$, and $\sigma(s)..\rho$ connecting $\sigma(s)$ and the root node ρ of the whole parse tree are used as features. These features provide syntactic "vertical context" which shows the generation history of the source phrases on the parse tree. In Fig. 6.2, the path features are "ADVP VP," "VP VP," and "VP IP" for s_1, s_2 and s respectively.
- *Constituent Boundary Matching Features* (CBMF). These features are to capture the relationship between a source phrase s and $\tau(s)$ or $\tau(s)$'s subtrees. There are three different scenarios[1]: (1) *exact match*, where s exactly matches the boundaries of $\tau(s)$ (Fig. 6.3a), (2) *inside match*, where s exactly spans a sequence of $\tau(s)$'s subtrees (Fig. 6.3b), and (3) *crossing*, where s crosses the boundaries of one or two subtrees of $\tau(s)$ (Fig. 6.3c). In the case of (1) or (2), we set the value of this feature to $\sigma(s)$-M or $\sigma(s)$-I respectively. When the left part of s crosses the boundaries of the sub-constituent ϵ_l, we set the value to $\sigma(\epsilon_l)$-LC; If the right part of s crosses the boundaries of the sub-constituent ϵ_r, we set the value to $\sigma(\epsilon_r)$-RC; If both, we set the value to $\sigma(\epsilon_l)$-LC-$\sigma(\epsilon_r)$-RC. Refer to Fig. 6.2 for illustration. The source phrase s_1 exactly matches the constituent ADVP, therefore CBMF is "ADVP-M". The source phrase s_2 exactly spans two sub-trees VV and AS of VP, therefore CBMF is "VP-I". Finally, the source phrase s cross boundaries of the lower VP on the right, therefore CBMF is "VP-RC".

6.1.4 Integrating the SDB Model into SMT

We integrate the SDB model into SMT to help the decoder perform syntax-driven bracketing. In particular, we add a new feature into the log-linear model: $P_{\text{SDB}}(b|T, \tau(.))$. This feature is computed by the SDB model described in the Eqs. (6.3) or (6.4), which estimates a probability that a source span is translated as a unit within particular syntactic contexts. If a source span can be translated as a unit, the feature will give a higher probability even though this span violates boundaries of a constituent. Otherwise, a lower probability is given. Through this additional

---

[1] The three scenarios that we define here are similar to those used by Lü et al. (2002).

feature, we want the decoder to prefer hypotheses that translate source spans that can be translated as a unit, and avoid translating those that are discontinuous after translation. The weight of this new feature is tuned via minimum error rate training (Och 2003), which measures the extent to which this feature should be trusted.

Integrating the SDB model into SMT is straightforward. Whenever a translation rule that covers a source span (i, j) is applied, we calculated the bracketing probability of the source span according to the SDB model. Particularly, we take BTG-based SMT as an example. During decoding, whenever a BTG bracketing rule $(X \rightarrow [X_1 \ X_2] \text{or} X \rightarrow \langle X_1 \ X_2 \rangle)$ is used, the SDB model gives a probability to the span s covered by the rule, which estimates the extent to which the span is bracketable. For the unary SDB model, we only consider the features from $\tau(s)$. For the binary SDB model, we use all features from $\tau(s_1)$, $\tau(s_2)$ and $\tau(s)$ since the binary SDB model is naturally suitable to the binary BTG rules.

6.1.5 Comparing the SDB Model Against XP+

In order to compare the SDB model, especially the binary SDB model, against Marton and Resnik's (2008) best syntactic constraint XP+, we introduce a new statistical metric which measures the proportion of syntactic constituents[2] whose boundaries are consistently matched by the decoder during translation. This proportion, which we call *consistent constituent matching (CCM) rate*, reflects the extent to which translation outputs respect parse trees of the source language.

In order to calculate this rate, we output translation results as well as phrase alignments found by the decoder. Then for each multi-branch constituent c_i^j spanning from i to j on the source side, we check the following conditions:

- If its boundaries i and j are aligned to phrase segmentation boundaries found by the decoder.
- If all target phrases inside c_i^j's target span[3] are aligned to the source phrases within c_i^j and not to the phrases outside c_i^j.

If both conditions are satisfied, the constituent c_i^j is consistently matched by the decoder.

Table 6.1 shows the consistent constituent matching rates. Without using any source-side syntactic information, the baseline obtains a low CCM rate of 43.53 %, indicating that the baseline decoder violates source parse trees more than it respects.

By integrating syntactic constraints into decoding, we can see that both Marton and Resnik's XP+ and our SDB model achieve a significantly higher constituent matching rate, suggesting that they are more likely to respect source structures.

---

[2] We only consider multi-branch constituents.

[3] Given a phrase alignment $P = \{c_f^g \leftrightarrow e_p^q\}$, if the segmentation within c_i^j defined by P is $c_i^j = c_{i_1}^{j_1} ... c_{i_k}^{j_k}$, and $c_{i_r}^{j_r} \leftrightarrow e_{u_r}^{v_r} \in P$, $1 \leq r \leq k$, we define the *target span* of c_i^j as a pair where the first element is $\min(e_{u_1} ... e_{u_k})$ and the second element is $\max(e_{v_1} ... e_{v_k})$, similar to (Fox 2002).

Table 6.1 Consistent constituent matching rates reported on 1-best translation outputs on the NIST MT05

System	CCM Rate (%)
Baseline	43.5
XP+	74.5
BiSDB	72.4

The examples in Table 6.2 show that the decoder is able to generate better translations if it is faithful to source parse trees with syntactic constraints.

We further conduct a deep comparison of translation outputs of BiSDB versus XP+ with regard to constituent matching and violation. We found two significant differences that may explain why our BiSDB outperforms XP+. First, although the overall CCM rate of XP+ is higher than that of BiSDB, BiSDB obtains higher CCM rates for long-span structures than XP+ does, which are shown in Table 6.3. Generally speaking, violations of long-span constituents have a more negative impact on performance than short-span violations if these violations are toxic.

Table 6.2 Translation examples showing that both XP+ and BiSDB produce better translations than the baseline, which inappropriately violates constituent boundaries (within phrases in italic)

Src:	[[wei [yindu yang zaiqu minzhong]$_{NP}$]$_{PP}$ [fengxian [ziji] $_{NP}$ [yi fen aixin]$_{NP}$]$_{VP}$]$_{VP}$
Ref:	Show their loving hearts to people in the Indian Ocean disaster areas
Baseline:	⟨*love/aixin* [*for the/wei*⟨ [*people/minzhong* [*to/fengxian* [*own/ziji a report/yifen*]]]⟩ ⟨*in/zaiqu the Indian Ocean/yinduyang*⟩]⟩
XP+:	⟨[contribute/fengxian [its/ziji [part/yifen love/aixin]]] [for/wei ⟨the people/minzhong ⟨in/zaiqu the Indian Ocean/yinduyang⟩⟩]⟩
BiSDB:	⟨[[[contribute/fengxian its/ziji] part/yifen] love/aixin] [for/wei ⟨the people/minzhong ⟨in/zaiqu the Indian Ocean/yinduyang⟩⟩]⟩
Src:	[wujiaodasha [yi]$_{ADVP}$ [paiqian [[ershi jia]$_{QP}$ feiji] $_{NP}$ [zhi nanya]$_{PP}$]$_{VP}$]$_{IP}$ [,]$_{PU}$ [qizhong baokuo...]$_{IP}$
Ref:	The Pentagon has dispatched 20 airplanes to South Asia, including...
Baseline:	[[The Pentagon/wujiaodasha has sent/yipaiqian] [⟨*to/zhi*[[*South Asia/nanya*, /,] *including/qizhongbaokuo*]] [20/ershi plane/jiafeiji]⟩]]
XP+:	[The Pentagon/wujiaodasha [has/yi [sent/paiqian [[20/ershi planes/jiafeiji] [to/zhi South Asia/nanya]]]]] [,/, [including/qizhongbaokuo...]]
BiSDB:	[The Pentagon/wujiaodasha [has sent/yipaiqian [[20/ershi planes/jiafeiji] [to/zhi South Asia/nanya]]] [,/, [including/qizhongbaokuo...]]

Table 6.3 Consistent constituent matching rates for structures with different spans

System	CCM Rates (%)				
	<6	6–10	11–15	16–20	>20
XP+	75.2	70.9	71.0	76.2	82.2
BiSDB	69.3	74.7	74.2	80.0	85.6

Table 6.4 Translation examples showing that BiSDB produces better translations than XP+ via appropriate violations of constituent boundaries (within phrases in italic)

Src:	[[zai [[[meiguoguowuyuan yu baoer]$_{NP}$ [duanzan]$_{ADJP}$ [huitan]$_{NP}$]$_{NP}$ *hou*]$_{LCP}$]$_{PP}$*biaoshi*]$_{VP}$
Ref:	said after a brief discussion with Powell at the US State Department
XP+:	[⟨after/hou ⟨⟨[a brief/duanzan meeting/huitan] [with/yu Powell/baoer]⟩ [in/zai the US State Department/meiguoguowuyuan]⟩ said/biaoshi]
BiSDB:	⟨*said after/hou biaoshi* ⟨[a brief/duanzan meeting/huitan] ⟨ with Powell/yu baoer [at/zai the State Department of the United States/meiguoguowuyuan]⟩⟩⟩
Src:	[*xiang* [[jianli [weilai minzhu zhengzhi]$_{NP}$]$_{VP}$]$_{IP}$]$_{PP}$ [maichu le [guanjianxing de yi bu]$_{NP}$]$_{VP}$
Ref:	took a key step towards building future democratic politics
XP+:	⟨[a/le [key/guanjianxing step/deyibu]] ⟨forward/maichu [to/xiang [a/jianli [future/weilai political/minzhuzhengzhi democracy/minzhuzhengzhi]]]⟩⟩
BiSDB:	⟨[made a/maichule [key/guanjianxing step/deyibu]] [*towards establishing a/xiang jianli* ⟨democratic politics/minzhuzhengzhi in the future/weilai⟩]⟩

Second, different from XP+ that only punishes constituent boundary violations, our SDB model is able to encourage violations if these violations are done on bracketable phrases. We observed in many cases that by violating constituent boundaries BiSDB produces better translations than XP+ does, which on the contrary matches these boundaries. Consider the following example, where translations are found by XP+ and BiSDB respectively.

XP+: [to/ba ⟨[set up/sheli [for the/wei [navigation/hanghai section/jie]]] on July 11/qiyueshiyiri ⟩]

BiSDB: [to/ba ⟨[[set up/sheli a/wei] [marine/hanghai festival/jie]] on July 11/qiyueshiyiri⟩]

XP+ here matches all constituent boundaries, while BiSDB violates the PP constituent to translate the non-syntactic phrase "sheli wei". Table 6.4 shows more examples, where BiSDB successfully translates two non-syntactic phrases "hou biaoshi" and "xiang jianli" by violating their constituent boundaries. From these examples, we clearly see that appropriate violations are helpful and even necessary for generating better translations. By allowing appropriate violations to translate non-syntactic phrases according to particular syntactic contexts, our SDB model better inherits the strength of phrase-based approach than XP+.

6.2 Semantically Informed Argument Bracketing

As we mention in Chap. 4, argument reordering errors commonly occur in SMT systems. Yet another common error in argument translation is that arguments are wrongly translated into separate groups instead of a cohesive unit. We call this error

argument bracketing error. Figure 4.6 in Chap. 4 shows such an error. The first line
is the predicate-argument structure (PAS) of the source sentence in Chinese. The
second line shows the translation along with the phrase alignments generated by
the baseline BTG-based system that does not incorporate any bracketing models.
From the phrase alignments, we can obviously see that the ARG0 argument is translated into separate groups which are not adjacent on the target side. Sometimes
the translation of an argument may be interrupted by words outside the argument
while other times it should be translated as a unit. In this section, we discuss a
Semantically Informed Argument Bracketing Model (SIABM) that predicts whether
an argument should be translated as a unit or translated into separate discontinuous
groups.

6.2.1 Model

We build the argument bracketing model still based on the maximum entropy principle. The model is formulated as follows:

$$P_{\text{SIABM}}(b|\mathcal{C}(A)) = \frac{\exp(\sum_i \theta_i f_i(b, \mathcal{C}(A))}{\sum_{b'} \exp(\sum_i \theta_i f_i(b', \mathcal{C}(A))} \tag{6.5}$$

where $b \in \{bracketable, unbracketable\}$, $\mathcal{C}(A)$ is the context of argument A. The
binary features f_i will be introduced in the next section.

Given a source sentence with arguments $\{A_i\}_1^N$, the semantically informed argument bracketing model P_{B_s} is formulated as

$$P_{B_s} = \prod_{i=1}^{N} P(b_{A_i}|\mathcal{C}(A_i)) \tag{6.6}$$

where b_{A_i} is the binary indicator that denotes whether A_i is bracketable.

6.2.2 Features

The binary features f_i can be formulated as that shown in Eq. 4.3 of Chap. 4. The
contextual elements from $\mathcal{C}(A)$ are used as features, which include

- *Semantic Features*. They are the predicate, the semantic role, and the head word
  of argument A.
- *Lexical Features*. They consist of the leftmost word of argument A, the preceding
  two words of the leftmost word, the rightmost word, and the succeeding two words
  of the rightmost word.

Table 6.5 Features adopted in the semantically informed argument bracketing model

		Features of an argument A for bracketing
Semantic features		Its predicate A^p
		Its semantic role A^r
		Its head word A^h
Lexical features		The leftmost word of A: A_l
		The rightmost word of A: A_r
		The preceding two words of A_l: A_{l1}, A_{l2}
		The succeeding two words of A_r: A_{r1}, A_{r2}

Table 6.6 Semantic feature examples

$f(b, C(A)) = 1$ if and only if
b = bracketable and $C(A).A^p$ = jinxing
b = bracketable and $C(A).A^r$ = ARG0
b = bracketable and $C(A).A^h$ = youguan
b = bracketable and $C(A).A_l$ = youguan
b = bracketable and $C(A).A_{l1}$ = \$
b = bracketable and $C(A).A_{r2}$ = jinxing

Table 6.5 lists all features that are included in the semantically informed argument bracketing model while Table 6.6 shows some feature examples for the ARG0 argument in Fig. 6.4.

6.2.3 Training

To train the semantically informed argument bracketing model, we take the following four steps.

1. We first obtain predicate-argument structures for all source sentences according to the procedure shown in Sect. 4.1.3 of Chap. 4.

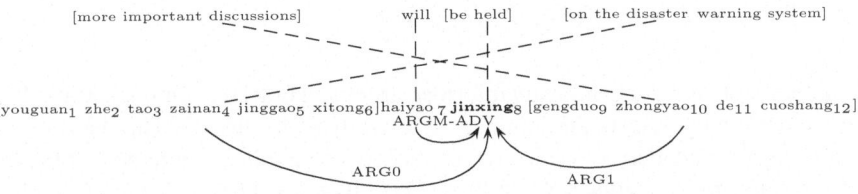

Fig. 6.4 An example of predicate-argument structure in Chinese and its aligned English translation. The *bold word* in Chinese is the verbal predicate. The *subscripts* on the Chinese sentence show the indexes of words from *left* to *right*

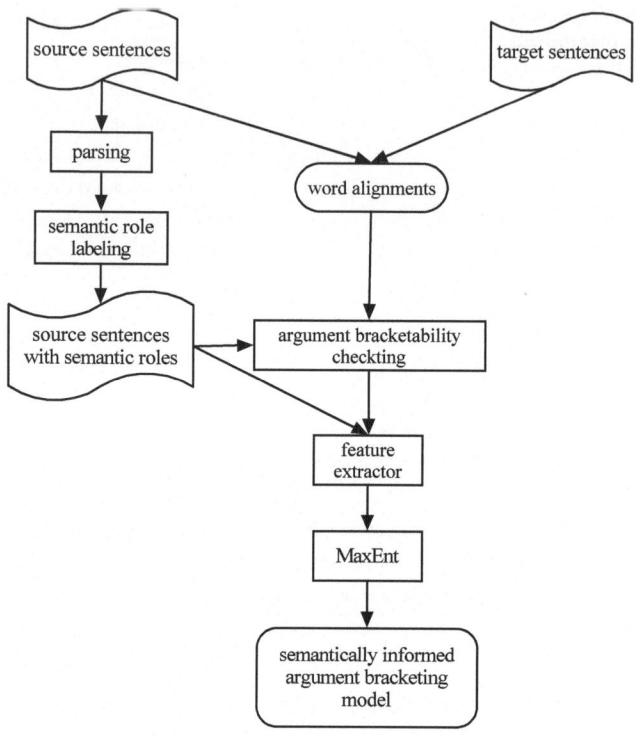

Fig. 6.5 The training process of the semantically informed argument bracketing model

2. For each argument in source-side predicate-argument structures, we determine whether it is bracketable according to word alignments.
3. We extract the semantic role, leftmost/rightmost words, and other items listed in Table 6.5 as features.
4. After all features are extracted, we use a maximum entropy toolkit to train the maximum entropy classifier as formulated in the Eq. (6.5).

We visualize these training steps in Fig. 6.5.

6.2.4 Integrating the Model into SMT

The integration of the semantically informed argument bracketing model into SMT is similar to the integration of the argument reordering model discussed in Chap. 4. Here we also face the challenge of misalignments between predicate-argument structures and structures of derivations. We still use BTG-based SMT as an example to show how this challenge can be addressed.

Table 6.7 Sample values for the function $\mathcal{A}(i, k, j, \tau)$ on the predicate-argument structure shown in Fig. 6.4

(i, k, j, τ)	$\mathcal{A}(i, k, j, \tau)$
$(1, 4, 6, \tau)$	ARG0
$(1, 4, 7, \tau)$	ARG0
$(1, 6, 7, \tau)$	NULL
$(9, 11, 12, \tau)$	ARG1

We first define a function $\mathcal{A}(i, k, j, \tau)$ on the source-side predicate-argument structure τ to find all arguments that either exactly align with the span (i, j) or cross the two neighboring sub-spans (i, k) and $(k + 1, j)$. Table 6.7 gives some examples for the function on the predicate-argument structure shown in Fig. 6.4. For instance, $\mathcal{A}(1, 4, 6, \tau) = $ ARG0 because ARG0 exactly covers the span $(1, 6)$ while $\mathcal{A}(1, 4, 7, \tau) = $ ARG0 because ARG0 crosses the two spans $(1, 4)$ and $(5, 7)$.

Then we define a function $\mathcal{P}(i, k, j, \tau)$ to calculate the bracketing probability for all arguments found by $\mathcal{A}(i, k, j, \tau)$ as follows:

$$\mathcal{P}(i, k, j, \tau) = \prod_{A \in \mathcal{A}(i,k,j,\tau)} P(b_A | \mathcal{C}(A)) \tag{6.7}$$

Figure 6.6 shows the integration algorithm in a deductive system. In order to know whether an argument is translated as a bracketable unit, we maintain word alignments for each phrase pair in the phrase table. Through the maintained word alignments we can easily track how an argument is translated. Whenever two neighboring spans (i, k) and $(k + 1, j)$ are merged by bracketing rules, we find all new arguments that either exactly cover the new span (i, j) or cross the two neighboring spans (i, k) and $(k + 1, j)$. According to the dynamic programming principle, we only need to calculate the bracketing probability for these arguments.

$$\frac{X \rightarrow e/f}{[X, i, j] : \mathcal{P}(i, \cdot, j, \tau)} \tag{6.8}$$

$$\frac{X \rightarrow [X_1, X_2] \text{ or } \langle X_1, X_2 \rangle \quad [X_1, i, k] : P_{B_s}(X_1) \quad [X_2, k + 1, j] : P_{B_s}(X_2)}{[X, i, j] : P_{B_s}(X_1) \cdot P_{B_s}(X_2) \cdot \mathcal{P}(i, k, j, \tau)}$$

$$\tag{6.9}$$

Fig. 6.6 Integrating the semantically informed argument bracketing model into BTG-based SMT

6.3 Summary and Additional Readings

The chapter elaborates two linguistically motivated bracketing models that explore syntactic and semantic knowledge to directly predict whether a source fragment (constituent or non-constituent) should be bracketed together and translated as a whole unit. The first model is the syntax-driven bracketing model that integrates various syntactic features into bracketing. For the syntax-driven bracketing,

- We introduce the algorithm to automatically learn bracketing instances from word-aligned bilingual data where source sentences are parsed.
- We develop two syntax-driven bracketing models: a unary model for a single phrase and a binary model for two neighboring phrases.
- We explore various syntactic features from source-side parse trees to determine whether a phrase is bracketable.

The second model focuses on argument bracketing, which predicts whether an argument should be translated as a bracketable unit or translated into separate discontinuous target phrases. For the argument bracketing,

- We incorporate both semantic and lexical features from predicate-argument structures on the source side into the bracketing model.
- We also present the algorithm that integrates the bracketing model into SMT.

We empirically validate the effectiveness of the syntax-driven bracketing model. The empirical evaluation of the model is reported in "A Syntax-Driven Bracketing Model for Phrase-Based Translation" (Xiong et al., *Proceedings of the Joint Conference of the 47th Annual Meeting of the ACL and the 4th International Joint Conference on Natural Language Processing of the AFNLP*, Suntec, Singapore, August 2–7, 2009; pp315–323.).

Additional Readings. Huang et al. (2010) introduces yet another approach to incorporate soft syntactic constraints into hierarchical phrase-based SMT by decorating each nonterminal with a real-valued feature vector. Cui et al. (2010) propose a joint rule selection model to select desirable translation rules for hierarchical phrase-based SMT with syntactic constraint features. Li et al. (2013) present a framework for SMT that first forces the decoder to generate syntactically constrained translations and then further enhances translations with semantic information.

Chapter 7
Translation Rule Selection with Document-Level Semantic Information

Abstract This chapter presents a framework for translation rule selection based on document-level semantic knowledge, particularly the gist of a document. Translation rule selection is a task of selecting appropriate translation rules for an ambiguous source-language segment. We represent the gist of a document as the topic of the document. Therefore we introduce two topic-based models for translation rule selection which incorporates global topic information into translation disambiguation. We associate each synchronous translation rule with source- and target-side topic distributions. With these topic distributions, we propose a topic dissimilarity model to select desirable (less dissimilar) rules by imposing penalties for rules with a large value of dissimilarity of their topic distributions to those of given documents. In order to encourage the use of nontopic specific translation rules, we also present a topic sensitivity model to balance translation rule selection between generic rules and topic-specific rules. Furthermore, we project target-side topic distributions onto the source-side topic model space so that we can benefit from topic information of both the source and target language. We integrate the proposed topic dissimilarity and sensitivity model into hierarchical phrase-based machine translation for synchronous translation rule selection.

In the last several chapters, we study reordering and bracketing from the perspective of linguistics and build linguistically motivated reordering and bracketing models for SMT. In this chapter, we will shift our attention to translation and investigate how we can appropriately select translation rules using document-level semantic knowledge.

Normally, we can learn a large number of translation rules from bilingual training data for a single source segment which occurs in different contexts. For example, Xiong et al. (2012) observe that each Chinese verb can be translated with more than 140 different translation rules on average. Therefore how to select an appropriate translation rule for an ambiguous source segment is a very crucial issue in SMT.

Traditionally the appropriateness of a translation rule is measured with multiple probabilities estimated from word-aligned data, such as bidirectional translation probabilities (Koehn et al. 2003). As such probabilities fail to capture local and global contexts of highly ambiguous source segments, they are not sufficient to select correct translation rules for these segments. Therefore various approaches have been proposed to capture rich contexts at the sentence level to help select proper translation

© Springer Science+Business Media Singapore 2015
D. Xiong and M. Zhang, *Linguistically Motivated Statistical Machine Translation*, DOI 10.1007/978-981-287-356-9_7

rules for phrase- (Carpuat and Wu 2007a) or syntax-based SMT (Chan et al. 2007; He et al. 2008; Liu et al. 2008). These studies show that local features, such as surrounding words, syntactic information and so on, are helpful for translation rule selection.

Beyond these contextual features at the sentence level, we conjecture that translation rules are also related to high-level global information, particularly the document gist. We represent the gist of a document as the topic of the document following Griffiths et al. (2007). In order to visualize the relatedness between translation rules and document topics (Hofmann 1999; Blei et al. 2003), we show four hierarchical phrase-based translation rules with their topic distributions in Fig. 7.1. From the figure, we can observe that

- First, translation rules can be divided into two categories in terms of their topic distributions: *topic-sensitive rules* (i.e., topic-specific rules) and *topic-insensitive rules* (i.e., non-topic specific or generic rules). The former rules, e.g., the translation rule (a), (b) and (d) in Fig. 7.1, have much higher distribution probabilities on a few specific topics than other topics. The latter rules, e.g., the translation rule (c) of Fig. 7.1, have an even distribution over all topics.
- Second, topic information can be used to disambiguate ambiguous source segments. In Fig. 7.1, translation rule (b) and (c) have the same source segment.

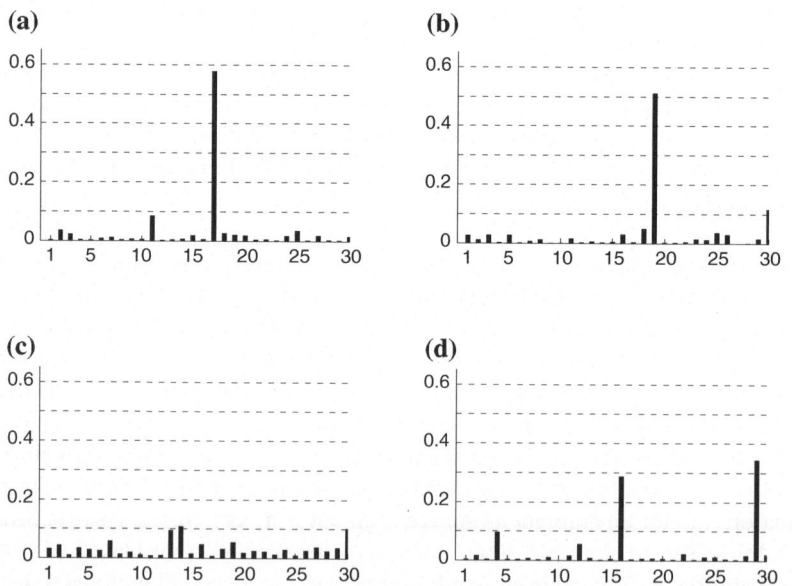

Fig. 7.1 Four synchronous rules with topic distributions. Each sub-graph shows a rule with its topic distribution, where the X-axis shows the topic index and the Y-axis the topic probability. Notably, the rule (**b**) and rule (**c**) shares the same source Chinese string, but they have different topic distributions due to the different English translations. Zuozhan nengli ⇒ operational capability (**a**), jiyu X_1 ⇒ grants X_1 (**b**), jiyu X_1 ⇒ give X_1 (**c**), X_1 juxing huitan X_2 ⇒ held talks X_1 X_2 (**d**)

However their topic distributions are quite different. Rule (b) distributes on the topic about "international relations" with the highest probability, which suggests that rule (b) is much more related to this topic than other topics. In contrast, rule (c) has an even distribution over all topics. Therefore in a document on "international relations," rule (b) will be more appropriate than rule (c) for the source segment "jiyu X_1".

These two observations suggest that different translation rules have different topic distributions and document-level topic information can be used to benefit translation rule selection.

In this chapter, we introduce a framework for translation rule selection that exactly capitalizes on document-level semantic topic information. The topic-based translation rule selection framework associates each translation rule with a topic distribution (rule-topic distribution) on both the source and target side. Each source document is also annotated with its corresponding topic distribution (document-topic distribution). Dissimilarity between the document-topic distribution and rule-topic distribution is calculated and used to help select translation rules that are related to documents in terms of topics. In particular,

- Given a document to be translated, we use a topic dissimilarity model to calculate the dissimilarity of each translation rule to the document based on their topic distributions. Our translation system will penalize candidate translations with high dissimilarities.[1]
- The dissimilarity between a topic-insensitive translation rule and a given source document computed by our topic dissimilarity model is often very high as documents are normally topic-sensitive. We do not want to penalize these generic topic-insensitive rules. Therefore, we further propose a topic sensitivity model which rewards topic-insensitive rules so as to complement the topic dissimilarity model.
- We associate each translation rule with a rule-topic distribution on both the source and target side. In order to calculate the dissimilarity between target-side rule-topic distributions of translation rules and source-side document-topic distributions of given documents during decoding, we project the target-side rule-topic distributions of translation rules onto the space of source-side document topic model by one-to-many mapping.

We integrate the topic-based models into hierarchical phrase-based SMT (Chiang 2007) for translation rule selection. The rest of this chapter is organized as follows:

- Section 7.1 provides background knowledge about hierarchical phrase-based SMT and topic modeling.
- Section 7.2 elaborates the topic-based translation rule selection framework, including the topic dissimilarity and topic sensitivity model.

---

[1] Section 7.4 explains why our system penalizes candidate translations with high dissimilarities.

- Section 7.3 discusses how we estimate rule-topic and document-topic distributions and how we project target-side rule-topic distributions onto the source-side topic space in a one-to-many mapping fashion.
- Section 7.4 presents the integration of the topic-based translation rule selection models into hierarchical phrase-based SMT.
- Section 7.5 gives some suggestions for bilingual topic modeling from the perspective of machine translation.
- Finally, we summarize in Sect. 7.6 with additional readings.

7.1 Preliminaries

We establish, in this section, some background knowledge about both hierarchical phrase-based statistical machine translation and topic modeling.

7.1.1 Hierarchical Phrase-Based SMT

In hierarchical phrase-based SMT (Chiang 2005), translation rules extracted from word-aligned training data are synchronous context-free grammar rules, which can be denoted as follows:

$$X \rightarrow \langle \alpha, \beta, \sim \rangle \qquad (7.1)$$

where X is an undifferentiated nonterminal, α and β are strings of terminals and nonterminals[2] on the source and target side, respectively, $\sim$ denotes the one-to-one mapping between nonterminals in α and nonterminals in β. In addition to the rules that are extracted from bilingual training data, two special rules are also introduced into hierarchical phrase-based SMT.

$$
\begin{aligned}
S &\rightarrow \langle X_{\sim 1}, X_{\sim 1} \rangle \\
S &\rightarrow \langle S_{\sim 0} X_{\sim 1}, S_{\sim 0} X_{\sim 1} \rangle
\end{aligned}
\qquad (7.2)
$$

These two rules are used to serially concatenate nonterminal Xs in a monotonic manner to form an initial symbol S, the start symbol of the grammar of hierarchical phrase-based SMT.

The log-linear model of hierarchical phrase-based SMT can be formulated as follows:

$$w(\mathcal{D}) = \exp\left(\sum_{r \in D} \log(t(r)) + \lambda_{lm} \log P_{lm}(e) + \lambda_{wp}|e| + \lambda_{rp} I \right) \qquad (7.3)$$

---

[2] In order to simplify the decoder implementation, at most two nonterminals are allowed in hierarchical translation rules.

where $\mathcal{D}$ is a derivation defined as a set of triples (r, i, j), each of which denotes an application of a translation rule that spans words i from j on the source side. I is the number of translation rules in $\mathcal{D}$. The probability of a translation rule r is defined as

$$t(r) = P(\alpha|\beta)^{\lambda_1} P(\beta|\alpha)^{\lambda_2} P_{\text{lex}}(\alpha|\beta)^{\lambda_3} P_{\text{lex}}(\beta|\alpha)^{\lambda_4} \qquad (7.4)$$

where the lexical translation probabilities $P_{\text{lex}}(\alpha|\beta)$ and $P_{\text{lex}}(\beta|\alpha)$ estimate the probabilities that the words in α translate the words in β in a word-by-word manner (Koehn et al. 2003).

7.1.2 Topic Modeling

Topic modeling is used to discover topics that occur in a collection of documents. Both Latent Dirichlet Allocation (LDA) (Blei et al. 2003) and Probabilistic Latent Semantic Analysis (PLSA) (Hofmann 1999) are topic models. As LDA is the most widely used topic model, we exploit it to mine topics for our translation rule selection.

LDA views each document as a mixture of various topics, each of which is a probability distribution over words. More particularly, LDA works in a generative process as follows.

- For each document D_j, sample a document-topic distribution (per-document topic distribution) θ_j from a Dirichlet distribution $\text{Dir}(\alpha)$: $\theta_j \sim \text{Dir}(\alpha)$;
- for each word $w_{j,i}$ of N_j words in the document D_j,

  – Sample a topic assignment $z_{j,i} \sim \text{Multinomial}(\theta_j)$;
  – Sample the word $w_{j,i} \sim \text{Multinomial}(\varphi_{z_{j,i}})$ where $\varphi_{z_{j,i}}$ is the per-topic word distribution of topic $z_{j,i}$ drawn from $\text{Dir}(\beta)$.

Figure 7.2 displays the graphic representation of the LDA model.

Fig. 7.2 Graphical model representation of LDA

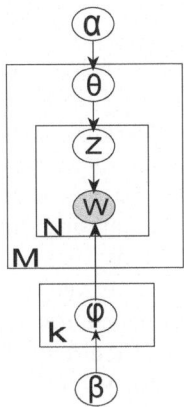

Generally speaking, LDA contains two groups of parameters. The first group of parameters characterizes document-topic distributions (θ_j), which record the distribution of each document over topics. The second group of parameters is used for topic-word distributions (φ_k), which represent each topic as a distribution over words.

Given a document collection with observed words $\mathbf{w} = \{w_{j,i}\}$, the goal of LDA inference is to compute the values for these two sets of parameters θ and φ as well as the latent topic assignments $\mathbf{z} = \{z_{j,i}\}$. The inference is complicated due to the latent topic assignments $\mathbf{z}$. An efficient inference algorithm that has been proposed to address this problem is Collapsed Gibbs Sampling (Griffiths and Steyvers 2004), where the two sets of parameters θ and φ are integrated out of the LDA model, and only the latent topic assignments $\mathbf{z}$ are sampled from $P(\mathbf{z}|\mathbf{w})$. Once we obtain the values of $\mathbf{z}$, we can estimate θ and φ by recovering their posterior distributions given $\mathbf{z}$ and $\mathbf{w}$. In Sect. 7.3, we will use these two sets of estimated parameters and the topic assignments of words to calculate the parameters of our models.

7.2 Topic-Based Dissimilarity and Sensitivity Models

In this section, we elaborate the topic-based models for translation rule selection, including a topic dissimilarity model and a topic sensitivity model.

7.2.1 Topic Dissimilarity Model

Sentences should be translated in accordance with their topics (Zhao and Xing 2006, 2007; Tam et al. 2007). Take the translation rule (b) in Fig. 7.1 as an example. If the source side of rule (b) occurs in a document on "international relations", we hope to encourage the application of rule (b) rather than rule (c). This can be achieved by calculating the dissimilarity between probability distributions of a translation rule and a document over topics.

In order to calculate such a topic dissimilarity for translation rule selection, we associate both the source and target side of a translation rule with a *rule-topic distribution* $P(z_\diamond|r_\diamond)$, where $\diamond$ is the placeholder for the source side f or target side e, $r_\diamond$ is the source or target side of a translation rule r, and $z_\diamond$ is the corresponding topic of $r_\diamond$. Therefore each translation rule has two rule-topic distributions: $P(z_f|r_f)$ on the source side and $P(z_e|r_e)$ on the target side.

Supposing there are K topics, the two distributions can be represented by a K-dimension vector. The kth component $P(z_\diamond = k|r_\diamond)$ denotes the probability of topic k given $r_\diamond$. The source- and target-side rule-topic distributions are separately estimated from training data. The estimation method is described in Sect. 7.3, where we also discuss the reason why we estimate them in a separate manner.

Analogously, we represent the topic information of a document d to be translated by a *document-topic distribution* $P(z|d)$, which is also a K-dimension vector.

The kth dimension $P(z = k|d)$ is the topic proportion for topic k in document d. Different from the rule-topic distribution, the document-topic distribution can be directly inferred by an off-the-shelf LDA tool.

Based on the defined rule-topic and document-topic distributions, we can measure the dissimilarity of a translation rule to a document so as to decide whether the rule is suitable for the document in translation. Traditionally, the similarity of two probability distributions is calculated by information measurements such as Jensen–Shannon divergence (Lin 2006) or Hellinger distance (Blei and Lafferty 2007).

Here we adopt the Hellinger distance (HD) to measure the topic dissimilarity, which is symmetric and widely used for comparing two probability distributions (Blei and Lafferty 2007). Given a rule-topic distribution $P(z_\diamond|r_\diamond)$ and a document-topic distribution $P(z|d)$, HD is computed as follows:

$$\text{HD}(P(z|d), P(z_\diamond|r_\diamond)) = \sum_{k=1}^{K} \left(\sqrt{P(z = k|d)} - \sqrt{P(z_\diamond = k|r_\diamond)} \right)^2 \qquad (7.5)$$

Let $\mathcal{D}$ be a derivation. Let $\mathbf{P}(\mathbf{z}|\mathbf{r})$ represent corresponding rule-topic distributions for all rules in $\mathcal{D}$. Our topic dissimilarity model $\text{Dsim}(P(z|d), \mathbf{P}(\mathbf{z}|\mathbf{r}))$ on a derivation $\mathcal{D}$ is defined on the HD of the Eq. (7.5) as follows:

$$\text{Dsim}(P(z|d), \mathbf{P}(\mathbf{z}|\mathbf{r})) = \sum_{r \in \mathcal{D}} \text{HD}(P(z|d), P(z_\diamond|r_\diamond)) \qquad (7.6)$$

Obviously, the larger the Hellinger distance between a candidate translation yielded by a derivation and a document, the larger the dissimilarity between them. With the topic dissimilarity model defined above, we aim to select translation rules that are similar to the document to be translated in terms of their topics.

7.2.2 Topic Sensitivity Model

Before we introduce the topic sensitivity model, let us revisit Fig. 7.1. We can easily find that the probability of rule (c) distributes evenly over all topics. This indicates that it is insensitive to topics, and can be therefore applied on any topics. In contrast, the distributions of the other three rules peak on a few topics. Generally speaking, a topic-insensitive rule has a fairly flat distribution over all topics, while a topic-sensitive rule has a sharp distribution over a few topics.

As a document typically focuses on a few topics, it has a sharp distribution over these topics. In other words, documents are normally topic-sensitive. Since the distribution of a topic-insensitive rule is fairly flat, the dissimilarity between a topic-insensitive rule and a topic-sensitive document will be very low. Therefore, our system with the proposed topic dissimilarity model will punish topic-insensitive rules.

However, topic-insensitive rules may be more preferable than topic-sensitive rules if neither of them are similar to given documents. For a document about a topic of "love", the rule (b) and (c) in Fig. 7.1 are both dissimilar to the document as rule (b) relates to the "international relations" topic and rule (c) is topic-insensitive. Nevertheless, since rule (c) occurs more frequently across various topics, we prefer rule (c) to rule (b) when we translate a document about "love".

To address such issue of the topic dissimilarity model, we further propose a topic sensitivity model. The model employs an entropy-based metric to measure the topic sensitivity of a rule as follows:

$$H(P(z_\diamond|r_\diamond)) = - \sum_{k=1}^{K} P(z_\diamond = k|r_\diamond) \times \log(P(z_\diamond = k|r_\diamond)) \qquad (7.7)$$

According to this equation, a topic-insensitive rule normally has a large entropy while a topic-sensitive rule has a smaller entropy.

Given a derivation $\mathcal{D}$ and rule-topic distributions $\mathbf{P(z|r)}$ for rules in $\mathcal{D}$, the topic sensitivity model is defined as follows:

$$\text{Sen}(\mathbf{P(z|r)}) = \sum_{r \in \mathcal{D}} H(P(z_\diamond|r_\diamond)) \qquad (7.8)$$

Incorporating the topic sensitivity model with the topic dissimilarity model, we enable the SMT decoder to balance the selection of topic-sensitive and topic-insensitive rules. Given rules with approximately equal values of topic dissimilarity, we prefer topic-insensitive rules.

7.3 Estimation

Unlike document-topic distributions that can be directly learned by LDA tools, we need to estimate rule-topic distributions for translation rules. As we want to exploit topic information of both the source and target language, we *separately* train two monolingual topic models on the source and target side, and learn correspondences between the two topic models via word alignments in the bilingual training data.

Particularly, we adopt two rule-topic distributions for each translation rule: (1) the source-side rule-topic distribution $P(z_f|r_f)$ and the (2) the target-side rule-topic distribution $P(z_e|r_e)$, both of which are defined in Sect. 7.2.1. These two rule-topic distributions are estimated using trained topic models in the same way (Sect. 7.3.1). Notably, only source-language documents are available during decoding. In order to compute the dissimilarity between the target-side rule-topic distribution of a translation rule and the source-side document-topic distribution of a given document, we need to project the target-side rule-topic distribution of a translation rule onto the space of the source-side topic model (Sect. 7.3.2).

We can also establish alternative approaches to the estimation of rule-topic distributions via multilingual topic models (Mimno et al. 2009; Boyd-Graber and

Blei 2009) or bilingual topic models that also infer word-to-word alignments in document pairs (Zhao and Xing 2006, 2007). The former multilingual topic models only require that documents in different languages are comparable in terms of content similarity. In contrast, the latter bilingual topic models require that documents are parallel, i.e., translations of each other, so as to capture word alignments.

The biggest difference between our method and these multilingual and bilingual topic models is that they use the same per-tuple topic distribution θ for all documents in the same tuple. We define the tuple as a set of documents in different languages. Topic assignments for words in these languages are naturally connected since they are sampled from the same topic distribution. In contrast, we assume that each document on the source/target side has its own sampled document-specific distribution over topics. Topic correspondences between the source and target document are learned by projection via word alignments. We visualize this difference in Fig. 7.3.

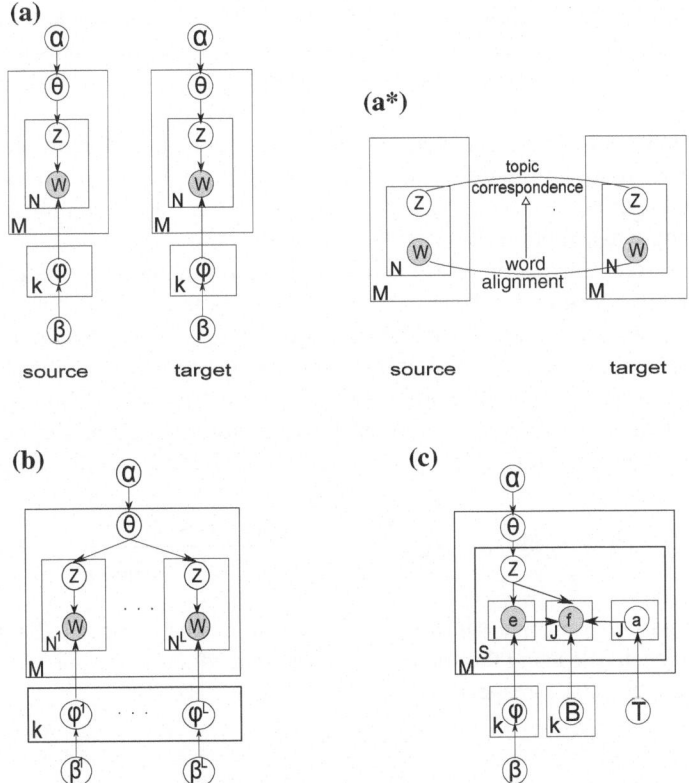

Fig. 7.3 Graphical model representations of our bilingual topic model (**a**), polylingual topic model of Mimno et al. (2009) (**b**) and bilingual topic model of Zhao and Xing (2007) (**c**) where S is the number of parallel sentence pairs in a document, a is the word alignment between a source and target sentence. For simplicity, we do not display HMM transitions among word alignments a. Subfigure (**a***) shows how we build topic correspondences between the source and target language after source and target topics are separately learned as shown in (**a**)

Yet another difference between our models and the topic-specific lexicon translation model of Zhao and Xing (2007) is that they use their bilingual topics to improve SMT at the word level instead of the rule level. Since a synchronous rule is rarely factorized into individual words, we believe that it is more reasonable to incorporate the topic model directly at the rule level rather than the word level.

Tam et al. (2007) also construct two monolingual topic models for parallel source and target documents. They build the topic correspondences between source and target documents by enforcing a one-to-one topic mapping constraint. We project target-side topics onto the space of the source-side topic model in a one-to-many fashion.

7.3.1 Rule-Topic Distribution Estimation

We estimate rule-topic distributions from word-aligned bilingual training corpus with document boundaries explicitly given. The source- and target-side rule-topic distributions are estimated in the same way. Therefore, for simplicity, we only describe the estimation of the source-side rule-topic distribution $P(z_f|r_f)$ of a translation rule in this section.

The estimation of rule-topic distributions is analogous to the traditional estimation of rule translation probabilities (Chiang 2007). In addition to the word-aligned corpus, the input for rule-topic distribution estimation also contains source-side document-topic distributions inferred by LDA tool.

We first extract translation rules from bilingual training data in a traditional way. When the source side of a translation rule r_f is extracted from a source-language document d_f with a document-topic distribution $P(z_f|d_f)$, we obtain an instance $(r_f, P(z_f|d_f), \epsilon)$, where ϵ is the fraction count of an instance as described by Chiang (2007). In this way, we can collect a set of instances $\mathcal{I} = \{(r_f, P(z_f|d_f), \epsilon)\}$ with different document-topic distributions for each translation rule. Using these instances, we calculate the probability $P(z_f = k|r_f)$ of r_f over topic k as follows:

$$P(z_f = k|r_f) = \frac{\sum_{I \in \mathcal{I}} \epsilon \times P(z_f = k|d_f)}{\sum_{k'=1}^{K} \sum_{I \in \mathcal{I}} \epsilon \times P(z_f = k'|d_f)} \tag{7.9}$$

Based on this equation, we can obtain two rule-topic distributions $P(z_f|r_f)$ and $P(z_e|r_e)$ for each rule using the source- and target-side document-topic distributions $P(z_f|d_f)$ and $P(z_e|d_e)$, respectively.

7.3.2 Target-Side Rule-Topic Distribution Projection

As described in the previous section, we also estimate target-side rule-topic distributions. However, we cannot directly use the Eq. (7.5) to calculate the dissimilarity between the target-side rule-topic distribution $P(z_e|r_e)$ of a translation rule and the source-side document-topic distribution $P(z_f|d_f)$ of a source-language document that is to be translated. In order to measure this dissimilarity, we need to project target-side topics onto the source-side topic space. The projection takes the following two steps.

- First, we calculate a correspondence probability $P(z_f|z_e)$ for each pair of a target-side topic z_e and a source-side topic z_f, which are inferred by the two separately trained monolingual topic models, respectively.
- Second, we project the target-side rule-topic distribution of a translation rule onto the source-side topic space using the correspondence probabilities learned in the first step.

In the first step, we estimate the topic-to-topic correspondence probabilities using co-occurrence counts of topic assignments of source and target words in the word-aligned corpus. The topic assignments of source/target words are inferred by the two monolingual topic models. With these topic assignments, we characterize a sentence pair (f, e) as $(\mathbf{z}_f, \mathbf{z}_e, \mathbf{a})$, where $\mathbf{z}_f$ and $\mathbf{z}_e$ are two vectors containing topic assignments for words in the source and target sentence f and e, respectively, and $\mathbf{a}$ is a set of word alignment links $\{(i, j)\}$ between the source and target sentence. Particularly, a link (i, j) represents that a source-side position i aligns to a target-side position j.

With these notations, we calculate the co-occurrence count of a source-side topic k_f and a target-side topic k_e as follows:

$$\sum_{(\mathbf{z}_f, \mathbf{z}_e, \mathbf{a})} \sum_{(i,j) \in \mathbf{a}} \delta(\mathbf{z}_{f_i}, k_f) * \delta(\mathbf{z}_{e_j}, k_e) \tag{7.10}$$

where $\mathbf{z}_{f_i}$ and $\mathbf{z}_{e_j}$ are topic assignments for words f_i and e_j, respectively, $\delta(x, y)$ is the Kronecker function, which is 1 if $x = y$ and 0 otherwise.

We then compute the topic-to-topic correspondence probability of $P(z_f = k_f|z_e = k_e)$ by normalizing the co-occurrence count as follows:

$$P(z_f = k_f|z_e = k_e) = \frac{\sum_{(\mathbf{z}_f, \mathbf{z}_e, \mathbf{a})} \sum_{(i,j) \in \mathbf{a}} \delta(\mathbf{z}_{f_i}, k_f) * \delta(\mathbf{z}_{e_j}, k_e)}{\sum_{(\mathbf{z}_f, \mathbf{z}_e, \mathbf{a})} \sum_{(i,j) \in \mathbf{a}} \delta(\mathbf{z}_{e_j}, k_e)} \tag{7.11}$$

Overall, after the first step, we obtain a topic-to-topic correspondence matrix $\mathbf{M}_{K_e \times K_f}$, where the item $M_{i,j}$ represents the probability $P(z_f = i|z_e = j)$. Figure 7.4 shows how we obtain the topic correspondence matrix.

In the second step, given the correspondence matrix $\mathbf{M}_{K_e \times K_f}$, we project the target-side rule-topic distribution $P(z_e|r_e)$ to the source-side topic space by multiplication as follows:

$$T(P(z_e|r_e)) = P(z_e|r_e) \cdot \mathbf{M}_{K_e \times K_f} \tag{7.12}$$

In this way, we get a second distribution for a translation rule in the source-side topic space, which we call *projected target-side topic distribution* $T(P(z_e|r_e))$.

Fig. 7.4 The process of
generating the topic
correspondence matrix

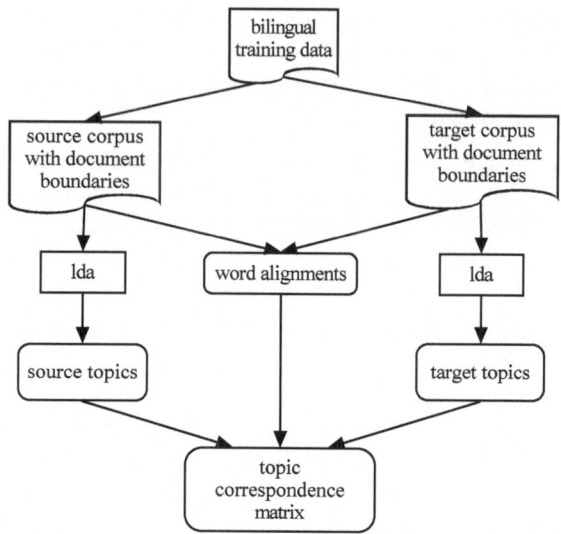

Word alignment noises may be introduced in the Eq. (7.10), which in turn may flatten the sharpness of the projected topic distributions calculated in the Eq. (7.12). In order to decrease the flattening effects of word alignment noises, we take the following action in practice: if the topic-to-topic correspondence probability $P(z_f = k_f | z_e = k_e)$ calculated via word alignments is less than $\frac{1}{K}$ where K is the predefined number of topics, we set it to 0 and then renormalize all other correspondence probabilities of the target-side topic k_e.

Obviously, our projection method allows one target-side topic z_e to align to multiple source-side topics. This is different from the one-to-one correspondence used by Tam et al. (2007). We investigate the correspondence matrix $\mathbf{M}_{K_e \times K_f}$ obtained from our training data. We find that the topic correspondence between the source and target language is not necessarily one-to-one. Typically, the correspondence probability $P(z_f = k_f | z_e = k_e)$ of a target-side topic mainly distributes over two or three source-side topics. Table 7.1 shows an example of a target-side topic with its three mainly aligned source-side topics.

7.4 Integration

We incorporate the introduced topic dissimilarity and sensitivity model as two new features into a hierarchical phrase-based system (Chiang 2007) under the log-linear discriminative framework (Och and Ney 2002). The dissimilarity values are positive as Hellinger distances are positive. The weight of this dissimilarity feature tuned by minimum error rate training will be negative. Therefore the log-linear model will favor those candidate translations with lower values of the dissimilarity feature (less

Table 7.1 An example of topic-to-topic correspondence

e-topic	f-topic 1	f-topic 2	f-topic 3
Enterprises	nongye(agriculture)	qiye(enterprise)	fazhan(develop)
Rural	nongcun(rural)	shichang(market)	jingji(economic)
State	nonmin(peasant)	guoyou(state)	keji(technology)
Agricultural	gaige(reform)	gongsi(company)	woguo(China)
Market	caizheng(finance)	jinrong(finance)	jishu(technique)
Reform	shehui(social)	yinhang(bank)	chanye(industry)
Production	baozhang(safety)	touzi(investment)	jiegou(structure)
Peasants	tiaozheng(adjust)	guanli(manage)	chuangxin(innovation)
Owned	zhengce(policy)	gaige(reform)	jiakuai(accelerate)
Enterprise	shouru(income)	jingying(operation)	gaige(reform)
$P(z_f|z_e)$	0.38	0.28	0.16

The last line shows the correspondence probability. Each column shows a topic represented by its top-10 topical words. The first column is a target-side topic, while the remaining three columns are source-side topics

dissimilar). In other words, translation rules that are more similar to the document to be translated in terms of their topics will be selected.

One possible side-effect of the integration of such a dissimilarity feature is that our system will favor translations generated by fewer translation rules against those generated by more translation rules because more translation rules result in higher dissimilarity (see the Eq. (7.6)). That is to say, the topic-based dissimilarity feature also acts as a translation rule count penalty on derivations. Fortunately, however, we also use a translation rule count feature (see the Eq. (7.3)) which normally favors translations yielded by a derivation with a large number of translation rules. This feature will balance against the mentioned side-effect of the introduced topic-based dissimilarity feature.

As each translation rule is associated with a source-side rule-topic distribution and a projected target-side rule-topic distribution during decoding, we add four features as follows.[3]

- Dsim($P(z_f|d)$, $\mathbf{P}(\mathbf{z}_f|\mathbf{r}_f)$) (or DsimSrc). Topic dissimilarity feature on rule-topic distributions of the source side.
- Dsim($P(z_f|d)$, $T(\mathbf{P}(\mathbf{z}_e|\mathbf{r}_e))$) (or DsimTrg). Topic dissimilarity feature on projected target-side rule-topic distributions.
- Sen($\mathbf{P}(\mathbf{z}_f|\mathbf{r}_f)$) (or SenSrc). Topic sensitivity feature on source-side rule-topic distributions.
- Sen($T(\mathbf{P}(\mathbf{z}_e|\mathbf{r}_e))$) (or SenTrg). Topic sensitivity feature on projected target-side rule-topic distributions.

The whole architecture of the system with these four features is shown in Fig. 7.5.

---

[3] Since the glue rule and rules of unknown words are not extracted from training data, we just set the values of the four features for these rules to zero.

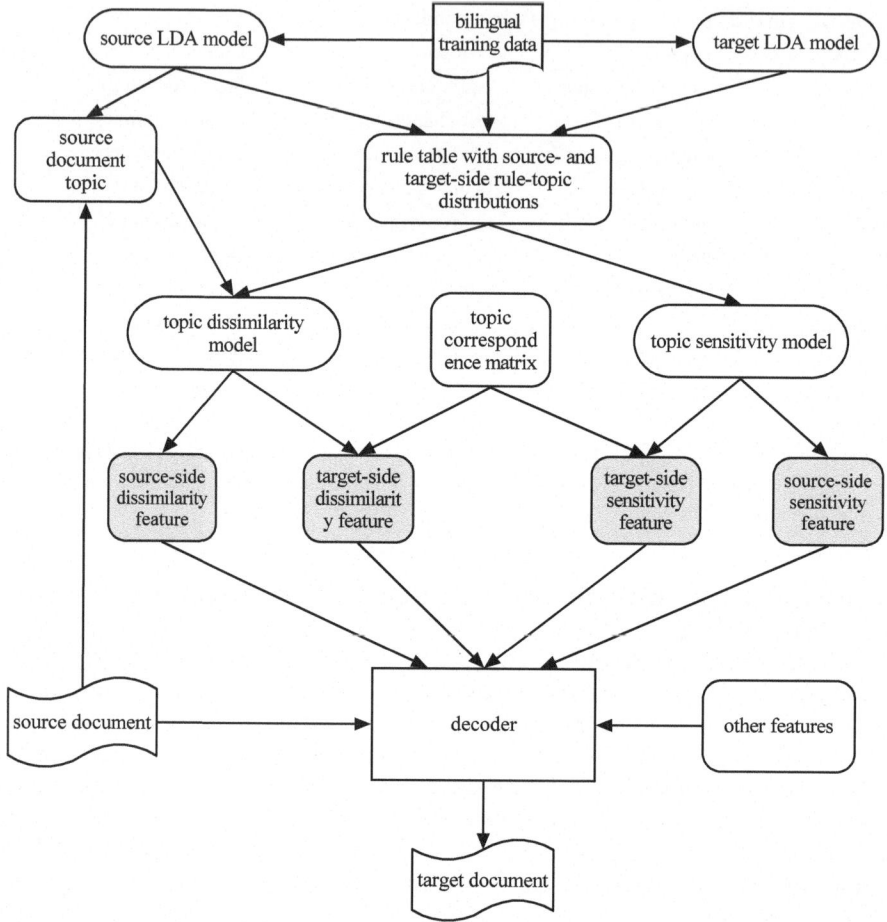

Fig. 7.5 The architecture of the hierarchical phrase-based SMT system with the four topic-based features

The source-side and projected target-side rule-topic distributions for translation rules can be calculated before decoding as described in the last section. During decoding, we first infer the topic distribution $P(z_f|d)$ for a given document of the source language. When a translation rule is adopted in a derivation, the scores of the four features will be updated correspondingly according to the Eqs. (7.6) and (7.8). Obviously, the computational cost of these features is rather small.

For topic-specific lexicon translation models (Zhao and Xing 2007; Tam et al. 2007), they first calculate topic-specific translation probabilities by normalizing the entire lexicon translation table and then adapt the lexical weights of translation rules correspondingly during decoding. This makes the decoder run slower. Therefore, comparing with previous topic-specific lexicon translation methods, our method provides a more efficient way for incorporating topic models into SMT.

7.5 Discussion on Bilingual Topic Modeling

Although topic models are widely adopted in monolingual text analysis, bilingual or multilingual topic models are less explored, especially those tailored for multilingual tasks such as machine translation. In this section, we try to provide some suggestions for bilingual topic modeling from the perspective of statistical machine translation as well as our practice on the integration of topic models into SMT. These suggestions are listed as follows.

- *Investigation on Topic divergences across different languages.* Cross-language divergences are pervasive and become one of big challenges for machine translation (Dorr 1994). Such language-level divergences hint that divergences at the topic or concept level may also exist across languages. This may explain why our one-to-many topic projection from the target side to the source side is better than the one-to-one mapping. Although Mimno et al. (2009) have studied on topic divergences using Wikipedia articles, we believe that a deeper and wider investigation on topic divergence is needed as it will shed new light on how we can build better bilingual topic models.
- *Adding more linguistic assumptions into topic modeling.* Practices in SMT show that integrating more linguistic knowledge into machine translation normally generates better translations (Chiang et al. 2008). We believe that adding more linguistic assumptions beyond bag-of-words will also improve topic modeling. A flexible topic modeling framework that allows us to integrate rich linguistic knowledge in the form of features will definitely further facilitate the application of topic models in natural language processing.
- *Joint modeling of topic induction and synchronous grammar induction.* Synchronous grammar induction for machine translation is a task of automatically learning translation rules from bilingual data (Blunsom et al. 2009; Xiao and Xiong 2013). As Bayesian approaches are successfully used in both topic modeling and synchronous grammar induction, joint modeling of them is an very interesting direction, which will also benefit grammar adaptation from one domain to another domain in machine translation.

7.6 Summary and Additional Readings

In this chapter, we have presented a topic-based translation rule selection framework which incorporates the topic information from both the source and target language for translation rule disambiguation. Particularly, we use a topic dissimilarity model to select appropriate translation rules for documents according to the similarities between translation rules and documents. We also adopt a topic sensitivity model to complement the topic dissimilarity model in order to balance translation rule selection between topic-sensitive and topic-insensitive rules. In order to calculate dissimilarities between source- and target-side topic distributions, we project topic distributions on the target side onto the source-side topic model space in a new and efficient way.

We integrate these two topic-based models into hierarchical phrase-based SMT. The experiment results of the two models are presented in "Topic-Based Dissimilarity and Sensitivity Models for Translation Rule Selection" (Zhang et al., *Journal of Artificial Intelligence Research*, 50:1–30, 2014). Experiment results on large-scale data validate that

- The introduced topic dissimilarity and sensitivity model are able to substantially improve translation quality in terms of BLEU and improve translation rule selection on various types of rules (i.e., phrase, monotone and reordering rules).
- The introduced method is better than previous topic-specific lexicon translation method in both translation quality and decoding speed.
- The proposed one-to-many projection method also outperforms various other methods such as one-to-one mapping, marginalization via word alignments and so on.
- If we want to use additional monolingual corpus to train topic models, we should first investigate whether the new monolingual corpus is similar to the test data in terms of topic distributions.

Additional Readings. The introduced topic-based dissimilarity and sensitivity models for translation rule selection are related to three categories of work in SMT: translation rule selection, topic models for SMT, and document-level translation. Here we introduce related approaches of the three categories and highlight the differences of our method from previous work.

Translation rule selection. As we mentioned before, translation rule selection is a very important task in SMT. Several approaches have been proposed for it recently. Carpuat and Wu explore both word and phrase sense disambiguation (WSD and PSD) for translation rule selection in phrase-based SMT (Carpuat and Wu 2007a, b). Their WSD and PSD system integrate sentence-level local collocation features. Experiments show that multi-word PSD can improve phrase selection. Also following the WSD line, Chan et al. (2007) integrate a WSD system into hierarchical phrase-based SMT for lexical selection or the selection of short phrases of length 1 or 2. Their WSD system also adopts sentence-level features of local collocations, surrounding words, and so on.

Different from lexical or phrasal selection using WSD/PSD, He et al. (2008) propose a maximum entropy based model for context-dependent synchronous rule selection in hierarchical phrase-based SMT. Local context features such as phrase boundary words and part-of-speech information are incorporated into the model. Liu et al. (2008) extends the selection method of He et al. to integrate a similar MaxEnt-based rule selection model into a tree-to-string syntax-based SMT system

(Liu et al. 2006). Their model uses syntactic information from source parse trees as features.

The significant difference between the introduced topic-based rule selection framework and previous approaches on translation rule selection is that we use global topic information to help select translation rules for ambiguous source segments rather than sentence-level local context features.

Topic models for SMT. Topic modeling (Hofmann 1999; Blei et al. 2003) is a popular technique for discovering underlying topic structures of documents. Recent years have witnessed that topic models have been explored for SMT. Zhao and Xing (2006, 2007) and Tam et al. (2007) have proposed topic-specific lexicon translation adaptation models to improve translation quality. Such models focus on word-level translations. They first estimate word translation probabilities conditioned on topics, and then adapt lexical translation probabilities of phrases by these topic-conditioned probabilities. Since modern SMT systems use synchronous rules or bilingual phrases to translate sentences, we believe that it is more reasonable to incorporate topic models for phrase or synchronous rule selection than lexical selection.

Gong et al. (2010) adopt a topic model to filter out phrase pairs that are not consistent with source documents in terms of their topics. They assign a topic for each document to be translated. Similarly, each phrase pair is also assigned with one topic. A phrase pair will be discarded if its topic mismatches the document topic. The differences from their work are twofold. First, we calculate the dissimilarities of translation rules to documents based on their topic distributions instead of comparing the best topics assigned to translation rules and those of documents. Second, we integrate topic information into SMT in a soft-constraint manner via the introduced topic-based models. They explore topic information in a hard-constraint fashion by discarding translation rules with unmatched topics.

Topic models are also used for domain adaptation on translation and language models in SMT. Foster and Kuhn (2007) describe a mixture model approach for SMT adaptation. They divide a training corpus into different domains, each of which is used to train a domain-specific translation model. During decoding, they combine a general domain translation model with a specific domain translation model that is selected according to various text distances calculated by topic model. Tam et al. (2007) and Ruiz and Federico (2011) use a bilingual topic model to project latent topic distributions across languages. Based on the bilingual topic model, they apply source-side topic weights onto the target-side topic model so as to adapt the target-side n-gram language model.

Document-level machine translation. Since we incorporate document topic information into SMT, our work is also related to document-level machine translation. Tiedemann (2010) integrates cache-based language and translation models that are built from recently translated sentences into SMT. Gong et al. (2011) further extend this cache-based approach by introducing two additional caches: a static cache that stores phrases extracted from documents in training data which are similar to the document in question and a topic cache with target language topic words. Xiao et al. (2011) try to solve the translation consistency issue in document-level translation by introducing a hard constraint where ambiguous source words are required to be consistently translated into the most frequent translation options. Ture et al. (2012) soften this consistency constraint by integrating three counting features into the decoder. These studies normally focus on the surface structure to capture inter-sentence dependencies for document-level machine translation while we explore the topic structure of a document for document translation.

Chapter 8
Translation Error Detection with Linguistic Features

Abstract This chapter discusses translation error detection with linguistic features. Automatic error detection is desired in the post-processing to improve machine translation quality. The previous work is largely based on confidence estimation using system-based features, such as word posterior probabilities calculated from N-best lists or word lattices. We propose to incorporate two groups of linguistic features, which convey information from outside machine translation systems, into error detection: lexical and syntactic features. We use a maximum entropy classifier to predict translation errors by integrating word posterior probability feature and linguistic features.

Translation hypotheses generated by an SMT system always contain both correct parts (e.g., words, n-grams, phrases matched with reference translations) and incorrect parts. Automatically distinguishing incorrect parts from correct parts is therefore very desirable not only for post-editing and interactive machine translation (Ueffing and Ney 2007) but also for SMT itself: either by rescoring hypotheses in the N-best list using the probability of correctness calculated for each hypothesis (Zens and Ney 2006) or by generating new hypotheses using N-best lists from one SMT system or multiple systems (Akiba et al. 2004; Jayaraman and Lavie 2005). In this chapter, we introduce a linguistically motivated model to automatically detect such incorrect parts in SMT-generated translations.

We restrict the "parts" to words. That is, we detect errors at the word level for SMT. A common approach to SMT error detection at the word level is calculating the confidence at which a word is correct. The majority of word confidence estimation methods follows three steps:

(1) Calculate features that express the correctness of words either based on SMT model (e.g., translation/language model) or based on SMT system output (e.g., N-best lists, word lattices) (Blatz et al. 2004; Ueffing and Ney 2007).
(2) Combine these features together with a classification model such as multi-layer perceptron (Blatz et al. 2004), Naive Bayes (Blatz et al. 2004; Sanchis et al. 2007), or log-linear model (Ueffing and Ney 2007).
(3) Divide words into two groups (correct translations and errors) by using a classification threshold optimized on a development set.

© Springer Science+Business Media Singapore 2015

D. Xiong and M. Zhang, *Linguistically Motivated Statistical Machine Translation*, DOI 10.1007/978-981-287-356-9_8

Sometimes the step (2) is not necessary if only one effective feature is used (Ueffing and Ney 2007); and sometimes the steps (2) and (3) can be merged into a single step if we directly output predicting results from binary classifiers instead of making thresholding decision.

Various features from different SMT models or system outputs are investigated (Blatz et al. 2004; Ueffing and Ney 2007; Sanchis et al. 2007; Raybaud et al. 2009). Experiment results show that they are useful for error detection. However, it is not adequate to just use these features as discussed by Shi and Zhou (2005) because the information that they carry is either from the inner components of SMT systems or from system outputs. To some extent, such information has already been considered by SMT systems. Hence finding external information sources from outside SMT systems is desired for error detection.

Linguistic knowledge is exactly such a good choice as an external information source. It has already proven effective in error detection for speech recognition (Shi and Zhou 2005). However, it is not widely used in SMT error detection. The reason is probably that people have yet to find effective linguistic features that outperform nonlinguistic features such as word posterior probability features (Blatz et al. 2004; Raybaud et al. 2009). In this chapter, we would like to show an effective use of linguistic features in SMT error detection.

We integrate two sets of linguistic features into a maximum entropy model and develop a MaxEnt-based binary classifier to predict the category (correct or incorrect) for each word in a generated target sentence. Experiment results show that linguistic features substantially improve error detection and even outperform word posterior probability features. Further, they can produce additional improvements when combined with word posterior probability features.

The rest of this chapter is organized as follows. In Sect. 8.1, we introduce our linguistic features as well as the word posterior probability feature. In Sect. 8.2, we elaborate our MaxEnt-based error detection model which combine linguistic features and word posterior probability feature together. In Sect. 8.3, we describe how we collect training data to train the MaxEnt-based error detection model. In Sect. 8.4, we introduce evaluation metrics for translation error detection. In Sect. 8.5, we present the architecture of the proposed error detection system and the procedure of testing and evaluating the system. Finally, we summarize this chapter with additional readings in Sect. 8.6.

8.1 Features

We explore two sets of linguistic features for each word in a machine-generated translation hypothesis. The first set of linguistic features are simple lexical features. The second set of linguistic features are syntactic features which are extracted from link grammar parse. To compare with the previously widely used features, we also investigate features based on word posterior probabilities.

8.1.1 Lexical Features

We use the following lexical features.

- wd: word itself
- pos: part-of-speech tag from a tagger[1] trained on WSJ corpus.

For each word, we look at previous n words/tags and next n words/tags. They together form a word/tag sequence pattern. The basic idea of using these features is that words in rare patterns are more likely to be incorrect than words in frequently occurring patterns. To some extent, these two features have similar function to a target language model or POS-based target language model.

8.1.2 Syntactic Features

High-level linguistic knowledge such as syntactic information about a word is a very natural and promising indicator to decide whether this word is syntactically correct or not. Words occurring in an ungrammatical part of a target sentence are prone to be incorrect. The challenge of using syntactic knowledge for error detection is that machine-generated hypotheses are rarely fully grammatical. They are mixed with grammatical and ungrammatical parts, which hence are not friendly to traditional parsers trained on grammatical sentences because ungrammatical parts of a machine-generated sentence could lead to a parsing failure.

To overcome this challenge, we select the *Link Grammar* (LG) parser[2] as our syntactic parser to generate syntactic features. The LG parser produces a set of labeled links which connect pairs of words with a link grammar (Sleator and Temperley 1993).

The main reason why we choose the LG parser is that it provides a robustness feature: *null-link* scheme. The null-link scheme allows the parser to parse a sentence even when the parser cannot fully interpret the entire sentence (e.g., including ungrammatical parts). When the parser fails to parse the entire sentence, it ignores one word each time until it finds linkages for remaining words. After parsing, those ignored words are not connected to any other words. We call them *null-linked words*.

Our hypothesis is that null-linked words are prone to be syntactically incorrect. We hence straightforwardly define a syntactic feature for a word w according to its links as follows:

$$\text{link}(w) = \begin{cases} \text{yes}, & w \text{ has links} \\ \text{no}, & \text{otherwise} \end{cases} \tag{8.1}$$

---

[1] Available via http://www-tsujii.is.s.u-tokyo.ac.jp/~tsuruoka/postagger/.

[2] Available at http://www.link.cs.cmu.edu/link/.

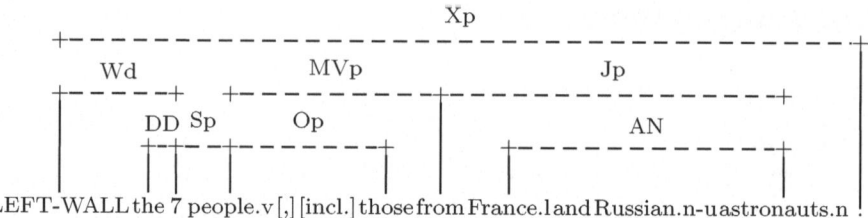

Fig. 8.1 An example of Link Grammar parsing results. (*Reference* The seven-member crew includes astronauts from France and Russia)

In Fig. 8.1 we show an example of a generated translation hypothesis with its link parse. Here links are denoted with dotted lines which are annotated with link types (e.g., Jp, Op). Bracketed words, namely "," and "including", are null-linked words.

8.1.3 Word Posterior Probability Features

The word posterior probability is calculated on N-best list, which is first proposed by (Ueffing et al. 2003) and widely used in (Blatz et al. 2004; Ueffing and Ney 2007; Sanchis et al. 2007).

Given a source sentence f, let $\{e_n\}_1^N$ be the N-best list generated by an SMT system, and let e_n^i is the ith word in e_n. The major work of calculating word posterior probabilities is to find the Levenshtein alignment (Levenshtein 1966) between the best hypothesis e_1 and its competing hypothesis e_n in the N-best list $\{e_n\}_1^N$. We denote the alignment between them as $\ell(e_1, e_n)$. The word in the hypothesis e_n which e_1^i is Levenshtein aligned to is denoted as $\ell_i(e_1, e_n)$.

The word posterior probability of e_1^i is then calculated by summing up the probabilities over all hypotheses containing e_1^i in a position which is Levenshtein aligned to e_1^i.

$$P_{\text{wpp}}(e_1^i) = \frac{\sum_{e_n:\ \ell_i(e_1,e_n)=e_1^i} P(e_n)}{\sum_1^N P(e_n)} \tag{8.2}$$

To use the word posterior probability in our error detection model, we need to make it discrete. We introduce a feature for a word w based on its word posterior probability as follows:

$$\text{dwpp}(w) = \lfloor -\log(P_{\text{wpp}}(w))/\text{df} \rfloor \tag{8.3}$$

where df is the discrete factor which can be set to 1, 0.1, 0.01, and so on.

"⌊ ⌋" is a rounding operator which takes the largest integer that does not exceed $-\log(P_{wpp}(w))/\mathrm{df}$. We optimize the discrete factor on a development set and find the optimal value is 1. Therefore a feature "dwpp = 2" represents that the logarithm of the word posterior probability is between -3 and -2;

8.2 Error Detection with a Maximum Entropy Model

As mentioned before, we consider error detection as a binary classification task. To formalize this task, we use a feature vector ψ to represent a word w in question, and a binary variable c to indicate whether this word is correct or not. In the feature vector, we look at 2 words before and 2 words after the current word position $(w_{-2}, w_{-1}, w, w_1, w_2)$. We collect features {wd, pos, link, dwpp} for each word among these words and combine them into the feature vector ψ for w. As such, we want the feature vector to capture the contextual environment, e.g., pos sequence pattern, syntactic pattern, where the word w occurs.

For classification, we employ the maximum entropy model (Berger et al. 1996) to predict whether a word w is correct or incorrect given its feature vector ψ.

$$P(c|\psi) = \frac{\exp(\sum_i \theta_i f_i(c, \psi))}{\sum_{c'} \exp(\sum_i \theta_i f_i(c', \psi))} \tag{8.4}$$

where f_i is a binary model feature defined on c and the feature vector ψ. θ_i is the weight of f_i. Table 8.1 shows some examples of our binary model features.

In order to learn the model feature weights θ for probability estimation, we need a training set of m samples $\{\psi^i, c^i\}_1^m$. The challenge of collecting training instances is that the correctness of a word in a generated translation hypothesis is not intuitively clear (Ueffing and Ney 2007). We will describe the method to determine the correctness of a word in Sect. 8.3, which is broadly adopted in previous work.

Table 8.1 Examples of model features

Feature	Example
wd	$f(c, \psi) = \begin{cases} 1, & \psi.w.\mathrm{wd} = \text{"."}, c = correct \\ 0, & \text{otherwise} \end{cases}$
pos	$f(c, \psi) = \begin{cases} 1, & \psi.w_2.\mathrm{pos} = \text{"NN"}, c = incorrect \\ 0, & \text{otherwise} \end{cases}$
link	$f(c, \psi) = \begin{cases} 1, & \psi.w.\mathrm{link} = no, c = incorrect \\ 0, & \text{otherwise} \end{cases}$
dwpp	$f(c, \psi) = \begin{cases} 1, & \psi.w_{-2}.\mathrm{dwpp} = 2, c = correct \\ 0, & \text{otherwise} \end{cases}$

We tune our model feature weights using an off-the-shelf MaxEnt toolkit.[3] To avoid overfitting, we optimize the Gaussian prior on the development set. During test, if the probability $P(\text{correct}|\psi)$ is larger than $P(\text{incorrect}|\psi)$ according to the trained MaxEnt model, the word is labeled as correct otherwise incorrect.

8.3 Data Collection

In order to train the translation error detector for an SMT system as described in the last section, we need to collect training instances for the MaxeEnt classifier. We use the SMT system to translate all source sentences of a bilingual corpus. To obtain the linkage information of the generated target translations, we run the LG parser on these translations. For those sentences that cannot be fully parsed by the LG parser, the LG parser will use the null-link scheme to generate null-linked words.

To determine the true class of a word in a generated translation hypothesis, we follow (Blatz et al. 2004) to use the word error rate (WER). We tag a word as correct if it is aligned to itself in the Levenshtein alignment between the hypothesis and the nearest reference translation that has minimum edit distance to the hypothesis among four reference translations. Figure 8.2 shows the Levenshtein alignment between a machine-generated hypothesis and its nearest reference translation. The "Class" row shows the label of each word according to the alignment, where "c" and "i" represent correct and incorrect respectively.

There are several other metrics to tag single words in a translation hypothesis as correct or incorrect, such as PER where a word is tagged as correct if it occurs in one of reference translations with the same number of occurrences, and *Set* which is a less strict variant of PER, ignoring the number of occurrences per word. In Fig. 8.2, the two words "last year" in the hypothesis will be tagged as correct if we use the PER or Set metric since they do not consider the occurring positions of words. We follow Ueffing and Ney (2007) to use the m-WER, which is stricter than PER and Set. It is also stricter than normal WER metric which compares each hypothesis to all references, rather than the nearest reference.

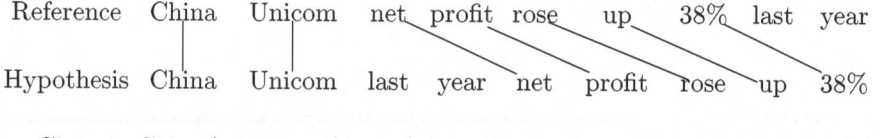

Fig. 8.2 Tagging a word as correct/incorrect according to the Levenshtein alignment

---

[3] http://homepages.inf.ed.ac.uk/s0450736/maxenttoolkit.html.

8.4 Evaluation Metrics

To evaluate the overall performance of the error detection, we use the commonly used metric, classification error rate (CER) to evaluate our classifiers. CER is defined as the percentage of words that are wrongly tagged as follows

$$CER = \frac{\# \text{ of wrongly tagged words}}{\text{Total } \# \text{ of words}} \tag{8.5}$$

The baseline CER is determined by assuming the most frequent class for all words. Since the ratio of correct words in both the development and test sets is lower than 50%, the most frequent class is "incorrect". Hence the baseline CER in our experiments is equal to the ratio of correct words as these words are wrongly tagged as incorrect.

We also use precision and recall on errors to evaluate the performance of error detection. Let n_g be the number of words of which the true class is incorrect, n_t be the number of words which are tagged as incorrect by classifiers, and n_m be the number of words tagged as incorrect that are indeed translation errors. The precision Pre is the percentage of words correctly tagged as translation errors.

$$Pre = \frac{n_m}{n_t} \tag{8.6}$$

The recall Rec is the proportion of actual translation errors that are found by classifiers.

$$Rec = \frac{n_m}{n_g} \tag{8.7}$$

F measure, the tradeoff between precision and recall, is also used.

$$F = \frac{2 \times Pre \times Rec}{Pre + Rec} \tag{8.8}$$

8.5 Architecture of Translation Error Detection System

In this section, we introduce the system architecture of the proposed translation error detection as well as the procedure of using this system to detect errors on a given test. Figure 8.3 shows the whole architecture of the error detection system. Our goal is to train a translation error detector for an SMT system $\mathcal{S}$. As described in Sect. 8.3, we first collect training instances (i.e., extracting features for the detector) as follows.

- Translating source sentences using the SMT system $\mathcal{S}$ and outputting the best translations and word posterior probabilities as described in Sect. 8.1.3.

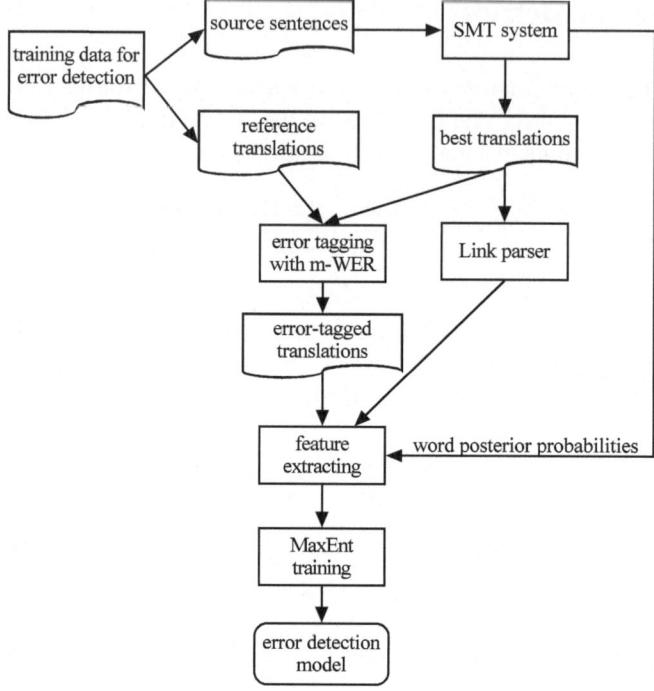

Fig. 8.3 The architecture of the translation error detection system

- Tagging each word in the best translations with labels of "correct" or "incorrect" by comparing the word to the reference translations according to the m-WER metric.
- Parsing the best translations with the LG parser to obtain the linkage information.
- Extracting the three groups of features defined in Sect. 8.1 based on error-tagged translations, linkage information and output word posterior probabilities.

Once we collect all features, we can easily train a MaxEnt classifier as our error detector for the SMT system S.

We can use the trained error detector to detect translation errors for the SMT system S on a test set. Figure 8.4 visualizes the procedure of testing and evaluating the error detector. Similar to the training procedure shown in Fig. 8.3, we first use the SMT system S to translate the test set and obtain the best translations as well as other information. Based on these outputs, we can obtain features and use the trained error detector to detect translation errors with these features on the best translations. In order to evaluate the error detector, we compare the detected errors with the errors tagged according to the reference translations of the test set.

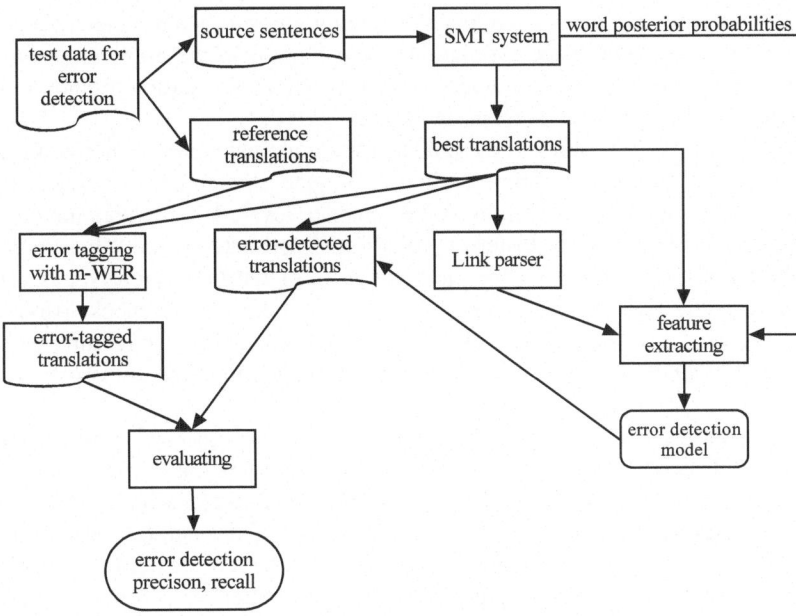

Fig. 8.4 The procedure of testing and evaluating the trained error detector

8.6 Summary and Additional Readings

In this chapter, we have presented a maximum entropy-based approach to automatically detect errors in translation hypotheses generated by SMT systems. We incorporate two sets of linguistic features together with word posterior probability-based features into error detection.

The extracted linguistic features are quite compact, which can be learned from a small training set. Furthermore, The learned linguistic features are system-independent. Therefore our approach can be used for other machine translation systems, such as rule-based or example-based system, which generally do not produce N-best lists.

Experiments of the maximum entropy-based error detection method are reported in "Error Detection for Statistical Machine Translation Using Linguistic Features" (Xiong et al., *Proceedings of the 48th Annual Meeting of the Association for Computational Linguistics*, Uppsala, Sweden, 11–16 July 2010; pp. 604–611.). Experiment results validate that linguistic features are very useful for error detection: (1) they by themselves achieve a higher improvement in terms of both CER and F measure than word posterior probability features; (2) the performance is further improved when they are combined with word posterior probability features.

Additional Readings. Here we present an overview of confidence estimation (CE) for machine translation at the word level. As we are only interested in error detection, we focus on work that uses confidence estimation approaches to detect translation errors. Of course, confidence estimation is not limited to the application of error detection, it can also be used in other scenarios, such as translation prediction in an interactive environment (Gandrabur and Foster 2003) .

In a JHU workshop, Blatz et al. (2004) investigate using neural networks and a naive Bayes classifier to combine various confidence features for confidence estimation at the word level as well as at the sentence level. The features they use for word-level CE include word posterior probabilities estimated from N-best lists, features based on SMT models, semantic features extracted from WordNet as well as simple syntactic features, i.e., parentheses and quotation mark check. Among all these features, the word posterior probability is the most effective feature, which is much better than linguistic features such as semantic features, according to their final results.

Ueffing and Ney (2007) exhaustively explore various word-level confidence measures to label each word in a generated translation hypothesis as correct or incorrect. All their measures are based on word posterior probabilities, which are estimated from (1) system output, such as word lattices or N-best lists and (2) word or phrase translation table. Their experimental results show that word posterior probabilities directly estimated from phrase translation table are better than those from system output except for the Chinese-English language pair.

Sanchis et al. (2007) adopt a smoothed naive Bayes model to combine different word posterior probability-based confidence features which are estimated from N-best lists, similar to (Ueffing and Ney 2007).

Raybaud et al. (2009) study several confidence features based on mutual information between words and n-gram and backward n-gram language model for word-level and sentence-level CE. They also explore linguistic features using information from syntactic category, tense, gender, and so on. Unfortunately, such linguistic features neither improve performance at the word level nor at the sentence level.

The approach presented in this chapter departs from the previous work in two major respects.

- We exploit various linguistic features and show that they are able to produce larger improvements than widely used system-related features such as word posterior probabilities. This is in contrast to some previous work. Yet another advantage of using linguistic features is that they are system-independent, which therefore can be used across different systems.
- We treat error detection as a complete binary classification problem. Hence we directly output prediction results from our discriminatively trained classifier without optimizing a classification threshold on a distinct development set beforehand.[4] Most previous approaches make decisions based on a pre-tuned classification threshold τ as follows:

---

[4] This does not mean we do not need a development set. We do validate our feature selection and other experimental settings on the development set.

$$\text{class} = \begin{cases} \text{correct,} & \Phi(\text{correct}, \theta) > \tau \\ \text{incorrect,} & \text{otherwise} \end{cases}$$

where Φ is a classifier or a confidence measure and θ is the parameter set of Φ. The performance of these approaches is strongly dependent on the classification threshold.

With respect to machine translation error detection at the sentence level, Bach et al. (2011) introduce a method to measure the goodness of a given sentence by taking an average over all goodness values of words in this sentence. They also use various linguistic features, such as POS tags, dependency structures, to assess the goodness of a single word. Felice and Specia (2012) propose yet another sentence-level translation quality assessment model built as a regression task, where a total of 70 linguistic features are used.

Chapter 9
Closing Remarks

Abstract This chapter concludes this book with a review of linguistically motivated SMT, especially those linguistically motivated models and algorithms introduced in this book from a linguistic perspective. We also discuss future directions for linguistically motivated SMT in this chapter.

The past two decades have witnessed that a wide variety of SMT formalisms have been proposed and developed, such as word-, phrase-, and tree-based SMT. In order to further enhance these SMT formalisms, we have introduced and discussed a series of models and algorithms in the preceding chapters. These linguistically motivated models and algorithms incorporate linguistic knowledge into reordering models, bracketing models, translation models as well as error detection for SMT. They have also proven useful in addressing the linguistic challenges of SMT discussed in Chap. 1.

This chapter, from a different perspective, provides a review of linguistically motivated SMT introduced in this book, especially those linguistically motivated models and algorithms (Sect. 9.1). We finally conclude this book with future directions of linguistically motivated SMT (Sect. 9.2).

9.1 Linguistically Motivated SMT: Review

In Chap. 1, we introduce four types of challenges for statistical machine translation from different linguistic levels. In this section, we will review the linguistically motivated models and algorithms elaborated in the proceeding chapters in terms of these linguistic challenges and linguistic knowledge that we use to address these challenges.

We incorporate *lexical knowledge* into linguistically motivated SMT to address issues caused by the lexical challenge. Specially, we introduce

- the boundary word-based reordering model that uses lexical boundary words of bilingual phrases to predict the order of two neighboring phrases on the target side
- two lexicalized bracketing models, i.e., the penalty model and bracketing strength model, both of which explore beginning and ending words of segments to determine whether segments are bracketable
- the translation error detection model that employs lexicon words as features to automatically detect errors in machine-generated translations.

© Springer Science+Business Media Singapore 2015
D. Xiong and M. Zhang, *Linguistically Motivated Statistical Machine Translation*, DOI 10.1007/978-981-287-356-9_9

Table 9.1 Models and algorithms for linguistically motivated SMT introduced in this book

Knowledge	Model	Algorithm	Chapter
Lexical	The boundary word-based reordering model	The reordering example extraction algorithm	3
	The bracketing penalty and strength model	The bracketable segment boundary learning algorithm	5
	The translation error detection model		8
Syntactic	The syntactically annotated reordering model	The annotation algorithm	3
	The syntax-driven bracketing model	The syntax-driven bracketing instances extraction algorithm	6
	The translation error detection model		8
Semantic	The semantically informed argument reordering model	The integration algorithm	4
	The semantically informed argument bracketing model	The integration algorithm	6
	The topic-based dissimilarity and sensitivity model	The topic projection algorithm	7

We also explore *syntactic knowledge* for linguistically motivated SMT in the following three different models: (1) the syntactically annotated reordering model that uses syntactic knowledge from source parse trees for long-distance phrase reordering, (2) the syntax-driven bracketing model that predicts whether a phrase is bracketable using rich syntactic features, and (3) the translation error detection model that utilizes syntactic features from a Link Grammar parser. Additionally, we also introduce a syntax-based reordering analysis framework to analyze phrase reordering based on parse trees.

Finally, we integrate sentence- and document-level *semantic knowledge* into linguistically motivated SMT. In particular, we present

- the semantically informed argument reordering model that capitalizes on semantic information from predicate-argument structures for argument reordering
- the semantically informed argument bracketing model that predicts whether an argument should be translated as a whole unit with semantic features
- the topic-based dissimilarity and sensitive models that incorporate document gists represented as topics for translation rule selection.

For ease of reference, we list all of these linguistically motivated models and associated algorithms in Table 9.1.

9.2 Linguistically Motivated SMT: Future Directions

Although the advancement from word-based SMT to syntax-based SMT produces significant improvements in translation quality, crucial meaning errors and lack of cross-sentence connections at discourse level still hurt the quality of SMT-generated translations. This requires that more high-level linguistic knowledge should be incorporated into SMT. Along the line of linguistically motivated SMT, we have witnessed two active movements recently: one toward combining semantics and SMT in an attempt to generate not only grammatical but also meaning-preserving translations (*semantic SMT*), and the other toward exploring discourse knowledge for document-level machine translation in order to capture intersentence dependencies (*document-level SMT*).

With respect to semantic SMT, we suggest that more attention should be paid to the following two directions.

- *Semantic representations in the context of SMT.* How semantics should be represented so that it is computable and easy to be incorporated into SMT? Generally we discuss semantics at two levels: lexical semantics and sentential semantics. Semantic SMT requires good representations at the two semantic levels. Recent developments in distributional semantic representations based on either generative topic models (Brody and Lapata 2009; Yao and Durme 2011) or neural networks-based models (Bengio et al. 2003; Mikolov et al. 2013) provide a good way to encode lexical semantics into vectors. But we need to adapt monolingual semantic space captured by these models to bilingual or multilingual semantic space. For example, Chap. 7 introduces a projection method for bilingual semantic representation adaptation. Additionally, we also need to investigate how we can obtain semantic representations of larger linguistic units (i.e., phrases or sentences) from those of smaller units (i.e., words or phrases). This is related to compositional semantics.
- *Semantic models built on bilingual semantic representations.* One interesting question to ask after we obtain semantic representations is how we can effectively incorporate semantic knowledge embedded in these representations into machine translation via semantic translation models. We can either follow what we do in syntax-based SMT to build various semantic tree-based models or establish new methodologies for building semantic models.

As we have mentioned in Chap. 1, sentences in a text are connected to each other via either surface links that are referred to as *cohesion* or underlying meaning connections that are called *coherence*. Halliday and Hasan (1976) further identify five categories of cohesion devices that create cohesion in texts: reference, substitution, ellipsis, conjunction, and lexical cohesion. The former four devices can be roughly grouped into grammatical cohesion in contrast to lexical cohesion that connects sentences in a text not through grammatical devices, but rather through lexical choices. This discourse-level knowledge should be incorporated into linguistically motivated SMT to capture cross-sentence dependencies and connectedness.

Future directions for document-level SMT include discourse representation in the context of machine translation, modeling lexical cohesion, and grammatical cohesion in document translation, producing coherence in document translation and so on.

Semantic SMT employs a variety of semantic knowledge in translation while document-level SMT captures cross-sentence discourse-level information for translation. Both of them can well fit into the general architecture of linguistically motivated SMT introduced in Chap. 1 (see Fig. 1.4). Some of the algorithms and models for knowledge learning and integrating introduced in this book may still be used or provide inspiration for future research in semantic and document-level SMT.

References

Akiba, Y., Sumita, E., Nakaiwa, H., Yamamoto, S., Okuno, H. G. (2004). Using a mixture of n-best lists from multiple MT systems in ranksum-based confidence measure for MT outputs. In Proceedings of the 20th International Conference on Computational Linguistics. Stroudsburg, PA, USA: Association for Computational Linguistics. Retrieved from http://dx.doi.org/10.3115/1220355.1220402 doi:10.3115/1220355.1220402

Al-Onaizan, Y., & Papineni, K. (2006, July). Distortion models for statistical machine translation. In Proceedings of the 21st International Conference on Computational Linguistics and 44th Annual Meeting of the Association for Computational Linguistics (pp. 529–536). Sydney, Australia. Retrieved from http://www.aclweb.org/anthology/P06-1067 doi:10.3115/1220175.1220242

Aziz, W., Rios, M., Specia, L. (2011, July). Shallow semantic trees for SMT. In Proceedings of the Sixth Workshop on Statistical Machine Translation (pp. 316–322). Edinburgh, Scotland: Association for Computational Linguistics. Retrieved from http://www.aclweb.org/anthology/W11-2136

Bach, N., Huang, F., Al-Onaizan, Y. (2011). Goodness: A method for measuring machine translation confidence. In Proceedings of the 49th Annual Meeting of the Association for Computational Linguistics: Human Language Technologies (Vol. 1, pp. 211–219). Stroudsburg, PA, USA: Association for Computational Linguistics. Retrieved from http://dl.acm.org/citation.cfm?id=2002472.2002500

Bengio, Y., Ducharme, R., Vincent, P., & Jauvin, C. (2003). A neural probabilistic language model. *Journal of Machine Learning Research*, *3*, 1137–1155.

Berger, A. L., Pietra, S. A. D., & Pietra, V. J. D. (1996). A maximum entropy approach to natural language processing. *Computational Linguistics*, *22*(1), 39–71.

Blatz, J., Fitzgerald, E., Foster, G., Gandrabur, S., Goutte, C., Kulesza, A., et al. (2004). Confidence estimation for machine translation. In Proceedings of the 20th International Conference on Computational Linguistics. Stroudsburg, PA, USA: Association for Computational Linguistics. Retrieved from http://dx.doi.org/10.3115/1220355.1220401 doi:10.3115/1220355.1220401

Blei, D. M., Ng, A. Y., Jordan, M. I., & Lafferty, J. (2003). Latent Dirichlet allocation. *Journal of Machine Learning Research*, *3*, 993–1022.

Blei, D. M., & Lafferty, J. D. (2007). A correlated topic model of science. *AAS*, *1*(1), 17–35.

Blunsom, P., Cohn, T., Dyer, C., Osborne, M. (2009, August). A Gibbs sampler for phrasal synchronous grammar induction. In Proceedings of the Joint Conference of the 47th Annual Meeting of the ACL and the 4th International Joint Conference on Natural Language Processing of the AFNLP (pp. 782–790). Suntec, Singapore: Association for Computational Linguistics. Retrieved from http://www.aclweb.org/anthology/P/P09/P09-1088

© Springer Science+Business Media Singapore 2015
D. Xiong and M. Zhang, *Linguistically Motivated Statistical Machine Translation*, DOI 10.1007/978-981-287-356-9

Boyd-Graber, J., & Blei, D. M. (2009). Multilingual topic models for unaligned text. *Proceedings of the Twenty-Fifth Conference on Uncertainty in Artificial Intelligence* (pp. 75–82). Arlington, VA, USA: AUAI Press.

Brants, T., Popat, A. C., Xu, P., Och, F. J., & Dean, J. (2007, June). Large language models in machine translation. In Proceedings of the 2007 Joint Conference on Empirical Methods in Natural Language Processing and Computational Natural Language Learning (EMNLP-CoNLL) (pp. 858–867). Prague, Czech Republic: Association for Computational Linguistics. Retrieved from http://www.aclweb.org/anthology/D/D07/D07-1090

Brody, S., & Lapata, M. (2009, March). Bayesian word sense induction. In Proceedings of the 12th Conference of the European Chapter of the ACL (EACL 2009). (pp. 103–111). Athens, Greece: Association for Computational Linguistics. Retrieved from http://www.aclweb.org/anthology/E09-1013

Brown, P. F., Pietra, S. A. D., Pietra, V. J. D., & Mercer, R. L. (1993). The mathematics of statistical machine translation: Parameter estimation. *Computational Linguistics, 19*(2), 263–311.

Callison-Burch, C., Fordyce, C., Koehn, P., Monz, C., Schroeder, J. (2007, June). (Meta-) evaluation of machine translation. In Proceedings of the Second Workshop on Statistical Machine Translation (pp. 136–158). Prague, Czech Republic. Retrieved from http://www.aclweb.org/anthology/W/W07/W07-0718

Carpuat, M., & Wu, D. (2007a). How phrase sense disambiguation outperforms word sense disambiguation for statistical machine translation. In Proceedings of the 11th Conference on Theoretical and Methodological Issues in Machine Translation (pp. 43–52).

Carpuat, M., & Wu, D. (2007b, June). Improving statistical machine translation using word sense disambiguation. In Proceedings of the 2007 Joint Conference on Empirical Methods in Natural Language Processing and Computational Natural Language Learning (EMNLP-CoNLL) (pp. 61–72). Prague, Czech Republic: Association for Computational Linguistics. Retrieved from http://www.aclweb.org/anthology/D/D07/D07-1007

Chan, Y. S., Ng, H. T., & Chiang, D. (2007, June). Word sense disambiguation improves statistical machine translation. In Proceedings of the 45th Annual Meeting of the Association of Computational Linguistics (pp. 33–40). Prague, Czech Republic: Association for Computational Linguistics. Retrieved from http://www.aclweb.org/anthology/P07-1005

Charniak, E., Knight, K., & Yamada, K. (2003). Syntax-based language models for statistical machine translation. In Proceedings of MT Summit IX. New Orleans: International Association for Machine Translation.

Cherry, C. (2008, June). Cohesive phrase-based decoding for statistical machine translation. In Proceedings of ACL-08: HLT (pp. 72–80). Columbus, Ohio. Retrieved from http://www.aclweb.org/anthology/P/P08/P08-1009

Chiang, D. (2005, June). A hierarchical phrase-based model for statistical machine translation. In Proceedings of the 43rd Annual Meeting of the Association for Computational Linguistics (pp. 263–270). Ann Arbor, USA.

Chiang, D. (2006). An introduction to synchronous grammars.

Chiang, D., Lopez, A., Madnani, N., Monz, C., Resnik, P., Subotin, M. (2005, October). The hiero machine translation system: Extensions, evaluation, and analysis. In Proceedings of Human Language Technology Conference and Conference on Empirical Methods in Natural Language Processing (pp. 779–786). Vancouver, British Columbia, Canada. Retrieved from http://www.aclweb.org/anthology/H/H05/H05-1098

Chiang, D., Marton, Y., Resnik, P. (2008, October). Online large-margin training of syntactic and structural translation features. In Proceedings of the 2008 Conference on Empirical Methods in Natural Language Processing (pp. 224–233). Honolulu, Hawaii: Association for Computational Linguistics. Retrieved from http://www.aclweb.org/anthology/D08-1024

Chiang, D. (2007). Hierarchical phrase-based translation. *Computational Linguistics, 33*(2), 201–228.

Chomsky, N. (1957). *Syntactic structures*. The Hague: Mouton.

Church, K. W., & Hanks, P. (1990). Word association norms, mutual information, and lexicography. *Computational Linguistics*, *16*(1), 22–29.

Collins, M., Koehn, P., Kucerova, I. (2005, June). Clause restructuring for statistical machine translation. In Proceedings of the 43rd Annual Meeting of the Association for Computational Linguistics (ACL'05) (pp. 531–540). Ann Arbor, Michigan: Association for Computational Linguistics. Retrieved from http://www.aclweb.org/anthology/P/P05/P05-1066

Cui, L., Zhang, D., Li, M., Zhou, M., Zhao, T. (2010). A joint rule selection model for hierarchical phrase-based translation. In Proceedings of the ACL 2010 Conference Short Papers (pp. 6–11). Stroudsburg, PA, USA: Association for Computational Linguistics. Retrieved from http://dl.acm.org/citation.cfm?id=1858842.1858844

Dorr, B. J. (1994). Machine translation divergences: A formal description and proposed solution. *Computational Linguistics*, *20*(4), 598–633.

Duchateau, J., Demuynck, K., & Wambacq, P. (2002, April). Confidence scoring based on backward language models. In Proceedings of ICASSP (pp. 221–224). Orlando, FL.

Felice, M., & Specia, L. (2012). Linguistic features for quality estimation. In Proceedings of the Seventh Workshop on Statistical Machine Translation (pp. 96–103). Stroudsburg, PA, USA: Association for Computational Linguistics. Retrieved from http://dl.acm.org/citation.cfm?id=2393015.2393027

Finch, A., & Sumita, E. (2009, August). Bidirectional phrase-based statistical machine translation. In Proceedings of the 2009 Conference on Empirical Methods in Natural Language Processing (pp. 1124–1132). Singapore: Association for Computational Linguistics. Retrieved from http://www.aclweb.org/anthology/D/D09/D09-1117

Foster, G., & Kuhn, R. (2007, June). Mixture-model adaptation for SMT. In Proceedings of the Second Workshop on Statistical Machine Translation (pp. 128–135). Prague, Czech Republic.

Fox, H. (2002, July). Phrasal cohesion and statistical machine translation. In Proceedings of the 2002 Conference on Empirical Methods in Natural Language Processing (pp. 304–3111). Retrieved from http://www.aclweb.org/anthology/W02-1039 doi:10.3115/1118693.1118732

Fung, P., Zhaojun, W., Yongsheng, Y., & Wu, D. (2006, December). Automatic learning of Chinese English semantic structure mapping. In IEEE/ACL 2006 Workshop on Spoken Language Technology (SLT 2006). Aruba.

Galley, M., Graehl, J., Knight, K., Marcu, D., DeNeefe, S., Wang, W., et al. (2006, July). Scalable inference and training of context-rich syntactic translation models. In Proceedings of the 21st International Conference on Computational Linguistics and 44th Annual Meeting of the Association for Computational Linguistics (pp. 961–968). Sydney, Australia: Association for Computational Linguistics.

Galley, M., Hopkins, M., Knight, K., & Marcu, D. (2004, May). What's in a translation rule? In Proceedings of the Human Language Technology Conference of the North American Chapter of the Association for Computational Linguistics: HLT-NAACL 2004 (pp. 273–280). Boston, MA, USA.

Gandrabur, S., & Foster, G. (2003). Confidence estimation for translation prediction. In Proceedings of the Seventh Conference on Natural Language Learning at HLT-NAACL 2003 (Vol. 4, pp. 95–102). Stroudsburg, PA, USA: Association for Computational Linguistics. Retrieved from http://dx.doi.org/10.3115/1119176.1119189 doi:10.3115/1119176.1119189

Gong, Z., Zhang, Y., & Zhou, G. (2010, October). Statistical machine translation based on LDA. In Proceedings of IUCS 2010 (pp. 286–290).

Gong, Z., Zhang, M., & Zhou, G. (2011, July). Cache-based document-level statistical machine translation. In Proceedings of the 2011 Conference on Empirical Methods in Natural Language Processing (pp. 909–919). Edinburgh, Scotland, UK.

Goodman, J. (1997). Global thresholding and multiple-pass parsing. In Proceedings of Conference on Empirical Methods in Natural Language Processing (pp. 11–25).

Goodman, J. (2001). *A bit of progress in language modeling extended version*. Microsoft Research : Technical Report.

Goodman, J. (1999). Semiring parsing. *Computational Linguistics*, *25*, 573–605.

Griffiths, T. L., & Steyvers, M. (2004 April). Finding scientific topics. In *Proceedings of the National Academy of Sciences*, *101*(Suppl. 1), 5228–5235.

Griffiths, T. L., Tenenbaum, J. B., & Steyvers, M. (2007). Topics in semantic representation. *Psychological Review*, *114*, 211–244.

Halliday, M., & Hasan, R. (1976). *Cohesion in English*. London: Longman.

Hassan, H., Sima'an, K., Way, A. (2007, June). Supertagged phrase-based statistical machine translation. In Proceedings of the 45th Annual Meeting of the Association of Computational Linguistics (pp. 288–295). Prague, Czech Republic: Association for Computational Linguistics. Retrieved from http://www.aclweb.org/anthology/P/P07/P07-1037

Hassan, H., Sima'an, K., & Way, A. (2008, December). A syntactic language model based on incremental CCG parsing. In Proceedings of IEEE Spoken Language Technology Workshop (pp. 205–208).

He, Z., Liu, Q., Lin, S. (2008, August). Improving statistical machine translation using lexicalized rule selection. In Proceedings of the 22nd International Conference on Computational Linguistics (COLING 2008) (pp. 321–328). Manchester, UK: Coling 2008 Organizing Committee. Retrieved from http://www.aclweb.org/anthology/C08-1041

He, Z., Meng, Y., Yu, H. (2010a, August). Learning phrase boundaries for hierarchical phrase-based translation. In Proceedings of COLING 2010: Posters (pp. 383–390). Beijing, China: Coling 2010 Organizing Committee. Retrieved from http://www.aclweb.org/anthology/C10-2044

He, Z., Meng, Y., & Yu, H. (2010b). Maximum entropy based phrase reordering for hierarchical phrase-based translation. In Proceedings of EMNLP (pp. 555–563).

He, Z., Meng, Y., Lü, Y., Yu, H., & Liu, Q. (2009). Reducing SMT rule table with monolingual key phrase. In Proceedings of ACL/AFNLP (Short Papers) (pp. 121–124).

He, X., Yang, M., Gao, J., Nguyen, P., Moore, R. (2008, October). Indirect- HMM-based hypothesis alignment for combining outputs from machine translation systems. In Proceedings of the 2008 Conference on Empirical Methods in Natural Language Processing (pp. 98–107). Honolulu, Hawaii: Association for Computational Linguistics. Retrieved from http://www.aclweb.org/anthology/D08-1011

Hofmann, T. (1999). Probabilistic latent semantic analysis. In Proceedings of UAI 1999 (pp. 289–296).

Huang, Z., Cmejrek, M., Zhou, B. (2010). Soft syntactic constraints for hierarchical phrase-based translation using latent syntactic distributions. In Proceedings of the 2010 Conference on Empirical Methods in Natural Language Processing (pp. 138–147). Stroudsburg, PA, USA: Association for Computational Linguistics. Retrieved from http://dl.acm.org/citation.cfm?id=1870658.1870672

Huang, Y., Zhang, M., Tan, C. L. (2012, November). Improved constituent context model with features. In Proceedings of the 26th Pacific Asia Conference on Language, Information, and Computation (pp. 564–573). Bali, Indonesia: Faculty of Computer Science, Universitas Indonesia. Retrieved from http://www.aclweb.org/anthology/Y12-1061

Jayaraman, S., & Lavie, A. (2005). Multi-engine machine translation guided by explicit word matching. In Proceedings of the ACL 2005 on Inter-active Poster and Demonstration Sessions (pp. 101–104). Stroudsburg, PA, USA: Association for Computational Linguistics. Retrieved from http://dx.doi.org/10.3115/1225753.1225779 doi:10.3115/1225753.1225779

Khalilov, M., & Sima'an, K. (2011, November). Context-sensitive syntactic source-reordering by statistical transduction. In Proceedings of 5th International Joint Conference on Natural Language Processing (pp. 38–46). Chiang Mai, Thailand: Asian Federation of Natural Language Processing. Retrieved from http://www.aclweb.org/anthology/I11-1005

Knight, K. (1999). Decoding complexity in word-replacement translation models. *Computational Linguistics*, *25*, 607–615.

Koehn, P. (2004, July). Statistical significance tests for machine translation evaluation. In Proceedings of EMNLP 2004 (pp. 388–395). Barcelona, Spain.

Koehn, P. (2009). *Statistical machine translation*. Cambridge: Cambridge University Press.

Koehn, P. (2012). Statistical machine translation system user manual and code guide [Computer software manual]. Retrieved from http://www.statmt.org/moses/manual/manual.pdf

Koehn, P., Axelrod, A., Mayne, A. B., Callison-Burch, C., Osborne, M., & Talbot, D. (2005, October). Edinburgh system description for the 2005 IWSLT speech translation evaluation. In Proceedings of the International Workshop on Spoken Language Translation 2005. Pittsburgh, USA.

Koehn, P., Och, F. J., & Marcu, D. (2003, May-June). Statistical phrase-based translation. In Proceedings of the 2003 Human Language Technology Conference of the North American Chapter of the Association for Computational Linguistics (pp. 58–54). Edmonton, Canada.

Komachi, M., & Matsumoto, Y. (2006). Phrase reordering for statistical machine translation based on predicate-argument structure. In Proceedings of the International Workshop on Spoken Language Translation:Evaluation Campaign on Spoken Language Translation (pp. 77–82).

Kumar, S., & Byrne, W. (2005, October). Local phrase reordering models for statistical machine translation. In Proceedings of Human Language Technology Conference and Conference on Empirical Methods in Natural Language Processing (pp. 161–168). Vancouver, British Columbia, Canada. Retrieved from http://www.aclweb.org/anthology/H/H05/H05-1021

Levenshtein, V. (1966). Binary codes capable of correcting deletions, insertions and reversals. *Soviet Physics Doklady, 10*, 707–710.

Li, C.-H., Li, M., Zhang, D., Li, M., Zhou, M., Guan, Y. (2007, June). A probabilistic approach to syntax-based reordering for statistical machine translation. In Proceedings of the 45th Annual Meeting of the Association of Computational Linguistics (pp. 720–727). Prague, Czech Republic. Retrieved from http://www.aclweb.org/anthology/P07-1091

Li, P., Liu, Y., Sun, M. (2013, October). Recursive autoencoders for ITG-based translation. In Proceedings of the 2013 Conference on Empirical Methods in Natural Language Processing (pp. 567–577). Seattle, Washington, USA: Association for Computational Linguistics. Retrieved from http://www.aclweb.org/anthology/D13-1054

Li, J., Resnik, P., & Daumé III, H. (2013, June). Modeling syntactic and semantic structures in hierarchical phrase-based translation. In Proceedings of the 2013 Conference of the North American Chapter of the Association for Computational Linguistics: Human Language Technologies (pp. 540–549). Atlanta, Georgia: Association for Computational Linguistics. Retrieved from http://www.aclweb.org/anthology/N13-1060

Li, J., Zhou, G., Ng, H. T. (2010, July). Joint syntactic and semantic parsing of Chinese. In Proceedings of the 48th Annual Meeting of the Association for Computational Linguistics (pp. 1108–1117). Uppsala, Sweden: Association for Computational Linguistics. Retrieved from http://www.aclweb.org/anthology/P10-1113

Lin, J. (2006, September). Divergence measures based on the Shannon entropy. IEEE Transactions on Information Theory, 37(1), 145–151. Retrieved from http://dx.doi.org/10.1109/18.61115 doi:10.1109/18.61115

Liu, D., & Gildea, D. (2010, August). Semantic role features for machine translation. In Proceedings of the 23rd International Conference on Computational Linguistics (COLING 2010) (pp. 716–724). Beijing, China: Coling 2010 Organizing Committee. Retrieved from http://www.aclweb.org/anthology/C10-1081

Liu, Q., He, Z., Liu, Y., Lin, S. (2008, October). Maximum entropy based rule selection model for syntax-based statistical machine translation. In Proceedings of the 2008 Conference on Empirical Methods in Natural Language Processing (pp. 89–97). Honolulu, Hawaii: Association for Computational Linguistics. Retrieved from http://www.aclweb.org/anthology/D08-1010

Liu, Y., Liu, Q., Lin, S. (2006, July). Tree-to-string alignment template for statistical machine translation. In Proceedings of the 21st International Conference on Computational Linguistics and 44th Annual Meeting of the Association for Computational Linguistics (pp. 609–616). Sydney, Australia. Retrieved from http://www.aclweb.org/anthology/P06-1077 doi:10.3115/1220175.1220252

Lopez, A. (2008, August). Statistical machine translation. ACM Computing Surveys, 40(3), 8:1–8:49. Retrieved from http://doi.acm.org/10.1145/1380584.1380586 doi:10.1145/1380584.1380586

Lü, Y., Li, S., Zhao, T., Yang, M. (2002). Learning Chinese bracketing knowledge based on a bilingual language model. In Proceedings of the 19th International Conference on Computational Linguistics (pp. 1–7). Retrieved from http://acl.ldc.upenn.edu/coling2002/proceedings/data/area-11/co-012.pdf

Marcu, D., Wang, W., Echihabi, A., Knight, K. (2006, July). SPMT: Statistical machine translation with syntactified target language phrases. In Proceedings of the 2006 Conference on Empirical Methods in Natural Language Processing (pp. 44–52). Sydney, Australia. Retrieved from http://www.aclweb.org/anthology/W/W06/W06-1606

Marton, Y., & Resnik, P. (2008, June). Soft syntactic constraints for hierarchical phrased-based translation. In Proceedings of ACL-08: LT (pp. 1003–1011). Columbus, Ohio. Retrieved from http://www.aclweb.org/anthology/P/P08/P08-1114

Mauser, A., Hasan, S., Ney, H. (2009, August). Extending statistical machine translation with discriminative and trigger-based lexicon models. In Proceedings of the 2009 Conference on Empirical Methods in Natural Language Processing (pp. 210–218). Singapore: Association for Computational Linguistics. Retrieved from http://www.aclweb.org/anthology/D/D09/D09-1022

Mccallum, A., & Freitag, D. (2000). Maximum entropy Markov models for information extraction and segmentation. In Proceedings of the Seventeenth International Conference on Machine Learning (pp. 591–598). Morgan Kaufmann.

Mi, H., Huang, L., Liu, Q. (2008, June). Forest-based translation. In Proceedings of ACL-08: HLT (pp. 192–199). Columbus, Ohio: Association for Computational Linguistics. Retrieved from http://www.aclweb.org/anthology/P/P08/P08-1023

Mikolov, T., Chen, K., Corrado, G., & Dean, J. (2013). Efficient estimation of word representations in vector space. In Proceedings of Workshop at ICLR.

Mimno, D., Wallach, H. M., Naradowsky, J., Smith, D. A., & McCallum, A. (2009, August). Polylingual topic models. In Proceedings of the 2009 Conference on Empirical Methods in Natural Language Processing (pp. 880–889). Singapore. Retrieved from http://www.aclweb.org/anthology/D/D09/D09-1092

Mylonakis, M., & Sima'an, K. (2008). Phrase translation probabilities with ITG priors and smoothing as learning objective. In Proceedings of the Conference on Empirical Methods in Natural Language Processing (pp. 630–639). Stroudsburg, PA, USA: Association for Computational Linguistics. Retrieved from http://dl.acm.org/citation.cfm?id=1613715.1613793

Mylonakis, M., & Sima'an, K. (2011). Learning hierarchical translation structure with linguistic annotations. In Proceedings of the 49th Annual Meeting of the Association for Computational Linguistics: Human Language Technologies (Vol. 1, pp. 642–652). Stroudsburg, PA, USA: Association for Computational Linguistics. Retrieved from http://dl.acm.org/citation.cfm?id=2002472.2002554

Navarro, G. (2001). A guided tour to approximate string matching. ACM Computing Surveys, 33(1), 31–88.

Och, F. J. (2002). Statistical machine translation: From single-word models to alignment templates. Unpublished doctoral dissertation, RWTH Aachen University, Germany.

Och, F. J. (2003, July). Minimum error rate training in statistical machine translation. In Proceedings of the 41st Annual Meeting of the Association for Computational Linguistics (pp. 160–167). Sapporo, Japan. doi:10.3115/1075096.1075117

Och, F. J., & Ney, H. (2002).2002. Discriminative training and maximum entropy models for statistical machine translation. In Proceedings of the 40th Annual Meeting of the Association for Computational Linguistics (pp. 295–302). Philadelphia, PA.

Och, F. J., Gildea, D., Khudanpur, S., Sarkar, A., Yamada, K., Fraser, A., et al. (2004, May 2-May 7). A smorgasbord of features for statistical machine translation. In D. M. Susan Dumais & S. Roukos (Eds.), HLT-NAACL 2004: Main Proceedings (pp. 161–168). Boston, Massachusetts, USA: Association for Computational Linguistics.

Och, F. J., Ueffing, N., & Ney, H. (2001). An efficient A* search algorithm for statistical machine translation. In Proceedings of Data-Driven Machine Translation Workshop (pp. 55–62).

Papineni, K., Roukos, S., Ward, T., & Zhu, W.-J. (2002, July). BLEU: A method for automatic evaluation of machine translation. In Proceedings of 40th Annual Meeting of the Association for Computational Linguistics (pp. 311–318). Philadelphia, Pennsylvania, USA. doi:10.3115/1073083.1073135

Petrov, S., Barrett, L., Thibaux, R., Klein, D. (2006, July). Learning accurate, compact, and interpretable tree annotation. In Proceedings of the 21st International Conference on Computational Linguistics and 44th Annual Meeting of the Association for Computational Linguistics (pp. 433–440). Sydney, Australia: Association for Computational Linguistics. Retrieved from http://www.aclweb.org/anthology/P/P06/P06-1055

Popovic, M., de Gispert, A., Gupta, D., Lambert, P., Ney, H., Mariño, J. B., et al. (2006, June). Morpho-syntactic information for automatic error analysis of statistical machine translation output. In Proceedings on the Workshop on Statistical Machine Translation (pp. 1–6). New York. Retrieved from http://www.aclweb.org/anthology/W/W06/W06-3101

Quirk, C., Menezes, A., & Cherry, C. (2005, June). Dependency treelet translations: syntactically informed phrasal SMT. In Proceedings of the 43rd Annual Meeting of the ACL (pp. 271–279). Ann Arbor, USA.

Raybaud, S., Lavecchia, C., Langlois, D., & Smaÿli, K. (2009, January). New confidence measures for statistical machine translation. In Proceedings of the International Conference on Agents and Artificial Intelligence (pp. 61–68). Porto, Portugal.

Roark, B., & Hollingshead, K. (2008, August). Classifying chart cells for quadratic complexity context-free inference. In Proceedings of the 22nd International Conference on Computational Linguistics (COLING 2008) (pp. 745–752). Manchester, UK: Coling 2008 Organizing Committee. Retrieved from http://www.aclweb.org/anthology/C08-1094

Rosenfeld, R., Carbonell, J., & Rudnicky, A. (1994). *Adaptive statistical language modeling: A maximum entropy approach*. Technical Report : Carnegie Mellon University.

Ruiz, N., & Federico, M. (2011, July). Topic adaptation for lecture translation through bilingual latent semantic models. In Proceedings of the Sixth Workshop on Statistical Machine Translation.

Saers, M., Nivre, J., Wu, D. (2009). Learning stochastic bracketing inversion transduction grammars with a cubic time biparsing algorithm. In Proceedings of the 11th International Conference on Parsing Technologies (pp. 29–32). Stroudsburg, PA, USA: Association for Computational Linguistics. Retrieved from http://dl.acm.org/citation.cfm?id=1697236.1697242

Sánchez, J. A., & Benedý, J. M. (2006). Stochastic inversion transduction grammars for obtaining word phrases for phrase-based statistical machine translation. In Proceedings of the Workshop on Statistical Machine Translation (pp. 130–133). Stroudsburg, PA, USA: Association for Computational Linguistics. Retrieved from http://dl.acm.org/citation.cfm?id=1654650.1654669

Sanchis, A., Juan, A., Vidal, E., & Informatics, D. D. S. (2007). Estimation of confidence measures for machine translation. In Procedings of Machine Translation Summit XI. Copenhagen, Denmark.

Shen, L., Xu, J., Weischedel, R. (2008, June). A new string-to-dependency machine translation algorithm with a target dependency language model. In Proceedings of ACL-08: HLT (pp. 577–585). Columbus, Ohio: Association for Computational Linguistics. Retrieved from http://www.aclweb.org/anthology/P/P08/P08-1066

Shi, Y., & Zhou, L. (2005, October). Error detection using linguistic features. In Proceedings of Human Language Technology Conference and Conference on Empirical Methods in Natural Language Processing (pp. 41–48). Vancouver, British Columbia, Canada: Association for Computational Linguistics. Retrieved from http://www.aclweb.org/anthology/H/H05/H05-1006

Shieber, S. M., Schabes, Y., & Pereira, O. C. N. (1995). Principles and implementation of deductive parsing. *Journal of Logic Programming, 24*, 3–36.

Sleator, D. D., & Temperley, D. (1993). Parsing English with a link grammar. In Proceedings of the Third International Workshop on Parsing Technologies (pp. 277–292). Retrieved from http://www.cs.cmu.edu/afs/cs.cmu.edu/project/link/pub/www/papers/ps/LG-IWPT93.ps

Stolcke, A. (2002, September). SRILM–an extensible language modeling toolkit. In Proceedings of the 7th International Conference on Spoken Language Processing (ICSLP 2002) (pp. 901–904). Denver, Colorado, USA.

Su, J., Liu, Y., Mi, H., Zhao, H., Lü, Y., Liu, Q. (2010). Dependency based bracketing transduction grammar for statistical machine translation. In Proceedings of the 23rd International Conference on Computational Linguistics: Posters (pp. 1185–1193). Stroudsburg, PA, USA: Association for Computational Linguistics. Retrieved from http://dl.acm.org/citation.cfm?id=1944566.1944702

Tam, Y.-C., Lane, I. R., & Schultz, T. (2007). Bilingual LSA-based adaptation for statistical machine translation. *Machine Translation*, *21*(4), 187–207.

Tiedemann, J. (2010, July). Context adaptation in statistical machine translation using models with exponentially decaying cache. In Proceedings of the 2010 Workshop on Domain Adaptation for Natural Language Processing (pp. 8–15). Uppsala, Sweden: Association for Computational Linguistics. Retrieved from http://www.aclweb.org/anthology/W10-2602

Tillman, C. (2004, May). A unigram orientation model for statistical machine translation. In Proceedings of the Human Language Technology Conference of the North American Chapter of the Association for Computational Linguistics (HLT-NAACL 2004): Short Papers (pp. 101–104). Boston, Massachusetts, USA.

Ture, F., Oard, D. W., & Resnik, P. (2012, June). Encouraging consistent translation choices. In Proceedings of the 2012 Conference of the North American Chapter of the Association for Computational Linguistics: Human Language Technologies (pp. 417–426). Montréal, Canada: Association for Computational Linguistics. Retrieved from http://www.aclweb.org/anthology/N12-1046

Ueffing, N., & Ney, H. (2007, March). Word-level confidence estimation for machine translation. Computational Linguistics, 33(1), 9–40. Retrieved from http://dx.doi.org/10.1162/coli.2007.33.1.9 doi:10.1162/coli.2007.33.1.9

Ueffing, N., Macherey, K., & Ney, H. (2003). Confidence measures for statistical machine translation. In Proceedings of MT Summit IX (pp. 394–401). Springer.

Wang, C., Collins, M., Koehn, P. (2007, June). Chinese syntactic reordering for statistical machine translation. In Proceedings of the 2007 Joint Conference on Empirical Methods in Natural Language Processing and Computational Natural Language Learning (EMNLP-CoNLL) (pp. 737–745). Prague, Czech Republic. Retrieved from http://www.aclweb.org/anthology/D/D07/D07-1077

Wellington, B., Waxmonsky, S., & Melamed, I. D. (2006). Empirical lower bounds on the complexity of translational equivalence. In Proceedings of the 44th Annual Conference of the Association for Computational Linguistics.

Wu, D. (1996, June). A polynomial-time algorithm for statistical machine translation. In Proceedings of the 34th Annual Meeting of the Association for Computational Linguistics (pp. 152–158). Santa Cruz, California, USA. Retrieved from http://www.aclweb.org/anthology/P96-1021 doi:10.3115/981863.981884

Wu, D. (2010). Alignment. In N. Indurkhya & F. Damerau (Eds.), *Handbook of natural language processing* (pp. 367–408). London: Chapman & Hall.

Wu, D., & Fung, P. (2009a, May). Can semantic role labeling improve SMT. In Proceedings of the 13th Annual Conference of the EAMT (pp. 218–225). Barcelona.

Wu, D., & Fung, P. (2009b, June). Semantic roles for SMT: A hybrid two-Pass model. In Proceedings of Human Language Technologies: The 2009 Annual Conference of the North American Chapter of the Association for Computational Linguistics, Companion Volume: Short Papers (pp. 13–16). Boulder, Colorado: Association for Computational Linguistics. Retrieved from http://www.aclweb.org/anthology/N/N09/N09-2004

Wu, D., & Ng, C. (1995). Using brackets to improve search for statistical machine translation. In Proceedings of PACLIC-IO, Pacific Asia Conference on Language, Information and Computation.

Wu, X., Sudoh, K., Duh, K., Tsukada, H., Nagata, M. (2011, November). Extracting Pre-ordering rules from predicate-argument structures. In Proceedings of 5th International Joint Conference on Natural Language Processing (pp. 29–37). Chiang Mai, Thailand: Asian Federation of Natural Language Processing. Retrieved from http://www.aclweb.org/anthology/I11-1004

Wu, D. (1997). Stochastic inversion transduction grammars and bilingual parsing of parallel corpora. *Computational Linguistics, 23*(3), 377–403.

Xia, F., & McCord, M. (2004, August). Improving a statistical MT system with automatically learned rewrite patterns. In Proceedings of the 20th International Conference on Computational Linguistics (COLING 2004) (pp. 508–514). Geneva, Switzerland.

Xiao, X., & Xiong, D. (2013, October). Max-margin synchronous grammar induction for machine translation. In Proceedings of the 2013 Conference on Empirical Methods in Natural Language Processing (pp. 255–264). Seattle, Washington, USA: Association for Computational Linguistics. Retrieved from http://www.aclweb.org/anthology/D13-1026

Xiao, X., Xiong, D., Liu, Y., Liu, Q., Lin, S. (2012, December). Unsupervised discriminative induction of synchronous grammar for machine translation. In Proceedings of COLING 2012 (pp. 2883–2898). Mumbai, India: The COLING 2012 Organizing Committee. Retrieved from http://www.aclweb.org/anthology/C12-1176

Xiao, T., Zhu, J., Yao, S., & Zhang, H. (2011, September). Document-level consistency verification in machine translation. In Proceedings of the 2011 MT Summit XIII (pp. 131–138). Xiamen, China.

Xiong, D., & Zhang, M. (2013, July). A topic-based coherence model for statistical machine translation. In Proceedings of the Twenty-Seventh AAAI Conference on Artificial Intelligence (AAAI-13). Bellevue, Washington, USA.

Xiong, D., Liu, Q., Lin, S. (2006, July). Maximum entropy based phrase reordering model for statistical machine translation. In Proceedings of the 21st International Conference on Computational Linguistics and 44th Annual Meeting of the Association for Computational Linguistics (pp. 521–528). Sydney, Australia: Association for Computational Linguistics. Retrieved from http://www.aclweb.org/anthology/P06-1066 doi:10.3115/1220175.1220241

Xiong, D., Liu, Q., Lin, S. (2007, June). A dependency treelet string correspondence model for statistical machine translation. In Proceedings of the Second Workshop on Statistical Machine Translation (pp. 40–47). Prague, Czech Republic: Association for Computational Linguistics. Retrieved from http://www.aclweb.org/anthology/W/W07/W07-0706

Xiong, D., Zhang, M., Li, H. (2010b, June). Learning translation boundaries for phrase-based decoding. In Human Language Technologies: The 2010 Annual Conference of the North American Chapter of the Association for Computational Linguistics (pp. 136–144). Los Angeles, California: Association for Computational Linguistics. Retrieved from http://www.aclweb.org/anthology/N10-1016

Xiong, D., Zhang, M., Li, H. (2012, July). Modeling the translation of predicate-argument structure for SMT. In Proceedings of the 50th Annual Meeting of the Association for Computational Linguistics (Vol. 1, Long Papers, pp. 902–911). Jeju Island, Korea: Association for Computational Linguistics. Retrieved from http://www.aclweb.org/anthology/P12-1095

Xiong, D., Zhang, M., Aw, A., Mi, H., Liu, Q., & Lin, S. (2008, January). Refinements in BTG-based statistical machine translation. In Proceedings of the Third International Joint Conference on Natural Language Processing (pp. 505–512). Hyderabad, India.

Xiong, D., Zhang, M., & Li, H. (2010a). Linguistically annotated reordering: Evaluation and analysis. *Computational Linguistics, 36*(3), 535–568.

Xiong, D., Zhang, M., & Li, H. (2011). A maximum-entropy segmentation model for statistical machine translation. *IEEE Transactions on Audio, Speech and Language Processing, 19*(8), 2494–2505.

Xue, N. (2008). Labeling Chinese predicates with semantic roles. *Computational Linguistics, 34*(2), 225–255.

Yamada, K., & Knight, K. (2001, July). A syntax-based statistical translation model. In Proceedings of 39th Annual Meeting of the Association for Computational Linguistics (pp. 523–530). Toulouse, France. Retrieved from http://www.aclweb.org/anthology/P01-1067 doi:10.3115/1073012.1073079

Yamamoto, H., Okuma, H., Sumita, E. (2008, June). Imposing constraints from the source tree on ITG constraints for SMT. In Proceedings of the ACL-08: HLT Second Workshop on Syntax and Structure in Statistical Translation (SSST-2) (pp. 1–9). Columbus, Ohio. Retrieved from http://www.aclweb.org/anthology/W/W08/W08-0401

Yao, X., & Durme, B. V. (2011, June). Nonparametric Bayesian word sense induction. In Proceedings of TextGraphs-6: Graph-based Methods for Natural Language Processing (pp. 10–14). Portland, Oregon: Association for Computational Linguistics. Retrieved from http://www.aclweb.org/anthology/W11-1102

Zens, R., & Ney, H. (2003). A comparative study on reordering constraints in statistical machine translation. In Proceedings of the Annual Meeting of the Association for Computational Linguistics (p. 144–151).

Zens, R., & Ney, H. (2006, June). Discriminative reordering models for statistical machine translation. In Proceedings on the Workshop on Statistical Machine Translation (pp. 55–63). New York City: Association for Computational Linguistics. Retrieved from http://www.aclweb.org/anthology/W/W06/W06-3108

Zens, R., Ney, H., Watanabe, T., & Sumita, E. (2004). Reordering constraints for phrase-based statistical machine translation. In Proceedings of the 20th International Conference on Computational Linguistics (COLING) (pp. 205–211).

Zhai, F., Zhang, J., Zhou, Y., Zong, C. (2012, December). Machine translation by modeling predicate argument structure transformation. In Proceedings of COLING (pp. 3019-3036). Mumbai, India.

Zhang, H., & Gildea, D. (2005, June). Stochastic lexicalized inversion transduction grammar for alignment. In Proceedings of the 43rd Annual Meeting of the Association for Computational Linguistics (ACL'05) (pp. 475–482). Ann Arbor, Michigan: Association for Computational Linguistics. Retrieved from http://www.aclweb.org/anthology/P05-1059 doi:10.3115/1219840.1219899

Zhang, H., & Gildea, D. (2006, July). Efficient search for inversion transduction grammar. In Proceedings of the 2006 Conference on Empirical Methods in Natural Language Processing (pp. 224–231). Sydney, Australia: Association for Computational Linguistics. Retrieved from http://www.aclweb.org/anthology/W/W06/W06-1627

Zhang, H., Gildea, D., Chiang, D. (2008, August). Extracting synchronous grammar rules from word-level alignments in linear time. In Proceedings of the 22nd International Conference on Computational Linguistics (Coling 2008) (pp. 1081–1088). Manchester, UK. Retrieved from http://www.aclweb.org/anthology/C08-1136

Zhang, D., Li, M., Li, C.-H., Zhou, M. (2007, June). Phrase reordering model integrating syntactic knowledge for SMT. In Proceedings of the 2007 Joint Conference on Empirical Methods in Natural Language Processing and Computational Natural Language Learning (EMNLP-CoNLL) (pp. 533–540). Prague, Czech Republic. Retrieved from http://www.aclweb.org/anthology/D/D07/D07-1056

Zhao, B., & Xing, E. P. (2006, July). BiTAM: bilingual topic admixture models for word alignment. In Proceedings of the COLING/ACL 2006 Main Conference Poster Sessions (pp. 969–976). Sydney, Australia. Retrieved from http://www.aclweb.org/anthology/P/P06/P06-2124

Zhao, B., & Xing, E. P. (2007). HM-BiTAM: Bilingual topic exploration, word alignment, and translation. In Proceedings of NIPS 2007.

Zhao, B., Eck, M., & Vogel, S. (2004, August 23-August 27). Language model adaptation for statistical machine translation via structured query models. In Proceedings of Coling 2004 (pp. 411–417). Geneva, Switzerland: COLING.

Zhao, B., Lee, Y.-S., Luo, X., Li, L. (2011, June). Learning to transform and select elementary trees for improved syntax-based machine translations. In Proceedings of the 49th Annual Meeting of the Association for Computational Linguistics: Human Language Technologies (pp. 846–855). Portland, Oregon, USA: Association for Computational Linguistics. Retrieved from http://www.aclweb.org/anthology/P11-1085

Zhou, G. (2004, August 23-August 27). Modeling of long distance context dependency. In Proceedings of COLING (pp. 92–98). Geneva, Switzerland: COLING.

Zollmann, A., Venugopal, A., & Vogel, S. (2008, October). The CMU syntax-augmented machine translation system: SAMT on Hadoop with n-best alignments. In Proceedings of International Workshop on Spoken Language Translation (IWSLT) (pp. 18–25). Hawaii, USA.

Index

Symbols
−LM decoder, 19
+LM decoder, 23

A
Argument, 72
Argument motion orientation, 73
Argument reordering category, 72

B
Backward language model integration, 27
Backward n-gram, 26
Backward n-gram language model, 26
Binary bracketing instance, 95
Block, 45
Boundary word reordering model, 50
Bracketable segment, 82, 83
Bracketable segment boundary, 82
Bracketing, 10
Bracketing model, 10, 87
Bracketing rule, 16
Bracketing strength, 88
Bracketing strength model, 88
Bracketing Transduction Grammar, 16
BTG-based SMT, 17, 38
BTG derivation, 18
BTG tree, 18

C
Chart cell, 20
Classification error rate, 131
Classifier-based eordering, 22
Coherence, 139
Cohesion, 139

Composite category, 55
Consistent constituent matching rate, 99
Cube pruning, 34

D
Document-level SMT, 139
Document-topic distribution, 112
Dynamic threshold pruning, 34, 36

E
Error detection, 125

F
Fixed threshold pruning, 34
Formally syntax-based SMT, 5
Forward n-gram, 26
Forward n-gram language model, 27
Fully reorderable node, 60

G
Grammatical cohesion, 139

H
Hard constraint, 87
Hierarchical grammar, 40
Histogram pruning, 34
Hypothesis recombination, 33

I
IBM constraint, 39
Inference rule, 19

© Springer Science+Business Media Singapore 2015
D. Xiong and M. Zhang, *Linguistically Motivated Statistical
Machine Translation*, DOI 10.1007/978-981-287-356-9